Into Africa Errata

Page 243

top of page should begin

"…one percent of U.S. gross domestic product, which they describe as…"

Into Africa
INTERCULTURAL INSIGHTS

Yale Richmond and Phyllis Gestrin

The InterAct Series
GEORGE W. RENWICK, Series Editor

Other books in the series:
WITH RESPECT TO THE JAPANESE
UNDERSTANDING ARABS
GOOD NEIGHBORS: COMMUNICATING WITH THE MEXICANS
BUENOS VECINOS
CONSIDERING FILIPINOS
BORDER CROSSINGS: AMERICAN INTERACTIONS WITH ISRAELIS
A FAIR GO FOR ALL: AUSTRALIAN/AMERICAN INTERACTIONS
ENCOUNTERING THE CHINESE
FROM *NYET* TO *DA*: UNDERSTANDING THE RUSSIANS
FROM *DA* TO YES: UNDERSTANDING THE EAST EUROPEANS
SPAIN IS DIFFERENT
EXPLORING THE GREEK MOSAIC
A COMMON CORE: THAIS AND AMERICANS

Also by Yale Richmond:
SOVIET-AMERICAN CULTURAL EXCHANGES: RIPOFF OR PAYOFF?
HOSTING SOVIET VISITORS: A HANDBOOK
U.S.-SOVIET CULTURAL EXCHANGES, 1958-1986: WHO WINS?
FROM *NYET* TO *DA*: UNDERSTANDING THE RUSSIANS
FROM *DA* TO YES: UNDERSTANDING THE EAST EUROPEANS

Into Africa
INTERCULTURAL INSIGHTS

Yale Richmond and Phyllis Gestrin

INTERCULTURAL PRESS, INC.

For information, contact:
Intercultural Press, Inc.
P.O. Box 700
Yarmouth, Maine 04096, USA
1-207-846-5168

Book design and production by Patty J. Topel
Cover design and chapter graphic by Patty J. Topel

Printed in the United States of America

02 01 00 99 98   2 3 4 5

Library of Congress Cataloging-in-Publication Data

Richmond, Yale.
   Into Africa: intercultural insights / Yale Richmond and Phyllis Gestrin.
      p. cm.—(InterAct series)
   Includes bibliographical references and index.
   ISBN 1-877864-57-9
   1. Africa. Sub-Saharan—Social life and customs. I. Gestrin, Phyllis. II. Title. III. Series.
DT352.4.R53   1998
967—dc21
                                97-38933
                                      CIP

Traditional African societies were sophisticated organisms, finely tuned to the exigencies of climate and environment in a harsh continent. In their communal relationships and elaborate links of mutual responsibility, with their generic love of children and respect for the aged, they cultivated a respect for human values and human worth far in advance of the materialistic West.

—Allister Sparks, *The Mind of South Africa*

Table of Contents

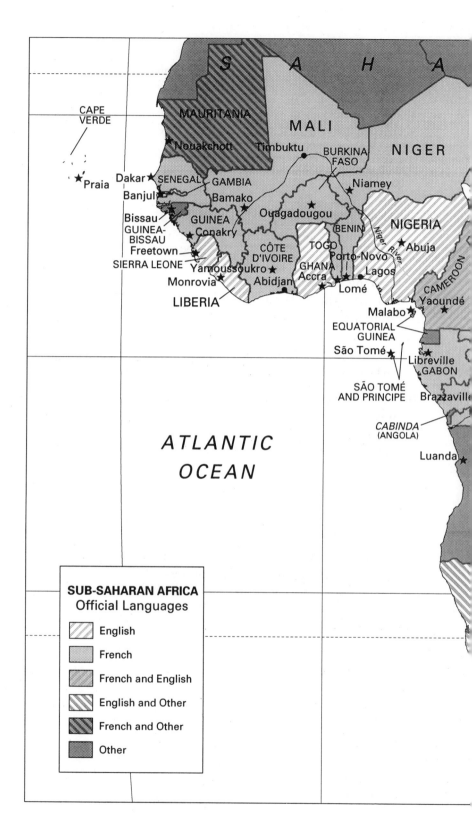

Preface

This book has been written for readers who will be going to sub-Saharan Africa to advise, consult, do business, work, study, or merely travel but who also want to understand the customs and cultures of the Africans they will be encountering and why they behave as they do.

Based on the personal experiences of the authors, interviews with Africans and expatriates knowledgeable about Africa, as well as on published studies, the book is intended to ease the newcomer's entry into Africa and provide the intercultural insights that will make a sojourn there more enjoyable as well as more productive.

There is, of course, no typical African, just as there is no typical American or European. Africa is a vast continent, more than three times the size of the United States, and with peoples of many cultures, languages, and religions. There are also sharp regional differences and within those regions a multitude of peoples with their own diversities. How, then, to write a book about understanding Africans?

Their differences notwithstanding, all Africans share many traits and traditions which visitors will encounter almost everywhere across the continent. As Columbia University anthropologist Elliot P. Skinner has put it:

Africanity, a term we use to mean the variety of indigenous customs, has provided Africans with answers to the basic questions of their existence, from how they came into being to how they cope with the problems of daily life. The solutions to these problems varied as specific African societies adapted to particular ecologies, but to a remarkable degree all African societies are similar.[1]

The same assertion was made earlier by Melville J. Herskovits, the founding father of African studies in the United States:

That considerable differences do exist...is as true as of any other major areas of the world. Yet the underlying similarities in its cultures, to say nothing of the historical contacts among its peoples as revealed by these similarities, give it a unity recognized not only by scholarly observers but also in the writings of the early explorers, missionaries and government officials.[2]

To cite some similarities, African traditional religions recognize a Supreme Creator and underscore the unity of the universe and the harmonious interaction of humans with their habitat. In communication, Africans value discretion and the use of aphorisms and oblique references to make a point. And, in contrast to the West where individual rights reign, African societies emphasize the importance of the extended family and the individual's integration into the community.

Business practices also will not vary much across the continent. In West, East, and Southern Africa (South Africa excepted), they will be remarkably similar—small and locally controlled markets, irregular enforcement of the law, and the discovery that a foreigner may be paying taxes but his local competitor is not.

The authors will focus first on the similarities across sub-Saharan Africa—the cultural characteristics that a visitor is likely to encounter in almost every country. This will be followed by practical advice for persons planning to visit the continent and to live, socialize, or do business there. Regional variations in cultural characteristics will next be discussed and illustrated by examples from individual countries. Chapters follow on conducting workshops for Africans and advice for travelers. Finally, some reflections on Africans and Americans and on "succeeding" in Africa.

Chapters should be read sequentially rather than at random, for in some cases they build on themes presented earlier. If readers should recognize some repetition in the advice given in the various chapters, this reflects an old African practice common to all oral traditions, where repetition is used for emphasis and as a reminder of what has been said before.

For convenience, *Africa* and *sub-Sahara* are used here synonymously with *sub-Saharan Africa*.

---

[1] Elliot P. Skinner, "The Triple Heritage of Lifestyles," in *The Africans: A Reader*, edited by Ali A. Mazrui and Toby Kleban Levine (New York: Praeger Scientific, 1986), 60.

[2] Melville J. Herskovits, *The Human Factor in Changing Africa* (New York: Alfred A. Knopf, 1962), 20.

Acknowledgments

Many people were interviewed for this book and shared their experiences with the authors. From those whom we have inadvertently failed to mention we ask forgiveness. Interviewees include Meri Ames, Mariama Bah, Cheryl and John Barton, Elio Bizarro, Carroll J. Bouchard, Max and Adina Boulét, Suzi Bouveron, Kandice Christian, John Paul Clark, Lydia Clemmons, John Deidrick, Phillipe Denichaud, Joseph DeStefano, Mamadou Dia, Manthita Tandia Diagana, Sambe Duale, Erin Eckert, Sarah Ford-Giossi, Robert and Mary Beth Gosende, Mouhamadou Guèye, Miriam Guichard, John Harris, Marge Horn, Lee Jennings, Nancy Keith, Stephen N. Kinoti, Ray Kirkland, Mamadou Konate, Nancy Lamson, Timothy G. Manchester, Wayne McDonald, Edward R. McMahon, Winifred Mixon, Poppy M. Mofolo, Yaseen and Aysha Mukadem, Joe Naimoli, Margaret Neuse, J. Daniel O'Flaherty, James Okanya, Dieudonné O. Ouedraogo, Dave Peterson, Susanne Prysor-Jones, Chahine Rassekh, Julie Owen Rea, Curtiss Reed Jr., Helene and Paul Rippey, Susan Ross, Idrissa Samba, Michael Samuels, Joel Schlesinger, Whitney Schneidman, Linda Semu, Michael Sheehan, Chakunja Sibale, Rhonda Smith, Charles Teller, Karen Tietjen, Pauline Vega, Howard Wallach, and Mitchell Warren.

A special thanks to readers who reviewed chapters: Kayode Apara, Hannah Baldwin, Shirley Buzzard, Leon Clark, Learned Dees, Francis Mading Deng, Christine Ann Djondo, Lynne and Ciro Franco, E. Gyimah-Boadi, Allan Kulakow, Harvey I. Leifert, Judith Timyan, Lalla Touré, and Richard Wall. Readers of the entire manuscript were Carroll J. Bouchard, Brenda Bowman, Momodou Darboe, Sara Pacqué-Margolis, Margaret and Steve McLaughlin, and Kitty Thuermer. Allan Kulakow helped to inspire the title. David and Kay Hoopes and Toby Frank were exemplary editors.

The views expressed are those of the authors and should not be seen as representing the opinions of organizations with which they have been associated. Any faults and omissions are our own.

Introduction

Hundreds of millions of Africans are lurching between an un-
workable Western present and a collapsing African past. Their
loyalties are stretched between predatory governments and dis-
integrating tribes, between arbitrary demands of dictators and
incessant pleadings of relatives, between commandments of the
Bible and obligations to the ancestors. At its heart, the great
experiment in modernity that continues to rattle Africa goes on
inside individuals, as they sort out new connections with their
families, their tribes, and their countries.
—Blaine Harden, *Africa*

Little more than a hundred years ago much of Africa was a
vast unknown. Distant and isolated from the rest of the
world, it was commonly called the "Dark Continent." But as
American Africanists Paul Bohannan and Philip Curtin tell
us, "...the darkness was our own ignorance, Europeans learned
about Africa late."[1]

Americans learned even later, and we might ask why Africa is still so little known to us and even less understood. As
Botswana president Sir Ketumile Masire said with surprise
after a lunch in Washington with U.S. congressional and
business leaders, "Some people know more than we know
[about Africa], and some know absolutely *nothing.*"[2]

On world maps, Africa may appear distant from the United States, but Dakar, Senegal's capital and a main gateway to West Africa, is less than seven hours by air from New York and is closer to the U.S. East Coast than is Paris. Africa, however, has not figured large in U.S. foreign policy except during the Cold War, when it was a locus of East-West rivalry and African governments were judged according to where they stood in the competition between the superpowers. Since the end of the Cold War, U.S. relations with individual governments have depended more on how those governments treat their own citizens.

Media coverage has emphasized Africa's negatives—droughts and famines, diseases and deaths, coups and wars—and, with the exceptions of the struggle against apartheid in South Africa, the U.S. peacekeeping effort in Somalia, civil war in Liberia, ethnic warfare in Rwanda and Burundi, and rebellion in the former Zaire (now Democratic Republic of Congo), the American public has paid little attention to Africa. For many African Americans, it took the television series "Roots" to arouse their curiosity.

Unknown as it still may be, sub-Saharan Africa, with its forty-eight countries, deserves our attention. More than three times the size of the United States, it has a population of more than 500 million. Nigeria, its most populous state, has more than 100 million; and Sudan, its largest country, is four times the size of Texas and nearly half as large as the United States. The Democratic Republic of Congo (hereinafter referred to as Congo) is as large as all of Western Europe. Sub-Sahara's potential for trade and investment is immense.

Incredibly rich in untapped natural resources, Africa has 90 percent of the world's cobalt reserves, 80 percent of the chrome, 50 percent of the gold, nearly half the platinum, and one-third the uranium. Nigeria is the fifth largest supplier of oil to the United States, and for those who are bedazzled by the glitter of diamonds, most of them come from southern Africa. Also with roots in Africa are the chocolate bars we savor, for Côte d'Ivoire is the world's largest producer of cocoa. And those expats who chafe over the frequent electricity outages in Africa may be consoled by learning that it has vast potential for hydroelectric power.

Sharp geographic differences distinguish the African landscape—arid deserts, tropical rain forests, highland savannas, fertile fields, and snowcapped mountains straddling the equator. Home to a multitude of ethnic groups, the peoples of sub-Sahara speak more than one thousand distinct languages and many more dialects.

Africa *is* different, and many aspects of its various cultures may seem strange at first. But when the differences are considered and explained, African patterns of behavior may not seem so strange after all. Many of them, in fact, are little different from what peoples in Europe and the Americas experienced in the not-too-distant past and may still be experiencing today, as the authors will at times point out.

---

[1] Paul Bohannan and Philip Curtin, *Africa and Africans*, 3d ed. (Prospect Heights, IL: Waveland Press, 1988), 3.

[2] *Washington Post*, 20 October 1995.

The African Community

Many factors have shaped the character of Africans, their values, and their institutions—geography, climate, ethnicity, language, religion, history, the economy, the legacy left by the colonialists, and, more recently, urbanization and Western ways.

Traditional Africa is indeed changing as more and more Africans move from the village to the city, where ancestral customs clash with new notions from Europe, Asia, and the Americas. Yet some 70 percent of sub-Saharans still live in small villages distant from big cities, observing many of the same traditions that generations of ancestors did before them. For those who move to the cities, the village remains a part of them. Africans, too, note that "you can't take the country out of the boy," although in African parlance, the saying becomes "the man moves to the city but takes the village with him." And so it is with the traditions of the village and its familial and kinship way of life that our book begins.

Communalism

A person is not a person without other people.
—Zulu proverb

1

"[I]n terms of African thought, life can be meaningful only in community, not in isolation," writes Ambrose Moyo, professor of religious studies at the University of Zimbabwe.[1] Traditional African societies are communal, as traditional societies have been almost everywhere, and individual needs and achievement, in contrast to the West, take second place to the needs of the many. A village, for example, may pool its resources to fund a bright boy's university studies in the expectation that he will return with a degree, a good job, and the resources to help support them; and the boy will honor that obligation. Indeed, as Hillary Clinton has suggested, in Africa it literally may take a village to educate a child.

Africa, moreover, is a harsh continent, with extremes of drought and heavy rainfall, famine and plenty, and Africans have had to learn to live in partnership with their environment rather than attempt to tame it—and consequently abuse it—as we have in the West. But to live in harmony with nature requires a communal effort with kith and kin, which leads us to the importance of the extended family, Africa's most immediate social unit. Whatever a person earns or achieves must be shared with other members of the extended family. What could be more considerate?

The Extended Family

> The family is a crowd.
>
> —Ashanti proverb

The extended family links its members through a broad network of mutual duties and responsibilities which shape almost every aspect of African life—work, leisure, finance, and even transportation. Whatever one person has is shared. What's mine is yours and what's yours is mine if we are both members of the same extended family. Its influence is pervasive, and for the foreigner, there is perhaps no aspect of African life more important to understand.

There is really no alternative in Africa to the extended family, says Akilagpa Sawyerr, Vice Chancellor of the University of Ghana:

> Its functioning is a major way to distinguish African society from that of Europe or the United States. And it is not going to go away. Every single person you meet in Africa who has got anything is sharing it with his kin.[2]

Far larger than the nuclear family, the African extended family is extended indeed. Among its members are parents and children, grandparents, uncles and aunts, in-laws, cousins of varying degrees, as well as persons not related by blood.

The titles of members of that "crowd" may be confusing to Americans and Europeans. An African will refer to an older person as auntie or uncle. Siblings of parents will be called father or mother rather than uncle or aunt. Cousins will be called brother or sister.

A household cook, for example, might one day say to his employer, "My mother has died and I must go to her funeral." Some time later, he might again say, "My mother has died." Both statements could be true because terms such as *mother*, *aunt*, or *cousin* may also be used for nonkinfolk with whom an African has a close relationship.

As confusing as these relationships may be, it can be a mistake to ask an African whether someone called "brother" has the same mother. Such queries can signal disapproval of the practice of polygyny (having more than one wife), which is common throughout Africa and a subject about which Africans do not appreciate foreign criticism.

Kinfolk and close companions provide a sense of community, security, and stability—people to turn to in difficult times or to provide housing when shelter is needed. The young, the old, and the frail in Africa are seldom without protection and a helping hand, which explains why so many Africans appear so secure and self-confident. "If relatives help each other," an Ethiopian proverb pronounces, "what evil can harm them?"

As former *Washington Post* correspondent Blaine Harden has described it:

> The extended family is a day-care, social security, and welfare system. It baby sits the children of working parents and keeps the elderly from feeling useless. It feeds the unemployed and gives refuge to the disabled and mentally ill. It pays for all this by redistributing resources between haves and have-nots...the extended family functions as a kind of home-grown glue. It holds together the world's poorest and most politically brittle continent.[3]

Those in the West who lament the breakup of the nuclear family and the decline in "family values" can learn some lessons from Africa.

But the extended family also has its drawbacks, say some Africans, for it can serve as a disincentive to capital accumulation and "getting ahead." When an African gets a job in the city and works in a cash economy, his entire family may regard him as a financial resource for paying the costs of its food, clothing, schooling, and other necessities. City dwellers will wonder why they should save if some day they may have to share their savings with relatives. Moreover, the country cousins who come to the city will expect their urban relatives to put them up, not just for a night or two but for months and years at a time.

As the first university graduate in his family, Kwasi Oduro, a sociologist at the University of Ghana, had an enviable teaching job in Accra, although his government salary was barely sufficient to support a wife and five children. Yet, they shared their two-bedroom house on the university campus with eleven "cousins of a sort," a number that was down from an earlier high of eighteen. His guests, as a rule, paid no rent and were fed for free, and some had been living with him for as long as two years. But when asked why he didn't turn them out, Oduro replied,

I suppose I should be thorough and dislodge all of these traditional obligations and call them humbug. I would be saved a lot of headache. But I cannot turn out anybody if there is space to sleep. You don't know what they will go to the village and say.[4]

Protecting one's assets against domestic depredation can have a major bearing on Africans who achieve some prosperity. On the other side of the continent, a story is told by a Somali medical doctor whose family in Mogadishu owned a large herd of camels that was being tended by relatives in the countryside. The herd was the family's main financial resource and their only means of accumulating assets without being constantly besieged by relatives. If the family's funds had been kept in a bank account and this had become known, many of their relatives would have felt free to ask for loans they would never repay. Camels, on the other hand, are a treasured possession in Somalia, an asset that no relative would ask his family to sell in order to lend him money. Similarly, Africans who work abroad and earn hard currency in the Middle East or Europe will often buy land or build houses back home to convert their funds into preservable assets.

This dilemma is captured poignantly by the Senegalese writer Sembene Ousmane in his book, *Le Mandat* (*The Money-Order*). An African receives a notice in the mail informing him that he is the recipient of a money order. Hearing of it, his relatives and friends come to borrow the money that he has not yet received. To avoid disappointing them, he borrows in order to lend, in anticipation of the fortune soon to follow. But when he finally receives the money order, he discovers that it's worth only a few francs. Unfortunately, he is now in debt for several hundred.

This downside of the extended family—its deterrence of savings and capital accumulation—has a psychological explanation, says Senegalese economist Mamadou Dia:

The first trait of African economic psychology is the tendency to favor conspicuous social consumptions and income redistribution over accumulations and investments.... Receiving and accommodating guests, feeding them and treating them well, are both admired and profitable behavior. Praise from his guests adds to the host's prestige and assures him of their help in the future.[5]

But "excess income," continues Dia, "simply leads to more lavish consumption habits and a widening of the circle of those benefiting from income redistribution." This disdain for accumulation, declares Dia, explains the tendency of traditional African enterprises to favor extension of investments over intensification of capital and greater productivity.[6] Multiply all the above examples by the millions and it is easy to understand why African countries have difficulty raising capital.

When Africans move to the city, they maintain ties to their ancestral villages, but the family system is nevertheless weakened as it comes in conflict with an urban way of life. The urban African faces an often difficult choice.

A story is told of a Western-trained Senegalese physician who had a lucrative practice in Dakar. Although urbanized, he would return to his ancestral village once a week to visit his parents and extended family, accompanied always by one or more of his children to show them their roots.

One of his sons later studied medicine in France, where he became engaged to an African student from the same ethnic group. The two lived the good life in France, vacationing on the Riviera, skiing in the Alps, and becoming thoroughly Frenchified. Yet, when the time came to marry, they returned to Senegal and had a traditional wedding in the ancestral village. Even so, after completing their studies in France and returning home, the young couple refused to live in the father's compound with his other children, as custom dictated, and declared their intention to break with other traditions as well— pursuing two careers and having only two children.

These are major departures for Africans, and in the conflict between the communalism of the village and the individualism of the city, the traditions of one African family had been breached.

Sense of Community

What belongs to me is destroyable by water or fire; what belongs to us is destroyable by neither water nor fire.

—Vais proverb

"In Africa we spend most of our time visiting and chatting," relates a Malawian doctor. But when he went to Edinburgh to study medicine, he was surprised to learn that the Scots spend most of their time on individual pursuits. A similar experience is reported by a black South African who studied in France. After a year in Paris he returned home because, as he explained to the authors, he found no sense of community there and had difficulty making friends. "I wanted to be friends with my fellow students after classes," he said, "but they made me feel that I was imposing on them."

Africans have a strong sense of belonging to a larger community where sharing, caring, and doing good for each other contribute to the greater good of the group. Those who do good do not necessarily expect to be repaid for each deed done, although they do hope to gain recognition when their good deeds are made public.

In Senegal, for example, when someone does something for you, you are expected to make it known. By publicly expressing appreciation to your benefactors, you celebrate their virtues and enhance their reputations. This is considered the right thing to do.

But Africans are especially praised for going beyond what society expects, not just for doing what is considered correct, which Americans might describe as "above and beyond the call of duty." A wealthy Muslim, for example, would not be praised for sending his mother to visit Mecca before she dies; he is *expected* to do so. But a poor man who has made sacrifices to send his mother *will* be praised.

Sharing and generosity are intrinsic to the African nature. An African student traveling by long-distance bus in the United States relates how he offered some of his sandwiches to the complete stranger in the next seat. The stranger, however, not sure whether the African was merely being polite, refused until the offer was repeated more compellingly. In Africa, where sharing is the norm, the stranger would have been obliged to accept on the first offer.

The caring and sharing ethic accompanies Africans as they move from the village to the city and enter the world of business and the professions. As Dia writes,

> Self-reliance and self-interest tend to take a back seat to group loyalty and the need to participate and belong.... Accordingly, a higher premium is set on interpersonal relations, which are...a prerequisite for effective professional and business interaction.[7]

Or as John Makhene of the South African Broadcasting Corporation (SABC) puts it so succinctly,

> African [black] culture is a "we" culture based on the community and communal experience.... Western [white] culture on the other hand is an "I" culture—it's far more individualistic.[8]

As a Westerner might describe it, to Africans, cooperation is more important than competition.

Reflecting their "we" culture, Africans will not hesitate to ask foreigners for personal information which would be considered private in their home countries. They may ask, for example, about the amount of a foreigner's salary, which among Africans may not be considered confidential. Most Americans will try to avoid such a question both because it is too personal and because to Africans with much lower incomes an American's salary might seem excessive. Such a question, however, might be answered by simply explaining that U.S. salaries are often higher than African salaries because we have other costs to cover such as cars, mortgages, taxes, health insurance, and savings for old age. Moreover, most of us do not have the extended family support system that Africans can turn to in time of need.

Also reflecting their communal ethic, Africans are reluctant to stand out in a crowd or to appear different from their neighbors or colleagues, a result of social pressure to avoid offense to group standards and traditions. But such traditions are not always immutable, as a villager in Côte d'Ivoire once learned.

Returning home to visit his pregnant wife, he found that she was ill and unable to draw water, and to help out he carried water for the household. But men in villages, by tradition, do not haul water, which is considered women's work. The other village men saw this as a threat to their status and pressured the husband to stop hauling water, which he refused to do. With his example, the tradition soon changed, and hauling water became acceptable for men in that village.

Along with their communalism, African societies are also hierarchical. Great deference is shown everywhere to age and status, although Africans within age-sets and social groups are egalitarian. This combination of hierarchy and egalitarianism will be encountered almost everywhere, but like many other cultural characteristics it can vary across the continent.

In Somalia, for example, when traveling on official business, drivers are usually invited to join in lunches with their passengers and to stay in the same accommodations. On a ten-hour trip from Mogadishu once, a Somali driver declared that he was tired, and without hesitation, he told one of his passengers, a senior Somali medical officer, that he would have to drive. Soon after, the doctor and the driver did indeed change places.

Congolese, by contrast, are more status conscious, as a U.S. public health adviser reports. While on tour in the countryside with Congo colleagues, she often stopped to visit local health officials and was invited to stay for lunch. Her African driver, however, was never invited to sit at the table but was told to go around back to the kitchen for something to eat.

The Expat and the Extended Family

> One does not remain for long in a town and yet remain uninvolved.
>
> —Yoruba proverb

The highest compliment made to an expatriate by an African is to be called "brother" or "sister." But does this mean that the expat has been accepted into an extended family? The answer is a qualified yes, *if* the expat is willing to be imposed upon and accept the responsibilities and obligations along with the benefits that go with membership in an African family. That's the downside.

Expats who help others in a family will be seen as patrons, and the family will likely come back for additional assistance. It works both ways, of course, and the expats are free to impose as well.

Obligations in Africa run deep, and foreigners will be expected to honor social obligations toward professional colleagues whom they may consider to be mere acquaintances. For one American woman, if she had declined to attend the wedding of an African secretary in an office where she was on short-term assignment, or failed to be at the funeral of the wife of an African from another office where she had worked some time before, the African colleagues involved would have been very upset.

The African family can also have surprising outreach, as an American woman learned when her African boyfriend in the United States invited his ex-wife's brother to share their apartment.

Foreigners should therefore not let themselves be drawn into an extended family unless they are prepared to play by African rules. Even those who have lived in Africa for several years and who may have become romantically involved with Africans will continue to be seen as outsiders unless they are willing to accept the responsibilities that go with the network of extended family and friends of Africa's communal societies.

Even after forming close friendships with Africans and feeling like "blood brothers," expats may still be regarded as outsiders. This should not be seen as a color barrier, because most Africans, with their sense of pride, self, and place, do not perceive color as a barrier to dealing with whites. But while their attitude toward outsiders transcends color, the "outsider syndrome" may nevertheless exist, as an American who lived in a guarded compound in Congo learned when all four wheels of her car were stolen one night. The theft must have taken time and made some significant noise, but none of the guards professed to have seen or heard anything.

While foreigners may be seen as outsiders, Africans can nevertheless be very protective of those they have befriended, especially women. The welfare of foreigners whom they know is a concern of Africans, who believe it would reflect badly on them should some harm befall their visitors. This concern includes accompanying a single woman, even where she may feel perfectly safe, and sitting with foreign friends who are ill.

One expat who was home once with a bad cold recalls being visited by an African colleague's mother who brought homemade cures of rendered fat from a sheep's-tail and honey mixed with garlic. The expat declined the sheep's tail fat but drank the honey with garlic; her cold was soon gone. And that was long before Western scientists discovered that garlic indeed has curative values.

Ethnicity and Diversity

> Tribalism is one of the most difficult African concepts to
> grasp, and one of the most essential in understanding Africa.
> —David Lamb, *The Africans*

Ethnicity is at the heart of African diversity. Ethnic groups,
commonly called tribes, embrace a number of local villages,
districts, lineages, and other social groupings that share common cultural values and are believed to descend from a common ancestor.

The term *tribe* (*tribu* in French), now considered pejorative
by some, was brought to Africa by Europeans in the nine-
teenth century in an attempt to classify Africans according to
language, culture, and history and, as one scholar has described it, "to fit the lines on the map."[9] Over generations,
however, one group of people may have adopted another's
language, pastoral nomads may have become farmers and vice
versa, and religions may have changed. But *tribe*, nevertheless, has come into common usage by the media, by many
historians and other scholars, and by Africans themselves
who do not see an insult in the use of the word.

In traditional African societies each ethnic group strove to
preserve the ways of its ancestors, and marriage outside the
tribe was rare. Today, however, mixed marriages are becoming more common and ethnic distinctions have blurred, particularly in urban areas as Africans move to the cities. But as
British anthropologist Colin M. Turnbull tells us,

> ...a respect for the ways of the ancestors *is* universal, and this
> respect encourages the desire to perpetuate these ways in the
> belief that this will bring good fortune in this life, if not in
> the next.[10]

Within the ethnic or clan system, there are bonds of compassion and powers of identity that may be inconceivable to

the Western mind. As one African has described it, "If I have walked for a very long way and am tired and can walk no further, I will collapse with exhaustion. But if someone says the name of my clan, I will get up and walk on."[11]

Chieftancy, one of the oldest institutions in Africa, not only survives but thrives, especially in anglophone countries where the British preserved local institutions and governed through them. Although abolished in some countries, chieftancy is a force to be reckoned with in countries where it still exists.

Ghanaian chiefs, for example, are recognized by the constitution, perform local administrative functions, and serve as judges in tribal courts recognized by law. "In Ghana," writes Dia, "...the chief is the symbol of unity among his people, the spiritual and secular head of the clan, the sovereign ruler, the commander-in-chief, and the highest judicial authority."[12]

As an indication of chieftancy prestige, many educated professionals are today giving up jobs in the city to return to their native regions as chiefs. Others are serving part-time, alternating between work in the city and the countryside. Nelson Mandela, for example, is a chief of the Thembu tribe. As president of South Africa, Mandela is at home in the world of politics and government but he is equally at home in village meetings with his ethnic elders and speaking his native Khosa language.

One African tradition regards the tribe as the human race and the village as the world. Ethnic ties, accordingly, are very strong. Politicians are expected to provide jobs for members of their ethnic group or clan; academic administrators are pressured to admit relatives as students; and businesspeople, to do favors for their kinfolk. Clan and ethnic ties, of course, are found in many if not all of the world's cultures, but they are particularly strong among Africans. Westerners living in Africa may find it difficult to understand and accommodate to how such ties can influence African behavior.

When Brian Davies, a Briton, was hired as managing director of the newly privatized Kenya Airways in 1992, he soon
learned that senior management posts were awarded on the
basis of political or ethnic affiliation, and the airline's management hierarchy mirrored not only the Kenyan civil service but also the country's social structure. Davies initially
underestimated the importance of ethnic allegiances:

> We would say we are only interested in the Kenya Airways
> tribe. But in fact we were ignoring reality. Tribe is a powerful
> aspect here that cannot be ignored. For example, people find
> it difficult to discipline someone from their own tribe. Things
> are getting better but we have to learn to live with that
> factor.[13]

But beyond the bounds of kinship and clan it can be a
different story. As the noted Kenyan political scientist and
author Ali A. Mazrui writes, "...the very fact that we have a
highly developed sense of responsibility towards our own
kinsmen...has resulted in diluting our capacity to empathize
with those that are much further from us."[14] In the West,
news of a natural catastrophe in another part of the world
brings forth floods of compassion and offers of assistance. The
African, adds Mazrui, is much more moved by the day-to-day
problems of a distant kinsman than a dramatic upheaval in a
remote part of the world.[15]

Allegiance, therefore, is primarily to kinfolk and not the
state, and many of Africa's ethnic groups are not yet reconciled to living together in one state. Such emphasis on ethnicity is one reason why so many African states have found
it difficult to build a national consensus and why many have
experienced explosions of ethnic violence. To understand
African politics, one must first understand African ethnicity.

Nigeria, with its more than one hundred million people,
has more than 270 linguistic groups, three major ethnic
groups, and several minor ones. A resident of Nigeria, if
asked in the United States what nation he is from, will

identify himself as a Nigerian. But the same man, if asked in Nigeria, will say that he is a Yoruba, Igbo, Hausa, Fulani, or one of the other ethnic groups.

The secession from Nigeria of the Christian Igbo (also written as Ibo) in 1967 and their creation of the oil-rich nation-state of Biafra led to a thirty-month civil war which caused hundreds of thousands of military and civilian casualties and divided many of the world's major powers, which took sides in the bitter and violent struggle. A similar polarizing rivalry developed in the 1990s when a military junta dominated by the Muslim Hausa and Fulani, which had seized political power in 1985, annulled an election in which a Yoruba had been chosen as president.

Ethnic diversity and discord are also found in other countries. Rwanda and Burundi have Hutu majorities and Tutsi minorities, and since independence the world community has been shocked by repeated surges of mass murder between the two ethnic groups in each country.

The mostly tall and lighter-skinned Tutsis, about 14 percent of the population in both countries, were traditionally herders. The Hutus, 85 percent of the people and cultivators by tradition, are mostly short and darker-skinned. In precolonial times, the two people lived together peacefully, although the pastoral Tutsis ruled as kings and chiefs and were dominant over the agricultural Hutus. Tutsi domination continued under the colonialists, first the Germans and then the Belgians, both of whom ruled through the Tutsi, giving them even more status and arousing increased Hutu resentment.

Over time, intermarriage between Tutsis and Hutus has reduced their physical differences, but disparities in status and wealth have continued, with Tutsis dominating the army, business, and civil service. The enmity, moreover, has persisted although the people of both ethnic groups are mostly Catholic, speak the same language, and have the same customs. During the 1972 ethnic violence in Burundi, some

150,000 Hutus were massacred by Tutsis. Violence begets violence, and in 1994 more than half a million Tutsis were slaughtered by Hutus in Rwanda over a two-month period. In the ethnic cleansing that followed, more than one million Rwandans, most of them Hutus, took refuge in neighboring Zaire and the carnage continued. From refugee camps in Zaire, Hutu militants staged cross-border raids against the Tutsi-led government in Rwanda, and Tutsi forces within Zaire raided the refugee camps and clashed with the Zairian military in Zaire's eastern border provinces. (See the section, "Coastal West and Central Africa," for subsequent developments.)

Ethnic diversity, however, is not the sole cause of African strife. Somalia, one of the few African countries with one ethnic group, one language, and one religion, has nevertheless seen fierce warfare between rival clans and warlords. And in Congo (Brazzaville), as the Republic of Congo is commonly known, the worst violence has been between closely related ethnic groups.

Tribalism is still very much a part of the African scene and is likely to remain so for the foreseeable future. Yet Africans, despite their many ethnic and linguistic differences, have more in common culturally than their diversity might indicate. In later chapters, we will be discussing how these similarities and dissimilarities may affect Western visitors in their business and social dealings with Africans.

The Colonial Legacy

...the European colonial system, brief but huge in its consequences....
 —Basil Davidson, *Africa in History*

When the European powers began to carve up Africa at the Berlin Conference of 1884-85, they imposed artificial and illogical boundaries based on the balance of power and their alliances in Europe but without regard for the ethnic, cultural, religious, and linguistic homogeneity that existed in Africa before their arrival. "[T]he colonial state was born out of wedlock," writes Mazrui, "and the sin is visited upon succeeding generations."[16]

The "scramble for Africa" began, and in a mere twenty years almost all of Africa, with the exception of Ethiopia and Liberia, was seized and colonized by Britain, France, Belgium, Germany, Portugal, Spain, and Italy. The boundaries they staked out separated, in some places, similar ethnolinguistic groups and, in other places, cobbled together in a single state peoples who were dissimilar and, in some cases, long-time adversaries. As Turnbull describes it:

> ...*nation* is still, in many areas, a foreign, meaningless term; the tribe is to them what the nation is to us, and the artificial boundaries drawn by colonial powers, often linking hostile tribes together and separating friendly ones, sometimes cutting a single tribe in two, mean nothing to the tribal African.[17]

The Gambia, for example, located in the middle of francophone West Africa, is a narrow, elongated state that follows the course of the Gambia River as it wends its way inland from the Atlantic. The anglophone Gambians, however, are ethnically and linguistically no different from the francophone Senegalese who live just across The Gambia's borders to the north, east, and south.

In Congo, the official language is French, but there are also four officially recognized African languages as well as many other languages and dialects spoken by the more than two hundred ethnic groups.

The stresses and strains caused by such ethnolinguistic crazy quilts have handicapped nation building in many states and delayed the development of a national consensus. Because an African's primary allegiance is to his village and clan and secondarily to his ethnic group, consensus is easily reached within tribes but much more difficult to attain between tribes.

Yet, as irrational as the artificial boundaries may be, they have rarely been a cause of conflict between states, and African political leaders, intent on nurturing nationalism, have shown no great interest in changing them. As British historians Roland Oliver and J. D. Fage point out,

> ...it is remarkable how sacrosanct the former colonial boundaries became for African statesmen, despite their earlier nationalist criticisms of them as artificial and ethnically divisive. The principle that each state should respect the sovereignty and the territorial integrity of the others was indeed enshrined in the Constitution of the Organization of African Unity....[18]

Whatever their faults, the current boundaries are considered untouchable by most African leaders and policymakers. Although Africa's development needs, as well as its cultures, often cut across borders, realigning them could start a slide down a slippery slope that could create a multitude of states, few of them viable. Nevertheless, some Africans today, noting that farmers and herders move freely across borders in search of water and grazing grounds much as their ancestors did in precolonial times, now advocate modifying the artificial borders to facilitate freedom of movement and regional cooperation between neighboring states. As the twentieth century draws to a close, African borders may be entering a period of transition toward greater fluidity, much as they were in precolonial times, when they were periodically redrawn.

The British policy of indirect colonial rule was adopted to maintain public security as cheaply and effectively as possible. Accordingly, the British interfered in local affairs only when necessary and supported traditional tribal leaders whose authority was left largely intact although subject to British review. Indirect British rule also led to the creation of an

African civil service that was better trained and numerically stronger than in the French colonies and provided a better basis for self-government. The records of the Belgians and Portuguese in this regard were the worst. As Newt Gingrich wrote (in his doctoral dissertation), "Belgium ran the Congo as a profitable business. It wanted the largest possible profit from the minimum investment of capital and manpower."[19]

In training for the civil service, the colonial powers, under a policy of "divide and conquer," often favored one ethnic group, usually a minority—in Nigeria, Igbo over Hausa, Fulani, and Yoruba; in The Gambia, Aku over Mandinka; and in Rwanda and Burundi, Tutsi over Hutu. Such favoritism gave these groups an advantage and laid the basis for ethnic conflict in later years.

The French, on the other hand, ousted most of the existing chiefs and appointed French-educated Africans in their place, passing political power to a small elite group that they had created in their own image—educated in French schools, speaking good French, and with tastes typically French. The existence of this elite helps to explain France's special relationship with its former African colonies and accounts for the French ambiance in many cities of francophone Africa.

French government in the colonies, moreover, was highly centralized, as in metropolitan France, and its cultural policy was assimilationist, seeking, as many have described it, to make Africans culturally into black French people. In so doing, they prepared the foundation for nationhood in each of their colonies and at the same time fostered a common identity among the cultural elites of francophone Africa.

"[W]hile Britain trained bureaucrats," writes American correspondent David Lamb, "France trained leaders."[20] Moreover, maintains Lamb, "...the legacy of French colonialism is much stronger in Africa today than that of Britain. France, in fact, retains extraordinary influence today in its former colonies, and in many cases remains the paramount economic and cultural force dominating their affairs."[21]

European forms of government are another legacy of colonialism. In the early years of independence the new African governments were modeled after those of the colonial powers, which all too often provided a poor match with African traditions. And although the reins of government were handed over to Africans, the former colonial powers, especially the French, played a major role in determining who held those reins and for how long.

Independence, moreover, came swiftly and without adequate preparation. Faced with ethnic divisions, a lack of self-governing experience on the national scale, overwhelming economic problems, and inflated expectations for the future, many of the new countries have seesawed between military and civilian rule on the one hand, and one-party and multi-party governments on the other, often with extremes of dictatorship and anarchy. As Mazrui explains, "...although one can teach other people how to speak the English language, or how to practice Christianity, one cannot teach them how to govern themselves. That they must learn for themselves."[22]

Also contributing to instability were the African armies left behind by the colonial powers, armies that have not hesitated to intervene in the political process by staging military coups. Writing of military governments, Wole Soyinka, Nigeria's Nobel laureate for literature, speaks of "...the ignoble and retrogressive role of the military in the African crisis, their wastrel, unaccounted-for spending, their corruption, their alienated apprehension of society and nationhood, and their brutal repression of civil aspirations."[23] The troops, moreover, are mostly underpaid and undereducated and often prey on innocent civilians. These armies, says Ghanaian historian A. Adu Boahen, "...are the greatest millstones around the necks of African leaders, and the future of the continent is going to be determined very much on how these armies are dealt with."[24]

Government centralization and swollen bureaucracies are

also legacies of colonial rule. Power is concentrated in the capital cities, and when one group or tribe controls the center, it is often unwilling to share power. Dominated in many cases by a "Big Man" and backed by the military, the one-party governments and their burgeoning bureaucracies deter the development of democratic governance, stifle private initiative, and provide temptations to corruption.

The cultivation of cash crops for export at the expense of subsistence farming for domestic consumption is another legacy of colonialism. With the arrival of the colonists, single-crop economies became prevalent in many countries; and the use of land, labor, and other agricultural inputs to grow coffee, cocoa, cotton, peanuts, and tobacco diverted resources from family farms that formerly fed entire villages.

Until recently, it was fashionable to blame the colonial powers for Africa's misfortunes. To be sure, the colonials must share responsibility for Africa's current ills, but they ruled Africa for little more than half a century and many of Africa's wounds today are self-inflicted. All the blame, as many Africans have now come to realize, can no longer be placed on the colonials.

At meetings on development attended by Africans and foreign donor agencies, two diverse views on colonialism are often evident. One group seems to be saying, "Our problems are all due to colonialism. Why are you foreign donors not doing more for us?" A second group counters with, "We acknowledge our past problems and their causes but we must also take responsibility for our current difficulties."

This "discourse of recrimination," which he says is so familiar in Africa, is described by Paulin J. Hountondji, a professor of philosophy in Benin:

> ...we constantly tend to reject onto others the responsibility for all our misfortunes and misdeeds. Yesterday it was imperialism, colonialism and neo-colonialism, today it is the World Bank and the IMF, tomorrow it will probably be new reincarnations of the same demon.[25]

The main legacy of colonialism, however, is psychological, says Boahen, and

...manifests itself in the belief so prevalent among Africans... that government and all public property and finance belong, not to the people, but to the...government, and could and should therefore be taken advantage of at the least opportunity, a belief which leads to the often reckless dissipation and misuse of public funds and property.[26]

Another psychological impact, adds Boahen, is ostentatious and flamboyant lifestyles, because

...while the colonialists taught their...subjects the Protestant work ethic, the drive for worldly success, and the acquisitive instinct, they did not...inculcate in them the puritanical spirit which emphasized frugality and very little consumption.... Thus, while in Europe this full ethic led to the rise of capitalism...and with it the scientific and technological breakthrough, in the African colonies it only generated the ostentatious consumption habits which are still very much with us.[27]

The custom of consumption continues, claims Claude Ake, one of Nigeria's leading intellectuals, who laments his country's loss of the hard-work ethic that once made it an agricultural powerhouse and sent its sons and daughters to excel in universities throughout the world.

One of the most challenging problems is that we prefer to consume without producing. That is why we contest political power so fiercely. Political power gives us abundant coercive resources to appropriate and consume.[28]

Francophones, Anglophones, and Other "-phones"

> Francophone sub-Saharan Africa was born of an African mother and a European father; from the union of two old civilizations emerged a new civilization.
>
> —Patrick Manning,
> *Francophone Sub-Saharan Africa, 1880-1985*

Francophone and anglophone Africans do differ, and francophone Africa may indeed appear to be a new civilization, as maintained by Patrick Manning, a U.S. professor of history and African American studies. But while the differences will be apparent to visitors to the continent, one can hardly imagine an African saying, "We Francophones (or Anglophones) believe...." More likely, given the priority of ethnicity, it will be "We Wolof" or "We Ashanti."

Yet, whatever their views on colonialism, Africans do reflect many characteristics of the former colonial powers, and in more ways than they might suspect. Wherever the colonials ruled, they left an imprint on the culture and character of the urbanized Africans foreign visitors are most likely to encounter. In rural areas the Western imprint will be much less evident or even nonexistent.

Sub-Saharan Africa has a more or less equal number of francophone and anglophone countries—twenty francophone and eighteen anglophone. In addition, there are five lusophone (Portuguese-speaking) countries, and one Spanish-speaking. Some Italian is still spoken in Ethiopia, Eritrea, and Somalia; and German influence lingers in Togo, Cameroon, and Namibia. In the latter, moreover, German is widely spoken, and a visitor can walk streets named Kaiser Wilhelm Strasse. In Ethiopia Amharic is the official language; in Sudan, Arabic; and in Kenya and Tanzania, Kiswahili (along with English). In South Africa and Namibia the white Afrikaners, and many blacks as well, speak Afrikaans, a simplified version of the High Dutch brought by the original settlers in 1652. (For a listing of official languages in the various countries, see Appendix A.) In these pages, we focus on some of the differences which a visitor may encounter between the two major language groups, Francophone and Anglophone.

French and English serve not only as a lingua franca among a country's various ethnic groups but also as a common language with other African states and the international community. Without a common language most Africans would simply not be able to communicate with each other across ethnic or state lines. Knowing a European language, moreover, has long been recognized in Africa as a valuable tool for career and social advancement.

English and French, however, are not spoken everywhere, as visitors will soon learn. In francophone countries it is rather easy to find an African who speaks some English but in anglophone countries an African who speaks French is a rarity. Visitors who speak both English *and* French will have no difficulty communicating with Africans in large cities.

All of Britain's former sub-Saharan colonies have retained English as an official language, as all former French and Belgian colonies have retained French. Only in Cameroon are both French and English official languages. Even in Senegal, where most of the population speaks Wolof, French is the official language. But while only a small percentage of Africans in any country may speak French or English well, that elite has the political and economic power as well as the social standing. The rest of the population may speak a passable French or English or a creole French or pidgin English or, as is more likely, no European language at all.

In the elementary schools of francophone and anglophone Africa, instruction is in French or English, although in some countries it may be in local languages for the first few years. At the secondary level, however, as in higher education, English or French is universally the language of instruction. One difficulty with teaching in local languages is that not all of them are written or have printed literature and other teaching materials.

Universities and secondary schools in both francophone and anglophone Africa maintain the educational standards of metropolitan France, Belgium, and Britain. Their degrees and diplomas are recognized in most cases, and qualified students are able to continue their studies in Europe. African universities, moreover, often have a "sister" relationship with a French, Belgian, or British university that facilitates exchanges of students and faculty.

France has been particularly active in encouraging African students to study in France. In 1992, 74,941 African students (including North Africans) were enrolled in French institutions of higher education, more than half the total number of foreign students in France. For the United Kingdom the corresponding number was 9,325.[29]

But while the colonial influence begins with language and education, it also affects many other aspects of culture. To Americans, Anglophones can appear "veddy" British and Francophones *très français*.

Anglophones tend to dress more formally; in the cities, men wear shirts and ties to the office and often jackets as well. As Nelson Mandela explains, "While I abhorred the notion of British imperialism, I never rejected the trappings of British style and manners."[30] Mandela and many other anglophone leaders, especially in Southern and East Africa, often appear in public in their well-tailored, English-cut, three-piece suits, even when the high heat would call for cooler clothing. Francophones tend to dress more casually, but when they do dress formally, they will often wear traditional African dress which expats may misinterpret as casual.

In francophone countries visitors will find French restaurants and pâtisseries and shops with cheeses, pâtés, and other French delicacies. Anglophones are addicted to their morning and afternoon tea breaks. Francophones drive on the right, while Anglophones drive on the left, although some anglophone countries have recently shifted to right-hand drive. And some Francophones, when greeting close friends, follow the French custom of kissing alternate cheeks several times. (The number of kisses depends on local custom and can vary, even from city to city.) The differences, however, run much deeper than dress, driving, and greetings.

Mixed marriages, for instance, were quite common with the French but not with the British. An African could become a Frenchman but never a Brit. As U.S. sociologist Immanuel Wallerstein has observed, "Africans in England were never absorbed into English life, as Africans in Paris were absorbed into French life."[31] Educated Africans could serve in the French parliament, as some did, rising even to cabinet level in the government.

Religion also plays a role in differences between Francophones and Anglophones. With the exception of the Sahelian states, which have Muslim majorities, most of francophone sub-Sahara is Catholic whereas Protestantism is stronger in anglophone countries. Within francophone Africa, however, the French language has facilitated communication between Catholics and Muslims and has helped to avoid a polarization between the two religions.

Language and culture have long been important elements of French foreign policy, what the French call their *mission civilisatrice*. The French have worked hard at it and still do, as Jean-Pierre Cot, a former French Minister of [Foreign] Cooperation, has explained:

> There is no sector in which French cooperation is more attached than that of culture. The promotion and the dissemination of our language, the propagation of our ideas, of our art, and, more recently, of our technical knowledge, have always been our most important preoccupation.[32]

France's feelings for its former colonies are equally strong. Some 300,000 French citizens still live in Africa, and many French companies rely on Africa for their export markets. A virtual requirement for election to higher office in France, reports the *New York Times*, is a campaign trip to Africa, which is still referred to as France's *pré-carré* (domain).[33] French armed forces are still stationed in several of its former colonies, and France has military cooperation agreements with many of the others. Since 1964, writes the *Times*, "...France has intervened on the continent every other year on average," and its interventions have often served to maintain friendly governments in power.[34]

But such paternalistic practices are not appreciated by all French. Lionel Jospin, French Socialist Party candidate for president in 1995 (and who was named prime minister in 1997), has called for reform of France's relations with the continent, saying that France should "...begin to deal with Africa a bit more like we deal with other countries."[35] Many Africans, however, interpreted Jospin's remark as an attack on "the system of industrial kickbacks, political slush funds, and other forms of influence peddling that French critics say have long characterized France's relations with the continent."[36] After becoming prime minister, Mr. Jospin announced a thorough review of French policy toward Africa, which is expected to reduce the number of French troops in Africa and to change how France distributes its development assistance there.

The manner in which people converse *dans la francophonie* (in the francophone mode) can also differ from the anglophone. Educated Francophones enjoy posing ideas in philosophical terms. At meetings debate and formal presentations are relished, and everyone expects to have his or her say at the podium. Anglophones are more interested in the practical discussions that follow the theoretical talk.

Francophones often address the nuances of words and will debate which one best expresses an idea under discussion. To finalize a report, they may want to discuss the form, grammar, and spelling before taking up the substance. At one recent East African conference attended by Francophones and Anglophones, participants were divided into small discussion groups, but by the time the Anglophones had completed a good part of their assignments, the Francophones were still arguing over the titles of their flip charts.

Discourse with Francophones is also very cordial, and when they do disagree, it is done with politesse. If you hear the words *juste pour completer* (to complete [my remarks] properly), be prepared for a polite explanation of why your interlocutor disagrees with you.

Anglophones and Francophones also have their own ways of conducting the question and answer periods which follow formal presentations. Anglophones will usually take each question as it is asked and give the answer. Francophones, however, will "open a list"—that is, go around the room and record the names of persons who have questions and then go back and ask each questioner, one by one, to pose his or her question, at which time each question will be discussed in depth and answered. This takes longer and often annoys Anglophones. At one West African workshop a foreign observer found that the Francophones had difficulty formulating objectives, creating strategies, devising implementation plans, and working out schedules to achieve their objectives. The more pragmatic Anglophones at the workshop (Ghanaians in this case) were appalled by the difficulty their fellow Africans were having in devising strategies and plans.

Women's urban fashions also differ between Francophones and Anglophones. Francophone dress is more colorful, very chic, and stands out in a crowd. Women follow the changing fashions more closely, and even poor women are aware of what is in vogue with respect to embroidery patterns, how dresses are cut, and how cloth is tied around the waist. In Côte d'Ivoire cities, women wear tailored African dresses to work rather than the traditional *boubou* (long gown). Abidjan and Dakar are reputed to be the fashion capitals of sub-Saharan Africa.

The arts have also flourished in francophone Africa, assisted often by government funding. Dance companies, drawing on tribal traditions, have brought their artistry to audiences in African countries and throughout the world. Wood carving, basketry, and weaving have drawn critical acclaim both within Africa and further afield where they can be found in the shops and museums of Europe and the Americas. Also strong in francophone Africa have been the plastic arts, which influenced the creativity of a generation of Parisian-based artists such as Picasso, Braque, and Modigliani. And Congo's pop music, which combines local African music, Latin rhythms, Caribbean beats, and American jazz has proven popular throughout Africa and beyond. Popular at parties as well as discos, it makes you want to dance.

What all this adds up to for francophone Africa is a new cultural composite and a high level of artistry which have attracted world attention. As Patrick Manning describes it:

> The emergent francophone African culture worked through the medium of the French language, it facilitated the development and the communication of numerous national traditions, it emphasized the commonality of all in a cosmopolitan francophone African culture, and it reinforced a broader pan-African identity which extended to all of Africa and to the African diaspora in the New World and, increasingly, in Europe.[37]

Does it really matter to the rest of the world, and to the major powers in particular, whether an African today is anglophone or francophone? It apparently did in 1996 when the United Nations was searching for a successor to Secretary General Boutros Boutros-Ghali. U.N. Security Council members agreed that the successor should be an African, but the United States and Britain resolutely opposed candidates from French-speaking Africa, while France just as resolutely opposed an English speaker. After a week of sparring and informal straw votes, consensus eventually prevailed and Kofi Annan of anglophone Ghana (who also speaks French) was elected to the important post. He is the first sub-Saharan African to hold the position.

Religions and Folk Beliefs

> Religion permeates all aspects of African traditional socie-
> ties. It is a way of life in which the whole community is
> involved, and as such it is identical with life itself. Even
> antireligious persons still have to be involved in the lives of
> their religious communities....
>   —Ambrose Moyo, "Religion in Africa"

Africans are a very spiritual people. Life is short and difficult,
and Africans, like people everywhere, need beliefs to explain
and give meaning to the world they live in. Among their
beliefs are Christianity and Islam as well as traditional African religions which embrace spirits, divination, and magic.

Two-thirds of sub-Saharan Africa is either Muslim or
Christian. Islam prevails to the north in a broad band across
the continent, and in the east along the Indian Ocean. Christianity, both Catholic and Protestant, predominates in
Coastal West Africa, Central Africa, Southern Africa, and in
East Africa inland from the coast. Also common are independent African churches which broke away from established
churches during the colonial period in protest against their
European domination. The independents have their own lit-
urgy and beliefs, and audience participation is marked by
spirited prayer, pulsating musical styles, and what has been
aptly described as "joyful noise." Religion in Africa, notes
Harden, "...is more about joy than guilt."[38]

But Western churches, Catholic as well as Protestant, have
also adopted many African traditional practices. Priests and
ministers may dance around altars, and church music may
embody the beat of village drums. Religious offerings can
include gourds, grains, and fruit. Christian creeds have incorporated many aspects of traditional African religions, and
Islam has adopted or at least tolerated many folk practices.

Among the Fang people of Gabon, for example, the relationship between a boy and his father's brother is closer than
with the father himself, and uncles are responsible for raising

their nephews. Accordingly, when the Fang were converted to Christianity, they initially saw Jesus as the nephew rather than the son of God. And in their patrilineal society, according to Herskovits, "...where the mother-son relationship is not held to be important, the Virgin was believed to have been the daughter, wife and sister of Jesus rather than his mother."[39]

Christianity came to Africa mostly by sea, but Islam came overland (the east coast of Africa excepted), literally on the backs of camels, and has been more prevalent inland. A civilization and way of life as well as a religion, Islam was spread from Arabia and North Africa, in some places and times by jihad (holy war) conquests, and elsewhere, peacefully, by Muslim merchants traversing trade routes—down the coast of East Africa, up the Nile, across the Sahara, and eventually into West Africa. Today, the northern third of the continent is Muslim. The central third would also be Muslim were it not for the arrival of the Europeans who brought Christianity and slowed Islam's spread. Senegal, Mali, Guinea (Conakry), and Niger are 90 percent Muslim. Estimates of Nigeria's Muslim people range from one-third to an absolute majority, and it has a larger Muslim population than any single Arab country. Islam today is said to be the fastest-growing religion in Africa.

Christianity came with the white colonial powers which sought to transform traditional African societies and beliefs. Islam, by contrast, has been more of an indigenous phenomenon, since in sub-Sahara it was spread largely by Africans. Islam is also more in accord with the African proclivity for the practical—a propensity for the present as opposed to the hereafter. Islam, moreover, does not require a baptismal conversion and is more tolerant of traditional beliefs such as divination, magic, witchcraft, and sorcery, as long as the omnipotence of Allah is not questioned. New adherents can become Muslims over a period of years and even generations, while retaining many of their old beliefs and customs, such as polygyny, which Islam allows.

Africans being courted by Islam and Christianity, muses Mazrui, "...have had to choose between the discipline of being satisfied with only one wife and the discipline of being satisfied with only soft drinks." In many instances, adds Mazrui, "...the choice has not by any means been easy."[40] Despite Africa's tradition of multiple wives, many Africans today have opted for monogamy. Tanzania's founding father and first president, Julius Nyerere, for example, the son of a tribal chief with twenty-two wives, became a Catholic and had only one—for forty-three years as of this writing.[41]

Islam also brought many of its traditions to Africa. An important one is the observance of Ramadan during the ninth month of the Islamic lunar calendar, which marks the days when Allah in the seventh century began to reveal to the prophet Muhammad the Qur'an (Koran), the Muslim scripture. During this month-long period, observant Muslims fast and abstain from sexual and other sensual pleasures from dawn to dusk. Ramadan is also a period of self-discipline and reflection as well as late-night dining and socializing with family and friends after the fast is broken. During the day, however, business activity slows and office hours are curtailed.

Other Islamic traditions include the hajj, a pilgrimage to the holy city of Mecca, which every Muslim is expected to make at least once during a lifetime, if physically and financially possible. Men and women pray separately, and at some mosques women may be required to use a separate entrance. Whichever entrance is used, shoes should be removed. Also, alcoholic beverages and pork are proscribed, and it is considered impolite to drink in the presence of a Muslim. Those who must drink should ask permission first.

Traditional African religions based on the spirit world coexist side by side with Christianity and Islam and often compete with them. Indeed, the largest number of believers in sub-Saharan Africa today may consist of animists or followers of other traditional religions. Like all beliefs, traditional

African religions seek to explain the nature of the universe and the place of humans in it. They prescribe practices, ceremonies, sacred objects, and festivals to be observed. They define values and morals that determine how people should live and relate to each other. And they have their officials—priests, ritual elders, medicine men, diviners, and rainmakers.

Animism, a term mistakenly used to describe all traditional religions, is based on the belief that souls or spirits inhabit all natural phenomena. As with many other African religions, animism can count devout Christians as well as Muslims among its many adherents. "There is an amazingly close overlap between the basic ideas of Islam and Christianity, and of the African religions," Bohannan and Curtin have noted.[42]

A similar view is expressed by a prominent prince of the Roman Catholic Church. "Much of African belief is animism," says Francis Cardinal Arinze of Nigeria, "and animism is very close to Catholicism, so there is natural attraction, an affinity." In animism, continues the cardinal, "there is one God, spirits good and evil, worship of ancestors, rituals. I was born an animist."[43] Conversions to Christianity and Islam continue, but as Moyo maintains, "Africans will continue to preserve in their new faiths elements of the old, as they have always done."[44]

In Benin, a West African country whose inhabitants are mostly Roman Catholic, January 10 is a national holiday in honor of Vodu, the traditional animist religion of its people. Vodu, or *vodou*, the word for gods in the Fon language, is the forerunner of what we know as Vaudou in Haiti, and voodoo elsewhere in the Americas.

Whatever their religion, most Africans, including animists, believe in a Supreme Being, creator of heaven and earth, ruler of the universe, and in this sense they are monotheists. Every African language has a word for God. Atheism is alien, and as a Swahili proverb says, "All things are done by God." In West Africa, this God is called *Nyame* or some variation thereof; in Central and Southern Africa, various versions of the word *Nzambi* are used. In African terms, this God is seen as the "Great Ancestor" or "Big Chief."

Despite their belief in a Supreme Being, most Africans worship God through a pantheon of lesser divinities which, like God, may be male or female. In times of great danger, Africans will appeal to their God directly, but at other times they are more likely to call on lesser divinities such as the spirits of natural objects that may be close at hand. Living close to nature and in equilibrium with it, Africans have always held natural objects and phenomena in awe. Spirits of the sun, moon, sky, and weather as well as earth, rocks, water, and trees are believed to be created by God as intermediaries between God and humans, having much the same status that patron saints often have for Christians.

A hidden mystical power is believed to be available to these spirits as well as to certain human beings who can use it for good or evil. As John S. Mbiti, a Kenyan-born Anglican priest, explains,

> It is the knowledge of this mystical power which is used to help other people (especially in healing, rainmaking, finding the cause of misfortunes and troubles, detecting thieves, and so on) or to harm them. When it is used harmfully, it is regarded as evil magic, witchcraft or sorcery; and it may also be used in curses.[45]

Sounds strange? Not really, when we consider that many Westerners today believe in demons, hexes, spells, satanism, and other sinister forces, while in Russia belief in folk medicine, witchcraft, and psychic healing is still strong. As Herskovits has observed, "...the spell of the witches in 'Macbeth' would be understandable to any African without explanation."[46] Also understandable would be the efforts by clergymen from six Christian churches who gathered in Blanco, Texas, in 1996 to lead local residents in prayer for rain to end a drought that had devastated their farming community.[47] And Africans would also understand why, at the time of the winter solstice, many of us in the West still bring into our homes the trees which wood spirits in Europe were once believed to inhabit.

In his novel *Things Fall Apart*, the celebrated Nigerian writer Chinua Achebe describes how his hero, a village elder, had a "medicine house" where he kept wooden symbols of his personal god and ancestral spirits. "He worshipped them," wrote Achebe, "with sacrifices of kola nut, food and palm wine, and offered prayers to them on behalf of himself, his three wives, and eight children."[48]

Spirits also have feelings, and they are not always good and kind. If disturbed, they can inflict harm and cause sickness and death. A woman who fails to conceive may believe that she is being punished for her behavior by evil spirits and must do something to assuage them.

Belief in the spirits of forebears, a practice loosely described as ancestor worship (although "veneration" is a more accurate description) is also strong, and some African bishops have urged the Pope to include ancestor worship in the Catholic Church's ecumenical initiatives.

Africans live in a continuum of their family's existence that includes ancestors, the living, and future generations, and it is not unusual to be able to trace families back for as many as ten generations, based solely on oral history. Ancestral or human spirits, which Westerners might call souls or ghosts, include the recently deceased as well as the long gone. Remembered and revered, these ancestors are believed to reside close to their former homes, are considered a part of the family, and are consulted on important issues. Whatever concerns the family will also be of concern to the ancestors.

Because ancestors expect to be reborn into the same family, they can use their powers to ensure the survival and well-being of their lineage. "In African society," wrote *Life* magazine editor Robert Coughlan, "the new child does not 'take after' his late relative, he *is* that relative."[49] Or, as a Chaya proverb says, "He who leaves a child, lives eternally."

Ancestors must be shown respect and must not be offended, as Benin's newly elected president, Mathieu Kerekou, a born-again Christian, learned in 1996, when he omitted a reference to ancestors in taking his oath of office. When two citizens complained to the country's constitutional court, the court forced the new president to retake his oath of office, swearing to respect the constitution "before God, *the spirits of the ancestors* [italics added], the nation, and before the people...."[50]

If not treated properly, ancestor spirits may become angry and punish their descendants, and to play it safe family members may pour drinks for their ancestors or leave bits of food for them on the ground before the family itself sits down to eat. When opening a bottle of beer or gin, Africans may symbolically pour a few drops on the ground as a libation.

This is not strange either, when we consider that in Japan, one of the world's most technologically advanced countries, ancestor veneration is still practiced by followers of Shintoism, Japan's traditional faith since ancient times, and many Japanese farmers still believe that every natural object has a spirit. And in Russia today, Orthodox Christians bring their freshly baked *kulich*, the traditional Easter cake, to church to be blessed by a priest, and then deposit morsels on the graves of their ancestors.

Closer to home for Americans, Hispanic residents of San Antonio, Texas, observe *El Dia de Los Muertos* (Day of the Dead) on November 2, when they honor the dearly departed by placing their favorite snacks, smokes, and drinks on grave sites, a custom that predates the arrival of Europeans in the Americas. Ancestor worship and animism were practiced by the peoples of the Americas and Europe long before the arrival of Christianity, which should tell us something about how similar we humans are.

As might be expected in societies that revere ancestors and take care not to anger them, funerals in Africa are big social events, with bands, beer, entertainment, and lots to eat, all intended to give loved ones a proper send-off. Festive funerals mark not only the importance of ancestors and the reverence due them but also celebrate the strength of the family and the continuation of its lineage. Relatives and friends are expected to attend, and they can look forward to being well fed even if the family goes broke in the process. The older the deceased, the bigger and better the funeral, and the more costly.

Designer coffins are the rage in Ghana, hand-hewn in a shape appropriate to the occupation of the deceased—a loaf of bread for a baker, a fish for a fisherman, even a bush taxi for a cab driver. Anniversaries of deaths are also celebrated, almost like birthdays in the West, and to mark the death of a long-deceased ancestor a family may give a big dinner party.

Magic, sorcery, and witchcraft also figure prominently in the lives of Africans. "Witchcraft and sorcery," as Turnbull tells us, "are not the exotic things in Africa that they are to us; they are perfectly practical, understandable forces that can be wielded, to some extent, by almost anyone."[51]

Magic potions are meant to fertilize the infertile, protect the healthy, and succor the sick. Camara Laye, a Guinean member of the Malinke people, tells how his father kept a series of pots hanging over the head of his bed containing extracts from plants and the barks of trees. They were the most important things in the hut, writes Laye:

>...they contained the magic charms, those mysterious liquids that keep evil spirits at bay and, smeared on the body, make it invulnerable to black magic. My father, before he went to bed, never failed to smear his body with a little liquid, first one, then another, for each charm had its own peculiar property....[52]

Such practices persist in cities as well as villages. According to Herskovits, "Belief in magic, in the efficacy of aboriginal medicines, and in divination is, indeed, one of the most persistently and widely retained traditions in the African urban scene."[53]

Amulets are worn as protection against witchcraft and sorcery, which are believed to cause illness. Talismans protect their owners by giving strength, health, and magical powers. Soldiers smear bush "medicine" on their bodies to protect against bullets. Urbanites will sacrifice a goat in their driveways to thank ancestors for a new home.

Wole Soyinka tells how he once wanted to sacrifice a goat, not in Africa but in Chicago, where one of his plays was being staged. Everything had gone wrong, says Soyinka—his assistant director had a car accident on the way to the theater, a stagehand fell from the rigging and was seriously injured, and a leading lady broke her leg. Soyinka asked for a goat to be sacrificed, but since none could be found in Chicago in winter, he had to settle for a chicken, which was sacrificed under the stage. "And from that moment on," he recalls, "I don't know why, everything just started going right."[54]

In South Africa, an office employee who did not get along with one of his coworkers refused to share an office with him because a *nyanga* (herbal healer) had told him that his colleague had purchased a local herb and sprinkled its essence throughout their shared office to create discord.

Before condemning such customs as baseless superstitions, Westerners might recall that some of their own compatriots carry comparable talismans such as a rabbit's foot, four-leaf clover, and other good luck charms. Some wear copper bracelets to assuage the aches of arthritis while others blame their discomforts on changes in barometric pressure, although physicians can find no scientific basis for such practices and beliefs.

Related to witchcraft in Africa is a widely held belief that things do not happen unless someone wishes them to happen. The reaction to misfortune is to ask why and to place the blame for personal misfortune on the actions of wicked people, evil spirits, or witches and to seek the cause of the unfortunate happening and remove it.

If a person dies, the blame may be assigned to magic, sorcery, or witchcraft, and the accused will be severely punished. Those who do not grieve with sufficient emotion may be blamed for causing the death. If a headache is not curable by aspirin, Africans may ask, "Why do I have this headache only when I come to visit this particular house?" Since there is no logical answer, they may attribute it to a malevolent spirit, a vindictive ancestor, or an angry witch. To search out the cause of misfortune and deal with it, they may consult a traditional diviner who might prescribe a ritual offering, sacrifice, or prayer.

Fear of evil spirits also makes many Africans reluctant to stand out in a crowd lest someone put the evil eye or a hex on them. In some development projects, farmers have been reluctant to take the lead in applying new techniques, fearing that if they stand out in their village or appear to be better off than others, some jealous neighbor might cast an evil spell on them.

When, in 1995, the Ebola virus spread to Kikwit, a Congo city of 400,000, some local inhabitants thought that evil spirits had struck. Civil servants, market-stall owners, and farmers of the outlying suburbs of Kikwit were convinced that an American medical missionary stationed nearby was a *sorcier* (witch doctor) who changed himself into a hippopotamus and was responsible for the virus.[55]

Also in Congo, an international health agency had planned to open a community nursery so that village children would be fed and cared for when their mothers were working in the fields. But the mothers were reluctant to leave their children in the care of other village women, fearing that if a woman were jealous or had a grievance, she might put a hex on the children.

When a high West African government official believed that his predecessor had been hexed and possibly poisoned, he refused to use the deceased's office although it was more luxurious than his own. If someone has a leak in his water line that cannot be repaired, he may assume that his ancestors do not want him to have water.

Such beliefs in spirits and witchcraft are a reality in Africa, even among the well educated and highly placed, where almost everyone seems to call on some form of intermediary for spiritual or medical assistance. Among such intermediaries are diviners and traditional healers whom people throughout Africa are likely to consult when they are sick. The remedies they receive often relate to an ancestor or spirit whose anger must be assuaged by some action of the afflicted person.

But the diviner usually goes further, as British anthropologist Robin Horton explains, adding something "about human hatreds, jealousies, and misdeeds" that may have disturbed the social equilibrium and thereby raised the wrath of ancestors or spirits as well as bringing on the illness.[56] In this, the diviners and other intermediaries function much as counselors and therapists do in the West, and as modern medical doctors do who see psychic stress as a cause of bodily illness.

In parts of Southern Africa, such an intermediary is called a *sangoma*. But a sangoma is really a psychic specialist, says Kae Graham, an English nurse who has been working in South Africa since 1948. Graham, who lived among the Venda people for almost thirty years and became a traditional healer, explains, "I was interested in the psychological aspects of witch doctoring.... Everybody, at some time, needs some help. And that is what this business is all about."[57]

In Muslim West Africa, some intermediaries are called *marabouts* (holy men), of which there are three kinds—heads of religious sects, religious teachers, and spiritual advisers or what one would call in India a guru. Marabouts are consulted by those who believe that someone is trying to harm them or by sick persons seeking to learn the cause of their illness.

In Senegal, it is said, high government officials do not make important decisions without consulting their marabouts, which puts the Muslim holy men in the enviable position of knowing many important goings-on in the country. Also in Senegal, because of fear of spirits, certain things are never done. A pregnant woman should not be asked when she is due because, according to traditional beliefs, pregnant women and young children are very vulnerable to spirits. People or children in a group should not be counted by pointing with a finger because quantifying people publicly exposes them to the spirit world. Also, it is best not to ask how many children someone has or to say, when picking up a child, how heavy he or she seems. Anything that calls attention to a vulnerable being should be avoided.

Africans may be reluctant to discuss such folk beliefs with Westerners, at least until they know them well and believe they will be more accepting of local customs. Until such time, expats should avoid discussing traditional religions. Rather, accept them as elements of African cultures and traditions and recognize that we in the West also have our witch doctors—astrologers, clairvoyants, faith healers, mediums, psychics, and practitioners of other folk beliefs and occult sciences, some of whom practice in very high places.

Traditional medicine, moreover, once scorned in the Western world, is now being studied in the United States and other countries as a source of alternative therapies. Western medicine is also beginning to recognize the therapeutic value of the sense of community and connection to other people that is intrinsic to traditional societies but has been largely lost in the postindustrial West.

Despite Africa's diversity of religions and beliefs, a spirit of religious tolerance and ecumenism prevails, and different faiths coexist with little friction. Quite common, as Mazrui notes, are families where one brother may be Catholic, a sister Muslim, another sibling Anglican, and their parents animists. Religion, moreover, does not appear to influence politics. Senegal, a mainly Muslim country, had a Roman Catholic president, Léopold Sédar Senghor, for twenty years, and his Muslim successor, Abdou Diouf, has a Catholic wife.

Tanzania, a country with a plurality of Muslims over Christians, had a Catholic president, Julius Nyerere, for twenty-four years.[58]

Western missionaries are still active today in virtually all of Africa, where they run schools, clinics, and hospitals as well as provide for the spiritual needs of their followers. But as they age and are not replaced by other Westerners, most of the nuns, priests, and other clergy today are Africans. In Tanzania, every Catholic diocese now has an African bishop. New Western missionaries, moreover, particularly among Protestant churches, are likely to include laypeople who bring new skills, setting examples by their own lives rather than actively preaching a direct religious message.

Wondrous Women

> The one constant amid the changes that are transforming the character of a continent is the role of the African woman, a person whose physical and spiritual strength is nothing short of remarkable.
>
> —David Lamb, *The Africans*

Africa may be a man's world, but women are the glue that binds it together. In traditional societies, men were the warriors and hunters, and women, the home keepers and child bearers. Today most men no longer make war or hunt, but women still work and reproduce. In the villages they haul water, gather firewood, pound grain, cook food, care for children, wash clothes, and tend crops. When they move to the cities, women continue to perform some of these same tasks, considered traditional for women, while also holding down full-time jobs in offices and factories.

In parts of Africa with a short growing season, men and women contribute more or less equally to agricultural production. But in regions where the season is long, while men do the heavy work of clearing and plowing the land, women sow the seeds, tend the fields, harvest the crops, and bear the major burden for growing the family's food. Women also produce most of the food sold in local markets, whereas men grow most of the cash crops for export, such as coffee, cocoa, peanuts, and tobacco. Another gender-based division of labor can be seen in the marketplace, where women predominate as vendors, especially in Coastal West Africa.

As long as they fulfill their wifely duties, women in Coastal West Africa are given considerable freedom and allowed to engage in activities outside the home and to profit from them. In some of these countries, women dominate the markets and the retail trade, and some have become quite wealthy. Those who drive Mercedes-Benz cars are often referred to as "Mama Benz."

But in parts of West and Central Africa, where the tsetse fly—and the sleeping sickness it causes—makes it difficult if not impossible to keep beasts of burden, women literally function as their substitutes, carrying crops on their heads and backs from farm to market. Westerners wonder at the sight of African women gliding along under head loads, with no back-and-forth motion and seemingly without effort. For those who feel sorry for such women, head loading has been found to be the most efficient way of bearing loads and has no ill effects on the spine.

Despite the importance of women in farming, most agricultural development projects have worked only with men, in part because agricultural extension workers are mainly men but also because men are more likely to be the producers of cash crops. Donor agencies, however, now recognizing the deficiency, have been increasing their efforts of late to improve the agricultural productivity of women.

Where men leave their villages to work in the cities and mines or on remote farms, they return home only twice a year, to plow their fields and beget children. But when these migrant workers fail to return home, or when they start a second family elsewhere, families are fractured. As a consequence, millions of African households are run by women whose husbands live or work elsewhere, and women in rural areas often greatly outnumber men.

In class terms, this gender division of farm labor has resulted, as Mazrui describes it, in

> ...the emergence of a male proletariat on the one side and a female peasantry on the other; an urbanised male population and a more firmly rural female sector. This is particularly true of situations of migrant male labour—either to towns and cities or to mines. In mines in southern Africa a rigid gender apartheid is often enforced—wives are kept firmly in their ancestral rural areas while their men sweat in coal or gold mines hundreds of miles away.[59]

One exception to this gender division in labor is South Africa, where women have a decided advantage over men in being hired for skilled jobs in industry, such as machinists. True, women are usually paid less than men, but as industrial managers there explain it, women are more dependable workers and have higher productivity. They show up for work on time, take less sick leave, do not drink or do drugs, perform better on the job, and with their need to support families, they show more interest in training for advancement.

In their role as growers and preparers of food, women are seen as the nourishers of Africa. The hearth is held to be the woman's province from which men are excluded. In South Africa, however, men do share with Americans one household duty—it's the man's job to grill the meat in the backyard!

Despite the important work that African women perform, they have customarily been subservient to men, and women who rebel against such customs are not respected. In many traditional cultures women do not inherit land. In some rural areas a wife who comes to talk to her husband gets down on her knees, addresses him as "master," and as a sign of respect, does not look at him directly. In other cultures women genuflect when addressing men or do a little curtsy. A nurse, for example, may curtsy before a doctor, and a daughter may curtsy when giving something to her father. A not uncommon sight is a woman walking down a road with a load on her head, a baby on her back, another in her belly, and a third child holding her hand, while her unburdened husband walks a few paces ahead.

In many cultures, women eat after the men, and women in mixed male-female company are not addressed directly. In a first meeting, it may even be incorrect to speak personally with the wife at all. Girls everywhere are less likely to go to school than boys and are expected to remain at home, helping with household chores and tending to younger children. When girls do go to school, they usually end their schooling at a lower grade than boys.

When young women migrate to cities, this imbalance between the sexes, as well as financial need, often causes young women of lower economic status, who lack education and job training, to have sexual relationships with older men who are established in their work or profession and can afford to support a girlfriend or two.

Ideas of pulchritude in Africa differ from those of Europe and the Americas. In traditional African societies, plumpness is considered a sign of beauty, health, and wealth, and slimness as evidence of unhappiness or disease or that a woman is being mistreated by her husband. This view is changing as more and more Africans move from villages to cities and become aware that "less" is often better than "more." But, as Mazrui phrases it, "big buttocks...is still a standard preference in most parts of Black Africa."[60]

In a recent beauty contest in Dar es Salaam to select a Miss Bantu, contestants were required to have heavy legs, wide waists, and big buttocks as well as pretty faces. But as a Tanzanian journalist reported, "...spectators at the pageant complained that they had been tricked, that the girls were skinny and unattractive and that none of them had *wowowo* (big buttocks)."[61]

In many Western countries there is a more equal balance of power and status between the genders, and nonsexual relationships between genders are accepted. For Africans, however, friendship without sex between people of the opposite gender is difficult to comprehend. If a man spends time with a woman who is not his wife, everyone will assume that they are having sexual relations. People may recognize, at times, that a relationship between an African and an expatriate may be professional and not sexual, but women who are alone will still be seen as curiosities.

Other attitudes toward women in Africa may also cause Westerners to wonder. Spousal abuse is widespread and a significant cause of female morbidity and mortality. As Stephen Buckley reports in the *Washington Post*:

> From Sudan to South Africa, from Mali to Mozambique, spousal abuse is among sub-Saharan Africa's best-known and least-discussed secrets, a problem far more pervasive but much less addressed than other social ills, such as AIDS. Over the centuries in most African societies, battering one's wife has become both a right and a rite.[62]

According to a World Bank study, "Women are beaten or otherwise abused if they do not comply with men's sexual and childbearing demands..." and "[a] study in Kenya showed that 42 percent of women were 'beaten regularly.'" Moreover, adds the study, "Such violence includes sexual abuse of children, physical and sexual assaults, and certain culture-bound practices, such as female genital mutilation."[63]

Female circumcision, or excision as it is also known, is an old tradition that has attracted much attention as well as opposition in the West. Practiced in a broad band of sub-Saharan countries (plus Egypt) north of the equator, it is symbolically akin to male circumcision, which is widely practiced throughout Africa. The female version, however, is often anatomically much more extensive, and its consequences—physical, psychological, and sexual—are severe and long lasting. Not required by any religious doctrine, its origins are obscure, but it is believed to have begun in Egypt or the Horn of Africa more than two thousand years ago, long before the advent of Islam. Based more on culture than religion, it is practiced today by Muslims, Christians, animists, and one Jewish sect, the Falasha of Ethiopia.

Each year, millions of girls and young women undergo a traumatic procedure in which parts of their external genitals are cut or excised without anesthesia. "These women and girls," writes Nahid Toubia, a Sudanese woman surgeon who is a professor at Columbia University, "experience pain, trauma, and frequently severe physical complications such as bleeding, infections, or even death. Long-term physical complications are numerous, and there appear to be substantial psychological effects on women's self-image and sexual lives."[64]

The procedure, requested by the child's parents (and increasingly by conservative grandparents), is widely supported by African traditionalists, both female and male, who see it as a rite of passage that transforms a girl into a woman. Traditionalists also believe that it keeps girls pure for their marriage and wives faithful to their husbands. Parents claim, moreover, that without the procedure their daughters will be unable to find husbands. Opponents, however, see it as reducing women's sexual pleasure and further subordinating them to men. Many African countries have publicly opposed the procedure but rarely prohibit it by law. In 1996 the U.S. Congress passed legislation prohibiting the practice in the United States, and an immigration court has ruled that it can be a basis for seeking asylum.

Many African women's organizations resent the attention shown to female genital mutilation by well-meaning American and European women. African women, they say, have more severe problems to overcome, such as poverty and malnutrition. Recently, however, women's groups condemning the custom have been formed in several African countries. Westerners who want to become involved in efforts to change the practice are advised to work through such indigenous groups, which are prepared to take the lead.

Despite the social and financial constraints, women in recent years have increasingly become a political force in many countries of Africa. Since 1992, when Kenya ended single-party rule, women there have been elected to fifty local political posts, doubling the number previously held. In 1994 Agatha Muthoni Mbogo, age twenty-four, was elected mayor of Embu, a Kenyan city of 66,000 people. Uganda has had its first female vice president, and Burundi, a female foreign minister. Rwanda's prime minister (killed in the 1994 massacres) was a woman. In Tanzania, at least 15 percent of the National Assembly seats must be held by women. In South Africa, women's rights are explicitly protected in the constitution, and 25 percent of the federal legislators are women. In Eritrea, women were among the foremost fighters in the war for independence from Ethiopia, which is perhaps why 21 percent of legislators in that new state are women. In West and Central Africa, most francophone countries have a ministry of women's affairs which is almost always headed by a woman. And in 1996 Africa had its first woman head of state when former Liberian senator Ruth Perry was appointed to chair her country's interim ruling council until an election could be held the following year.

But these are exceptions. As in most traditional societies, African women are less likely to be found in positions of authority in government or the private sector, and where women do have power, it is usually wielded behind the scenes. In many cultures wives figure in family decisions, and the husband consults his wife (or wives) before making a major decision. As a Pedi proverb says, "The father is the head, and the mother is the neck that supports the head." One exception is Coastal West Africa, where, as noted previously, women have considerable economic independence and are quite self-sufficient. In some West African societies, more-over, in precolonial times women served as chiefs and led their people in battle, and some may still serve today as chiefs or heads of villages.

The increased activism of African women has had a price, however, according to Stephen Buckley, "...as governments frequently break up meetings of women's groups, and female politicians are often harangued about their personal lives." Women politicians and activists say they are bucking deeply ingrained cultural mores which teach that "...African women cook, clean, take care of children, plant and harvest crops and support their husbands. They typically do not inherit land, divorce their husbands, control their finances or hold political office."[65]

Is there a feminist movement in Africa? Among educated women there is now a nascent effort for gender equality, and a movement in Africa may indeed be in the making. But while African feminists do not regard men as adversaries, they are often falsely accused of not wanting to have any-thing to do with men, similar to the misperception in the West during the early days of feminism. African men, more-over, often associate gains in the status of women with losses in the status of men. In any event, radical feminism, like other forms of radicalism, is not welcome in Africa.

Conjugal Customs

With wealth, one wins a woman.

—Ugandan proverb

"Loneliness is not an indigenous African problem," write Bohannan and Curtin.[66] Most women in Africa marry, at a young age and usually to a man who is older. And for those younger women who are divorced or widowed, remarriage generally comes quickly. They may still be lonely, but they are not alone.

In the village, marriage follows naturally after puberty, and boys and girls know that they are expected to marry, usually to someone chosen by their families, and to have children. Indeed, in traditional African societies, marriage is seen as an arrangement between two contracting families rather than as the union of two individuals.

The age-old practice of bridewealth, as it is called—payment by the groom's family, in the form of money, cattle, or other objects of value and status—is common in most traditional African cultures. As U.S. anthropologist James H. Vaughan explains, bridewealth legitimizes the union much as a marriage certificate does in other societies. By compensating a family for the loss of one of its members and her labor, it gives both families a vested interest in the survival of the marriage.[67] Indeed, a woman often cannot leave an unhappy marriage without her family repaying the bridewealth, which many families cannot afford to do.

To Westerners such practices may seem archaic. But the family in Africa, adds Vaughan, is very often the primary economic unit of society, organized in a way that facilitates production, and marriage is best seen "...as a formal relationship between two groups of people rather than between two individuals...an alliance between two families through the conjugal union of a female from one with a male from the other."[68]

Bridewealth should not be equated with the "selling" of daughters, writes American sociologist April A. Gordon.

> Rather, it indicates the high value attached to women in African society; families must be compensated for the loss of their daughters and the wealth she will bring to her husband's family.[69]

Conjugal customs in Africa also differ between patrilineal and matrilineal societies. In patrilineal societies the children belong to the father's lineage, and in matrilineal, to the mother's, which gives matrilineal mothers more economic and social security. In divorce in matrilineal societies, for example, the woman has the right to her children, which assures her greater economic support in her old age. Also, a matrilineal woman, upon her first marriage, is less likely to move to her husband's village, as in a patrilineal society. If she marries a man who has not yet inherited land, he may move to her village and farm there. The vast majority of African lineage systems are patrilineal and there are many variations in customs, but in both systems men usually have control over land and inheritance and, as we have seen, play a dominant role in politics.[70]

Polygyny is also traditional and still common throughout much of Africa. Islam allows men to have up to four wives, but the custom of a man having more than one wife predates Islam and exists in almost all African cultures. Among the Pedi people of South Africa, for example, far from Muslim influence, a man can have as many wives as he desires and can afford. Men may often have a wife in the home village and a "steady" in the city (a *deuxième bureau* or second office, as it is called in francophone countries) as well as casual sexual partners on the side. So it has always been, and most African women realize that they can do little to change it. Some countries, influenced by Christianity, have passed laws outlawing polygyny but the legislation is usually not enforced.

Men and women often appear to be members of two different societies with few common interests. Married men socialize with their male friends or girlfriends, writes Chenjerai Hove, Zimbabwe's leading novelist, but seldom with their wives.[71] "Married women," he adds, "are doomed to stay at home, bored, but resigned to it."[72]

One practical way to reduce the incidence of polygyny, argues Florence Abena Dolphyne, a professor at the University of Ghana, is to encourage professional and vocational training for girls so that they marry at a later age, when it is possible for them to find husbands among their own age group. Such professional training will also mean that

> ...a woman will be reasonably economically independent, so that it would not be necessary for her to become a second or a third wife to a man simply because he is well-to-do and therefore able to provide for her.[73]

Such changes are coming slowly to Africa, but young women are less inclined than their mothers to accept polygyny.

If asked about polygyny, Africans may be uncomfortable, and Western visitors should not question it, as one U.S. visitor learned. The American had become close friends with a Guinean student in the United States. But when she went to Guinea to visit her friend's family, they feared that she would be shocked by the traditional village hut they lived in and the father's multiple wives—and were relieved when they found she was not. Perhaps she recalled that polygyny was practiced by some in the United States little more than one hundred years ago, and many American married men and women today have lovers on the side, although they are not accorded legal recognition as are multiple wives in Africa.

More important than even a wife are blood relations, says Samu M. Samu, a Malawian professor who is a cross-cultural trainer for Peace Corps volunteers in his country. In Malawi, for example, men name their mothers in wills but not their wives. For this reason, women believe it most important to have children. As the mother of her husband's child, a woman can then say to him, "I have your blood."[74] Indeed, it is only after the birth of a child that a woman is fully accepted as kinfolk by her husband's family.

Is there romantic love in Africa? The answer is a clear yes for Bohannan and Curtin, who say that romantic love occurs in an African familial situation about as commonly as it does in a European or American one. In traditional societies, they explain, children accede to parents' choice on spouse selection, but where the choice does not correspond with their own, they simply elope and get their parents' approval afterward. Africans seldom make their children marry someone they do not like, although they may refuse to refund bridewealth and thereby make daughters remain with husbands they no longer care for.[75]

Despite what may seem to be a wide cultural gap, many successful intercultural marriages have been made by Westerners, both male and female, who have returned home with African spouses. But Westerners who marry Africans should be prepared to make some cultural adjustments, beginning with the extended family. In a traditional family, they may be accepted but only if they change their ways and adapt to African society. With an urbanized family it may be easier, but not always. As Turnbull explains,

> To live in Africa as a European is easy enough, but to live there as a European and an African by marriage requires something special. There is a different way of thinking, arising out of the different beliefs and values, that can not be adopted as though it were just another custom.[76]

An American woman in Benin, for example, reports two needs of her African husband that she is unable to satisfy. Although her husband is "liberated" in many ways, he still expects her to "wait on him," and because of obligations to his family he needs to spend more time with them and is unable to spend as much time with her as she would like.

A woman without a husband, children, or family is something Africans have difficulty understanding, as earlier noted. Because marriage is considered a sacred duty, a woman without a man is a puzzle. "Marriage is the one experience," writes Mbiti, "without which a person is not considered to be complete, 'perfect,' and truly a man or a woman."[77] "Woman without man," says an Ethiopian proverb, "is like a field without seed." Also a puzzle in Africa is the dependent husband. An American who accompanies his wife on a research grant or as the spouse of a foreign service employee may be seen as an anomaly, and Africans may not know how to relate to him.

The first question asked of a single or unaccompanied foreign woman is usually "Are you married?" or "Where is your husband?" If the response is that she has no husband, the next question will be "But who is taking care of you?" A further question may be "Do you want to meet a nice local boy?" And an expat woman should not be surprised if her African friends send a local lothario around to keep her company.

African men are willing and able to use their considerable skills to romance women, and expats in Muslim regions may be asked, "Do you want to be my fourth wife?" Women should not take such proposals seriously, advise old Africa hands. In most cases, it is merely playful banter or a sign that an African finds the woman attractive, though it may also mean that he wants to sleep with her.

When one African jokingly asked an American woman if she would become his fourth wife, she replied, "Yes, if you will be my fourth husband," adding facetiously that in her country women are allowed four husbands. The admirer, quite startled, responded, "You don't understand; men have different needs here."

Another American was asked by a Somali woman if she wanted to marry a local man. The American, who was in fact quite smitten with the Somalis, replied jocularly that she didn't want a husband who goes to the office early in the morning and does not return until late in the evening after spending time with his male friends or a girlfriend. The Somali woman replied that she understood but that women of her country did not have that choice.

Sexual annoyances can be avoided by the foreign woman who displays her multiple roles as wife, mother, and professional. One American woman reports that when her husband joins her in the middle of an assignment to Africa, relations with her African colleagues turn warmer, and they become even closer when she tells them about her four children and the problems they cause.

Having children can also help with immigration officials, reports an American woman who was stopped on her departure from Africa because her passport did not show an entry stamp for the country she was leaving. The officials were not prepared to permit her departure until she mentioned that she was going home to her three (nonexistent) children. When she showed the officials the T-shirts and other items she had purchased as gifts (for her nieces and nephews), the officials were touched by a mother's love for her children and relented.

In Mali, once, a policeman stopped an American woman when she was driving and tried to shake her down for some money. Taking her driver's license, he said he would not return it until she paid. In response, the American told the police officer that she had infant twins at home and he was preventing her from returning to nurse them. The officer immediately returned her papers, saying with a smile, "This is for the twins." Since then, she has always carried photos of her twins when they were infants to show to any policeman who might stop her. The same technique gets her reduced prices in the markets. This tactic works well in Mali and other parts of Africa where twins are revered but would not have the same result in other regions where twins may be considered bad luck.

Despite such traditional attitudes toward women, female expats can function well in Africa. Those who behave like professionals will be treated like professionals, although at times it may be necessary for a woman to be more assertive to strengthen her credibility. In short, if you are a professional, act like a professional but remember the advantage you may have among Africans by also playing up your role as wife or mother.

First impressions are lasting, as in the West, and women should also dress like professionals, which in Africa means no short skirts or pants. In Muslim countries, moreover, tight or revealing clothes are taboo, and shoulders should be kept covered. Socks are also out, and showing legs and knees may be considered erotic. A glimpse of a woman's thighs, however fleeting, will be perceived as obscene.

One American who manages a development project in Botswana reports that she has no problems there as a woman and is shown the respect she is due. The Batswana, as the people of Botswana are known, she explains, know that there is discrimination against women outside as well as within Africa so they assume that a foreign woman who holds an important position must be highly qualified or otherwise would not be able to hold down her job.[78]

Westerners preparing the ground for women's development projects should tread carefully, particularly when discussing their proposals with African male officials who may resent an emphasis on exclusively female issues. Such projects are more likely to be approved if men are included or the projects are broadened to include the entire family. A female and male approach will be more effective.

Daunting Demographics

One child is no child.

—African proverb

The birth of a child is a joyous occasion throughout Africa, where having many children, especially boys, is considered a sign of wealth and status. This is understandable in a part of the world where mortality has always been high and additional hands have been needed to tend the crops and mind the herds. But there are cultural as well as economic reasons for large families.

Children assure the continuation of the family line, an important factor in traditional societies where belief in the rebirth of ancestors may be strong. High fertility also means more support for parents in their old age—the father in a patrilineal society, and the mother in a matrilineal. The desire for large families also supports the popularity of polygyny. Today, however, large families come at a high cost to all.

"Africa is the most successful producer of babies in recorded history," writes Harden, "and the world's least successful producer of food."[79] Population is growing at 3 percent a year but food production at only 2 percent, and the threat of famine is always on the horizon. At current growth rates, population is projected to double in twenty or so years. Among the countries with the highest growth rates are Angola, Côte d'Ivoire, Ethiopia, The Gambia, Nigeria, Tanzania, Uganda, and Congo.

The average infant mortality rate (deaths under age one per 1,000 live births) dropped from 152 in 1960 to 111 in 1992, due in part to increased immunization and the introduction of oral rehydration for treatment of infant diarrhea.[80] But while the mortality rate has declined, the overall growth rate remains high because the fertility rate—the number of births per woman—is more than six.

Population has been doubling every twenty-four years, and more than half of the population in most sub-Saharan countries is under the age of fifteen, a statistic that creates a built-in momentum for future population growth. The expected surge, moreover, will be accompanied by immense pressures for social services, food, and jobs at a time when governments will be facing many economic challenges and problems such as AIDS, rapid urbanization, environmental degradation, increased unemployment, disillusioned youth, and escalating crime. Population growth, which is outpacing economic expansion, is simply swamping African development efforts.

Family planning, however, is not popular in many places where it is seen by some Africans as an attempt to limit the continuation and growth of their clan. Others see it as a plot of the industrial nations to depopulate less developed countries. Moreover, in traditional societies, a woman's status and esteem depend on the number of children she is able to bear. A woman who seeks to limit the number of children she has may be found wanting by her husband's family and runs the risk of being divorced or having her husband take another wife.

Limiting a family's growth is therefore a sensitive issue. Large families ensure care for parents in their old age as well as more hands to tend the cattle, gather wood, haul water, or tend to the younger children while mothers work in the fields. In Muslim countries, men often father as many as twenty or more children.

Despite such handicaps, family planning has been increasing in many countries, albeit slowly, for mainly economic reasons, especially in the cities and among the better educated. Urbanization has reduced the need for more hands in agriculture, and the availability and costs of schooling are inducing parents to focus their limited resources on having fewer children. But some 70 percent of Africans still live on the land, and increased investment in rural areas and greater food production is now recognized as a must, not only to feed more people but also to stem the flow of migrants to the cities.

Despite the baby boom, you will seldom see a woman pushing a baby carriage or pram (as the British call it). Babies are usually carried by an older sister on her hip or by the mother with the baby deftly supported on her back by a wraparound shawl. In a case of reverse technology transfer, the Western Snugli baby carrier, designed by a former Peace Corps couple, has its origins in Togo, where they had served.

Schools and Rules

This is a nation that worships certificates. If you don't have a certificate, you don't have a job. No job means more crime,

more drugs, more poverty. No education means the poor will
be poor forever.

—G. K. Ikara,
Professor of Economics, University of Nairobi

Perhaps nowhere in the world is education seen more as the
key to success than in Africa. This is not surprising, since for
decades university—and sometimes secondary school—graduates were guaranteed government jobs. Today, a certificate
(diploma) no longer guarantees a job but it does put an
applicant ahead of the many others who may lack proper
credentials.

As elsewhere in the world, there are wide variations in
education between generations and social classes. Younger
people are likely to be more literate and better educated than
their elders, and urban children better schooled than rural.
Children in politically prominent and financially successful
families are far more likely to receive a first-class education
and be sent abroad for further study.

But here, too, there are variations. That prosperous-look-
ing elderly African sitting next to you on a plane bound for
Europe or the Americas may be illiterate and can surprise you
by asking for help in filling out his immigration card. Many
of those enterprising West African market women, so shrewd
and successful in business, cannot read or write.

Colonial regimes engaged in continuous controversy over
whether their subject people should be schooled, and to what
extent.[81] But since colonial administrations had few financial
resources, they were initially only too pleased to leave schooling to the Catholic and Protestant missionaries who, recognizing the value of literacy in evangelizing, established the
first Western-type schools for Africans and were among the
first to devise written forms for African languages. "Whatever any individual Westerner may think of the missionary
edifice," write Bohannan and Curtin, "every African knows
that it is to missionaries that they owe the beginnings of their

Western-style educational system."[82] Speakers of Lugandan certainly know it, for in their language the same word, *okusoma*, is used for "read" and "pray."

With their knowledge of local languages, missionaries opened elementary schools in areas around their mission stations where they taught the basics of reading, writing, and 'rithmetic, and prepared pupils for work in the colonial economies in such subordinate positions as blacksmiths, carpenters, and clerks. (A Gambian who went to study in England in the 1960s has told the authors how surprised he was to see Englishmen laying bricks. He had not known that white people also performed manual labor.) And, in an unforeseen development, the missionary schools also produced Africa's first generation of nationalists and political leaders.

During the 1920s the colonial governments began to show some interest in education for Africans, but their approaches differed. The British, reflecting their tradition of limiting the state role in schooling, chose to work through the mission schools, improving them through supervision, subsidies, and setting standards, and in a few cases providing support for eight- and twelve-year schools. The French, reflecting their home politics, ignored the mission schools and set up national systems of education similar to the state schools of France but for a relatively small number of Africans who would shoulder supporting, but subservient, roles in their colonial administrations.

"The French tradition of centralization and consistent logic applied to the needs of empire building," wrote Wallerstein, "imposed standardized patterns throughout French colonies; teaching personnel were interchangeable and the curricula of the schools—all of them in French—were alike."[83] French education, moreover, favored the theoretical over the technical, with consequences still seen today. "The emphasis of the French system," says Jacob Ngu, a former vice-chancellor of the University of Yaounde in Cameroon, "is acquiring knowledge for the sake of knowledge."[84]

Handwriting receives special attention in francophone schools where every student undergoes frequent dictation to help master French orthography and to be precise in penmanship.

Until the end of World War II, less than 5 percent of the African school-age population was enrolled in schools, and girls were largely excluded. Colonial education, as British historian Basil Davidson notes, "...was designed to do no more than provide a little primitive literacy and counting for hewers of wood and drawers of water."[85]

After World War II, in response to demands by Africans, more secondary schools were opened and universities were established almost everywhere, although their numbers were still small. In Kenya, Tanganyika, and Uganda at the time of independence in the late 1950s, adds Davidson, there were fewer than 2,000 secondary school graduates each year for a total population of some 24 million.[86] In the Belgian and Portuguese colonies it was even worse. In the Belgian Congo, under the slogan "No elites, no problems," the emphasis was on primary education and the training of elementary school teachers, with the consequence that higher education for Congolese was not available prior to 1954, either at home or abroad. In Portuguese Angola and Mozambique, writes Davidson, "...less than 1 percent of African populations ever saw the inside of a school, no matter how rudimentary, before the wars of resistance began in 1961."[87]

The French provided training for medical doctors and teachers in Africa, mainly in Dakar and Brazzaville, but study in France was the highest goal, and future African administrators were often sent to elite universities there. More resources, moreover, were put into secondary and tertiary (higher) education to train a smaller number of highly qualified people to help run the centralized colonial administrations.

The British also established schools and colleges in their colonies to train clerks, teachers, and civil servants, but, in contrast to the French, they spread their resources more equitably among all levels of the educational system, building from the bottom up and creating a larger pool of trained personnel, which they needed to pursue their policy of indirect rule through local leaders.

South Africa had its own peculiarities in education, and under apartheid there were five separate systems based on race and language—White Anglo, Afrikaner, Indian, Coloured (racially mixed), and Black. Since the end of apartheid in 1994, the racial integration of all South African education has been under way.

In the Muslim regions of Africa, Qur'anic schools have a long, centuries-old tradition of learning and scholarship. Wherever Islam spread, it also established schools and brought literacy in Arabic to the countryside as well as to the cities. As Bohannan and Curtin point out, "The introduction of Islam always meant the introduction of literacy, since Muslims (like Christians and Jews) are 'people of the book.'"[88] Islamic schools continue this tradition today, although functional literacy is not guaranteed and girls are often excluded from literary instruction.

Since independence, debate on education and the limited resources for its funding has been spirited, between supporters of secondary and tertiary education for a favored few and those who favor high-quality primary education for a larger number of children. In francophone countries, where centralization of education continues, the debate has focused on whether to broaden educational opportunities or to continue the elitist system inherited from the French. In anglophone countries, where education is more decentralized, there is more of a tradition of consultation with local authorities and parents on such issues. Many governments, moreover, have sought to use state schools to build a national consensus among their various ethnic and language groups.

Despite such debates, the expansion of education has been enormous throughout sub-Saharan Africa, especially in primary education, where overall enrollment increased 350 percent from 1965 to 1989. Enrollment rates (the percentage of population in schools), however, have not improved as much because of rapid population growth, and universal primary education is still an unmet goal. Only two of three school-age children, on average, attend primary school, but this seemingly high level of school attendance masks a wide variation among and within countries, ethnic groups, and sexes.[89]

School may be "free" in many countries but the required uniforms, books, and supplies are not, and their costs are a drain on the scarce resources of the average household. Many pupils do not have textbooks and may lack paper and pencils as well. In response to larger enrollments and increased budgetary pressures, governments are now asking families and communities to pay ever larger portions of the costs of schooling.

Educational facilities for elementary schools are rudimentary in rural regions of many countries and may not be available at all in more remote regions. In more urbanized areas, as many as 120 pupils may be crammed into poorly lit schoolrooms designed for forty, and morning and afternoon sessions are often used to alleviate overcrowding. In more rural areas children from ages eight to eighteen and grades one to eight may share the same classroom and have the same teacher for instruction. Building construction ranges from cement block to mud and wattle, and many schoolrooms have no chairs or desks. Pupils may have notebooks and the teacher, a chalkboard, but not much more; and textbooks, where they exist, are shared. The teacher, moreover, is likely to be un- or underqualified, with little more than a primary school education, underpaid, and largely unsupported by the ministry of education.[90] Schools in small towns will have outside toilets and no running water or electricity, and some villages have movable classrooms—pupils and teacher sit under one side of a big tree in the morning and the other side in the afternoon, when the sun shifts.

Whether to teach in a local or European language is a question continually debated across Africa. In most anglophone countries, instruction starts in a local language, and English is introduced later. In many francophone countries, however, instruction starts in French. In Ethiopia, instruction is provided in some fifteen local languages, a practice which many educators question. At the opposite extreme, in Tanzania, Kiswahili is the language of instruction in all state primary schools. In many countries, however, tense ethnic politics are played out in the educational arena, and the choice of a local language for schooling can become a political flash point for tribal tensions.

Western languages, however, predominate after primary school, not only because they prepare for more advanced study but also because they help to avoid ethnic strife. Although many Africans are multilingual, pupils and teachers in a school may not share a common language or even one that is mutually intelligible. Western language instruction, moreover, is sought by parents who want their children to have access to the jobs that bilingualism offers, as well as the possibility of entry into elite influence networks with resultant upward mobility.

Secondary school, however, no matter how desirable, is prohibitively expensive for most families. In the absence of a sufficient number of free state schools, students must often attend schools away from home which charge tuition and where students must be boarded or housed with a friend or member of the extended family. Consequently, only one in five African children attends secondary school, and if parents must choose between which children to send, boys are usually favored over girls and outnumber girls in secondary schools by more than two to one. In most Muslim regions, moreover, there is still strong opposition to secondary education for girls.

Higher education has seen phenomenal growth over the past thirty years, but in 1996 only 4 percent of Africans age twenty to twenty-four attended colleges and universities. At the time of independence, sub-Saharan Africa (not counting South Africa) had only six universities and some of the new states had less than a hundred graduates. Those privileged few students were well treated—no tuition costs or fees, free room and board, books and materials, and even pocket money. Today, sub-Sahara has more than a hundred universities, almost all of them (and their students) fully funded by the state. And therein lies the problem.

Cash-strapped governments can no longer afford the costs of subsidizing higher education, and reductions in funding and the imposition of fees for students have sparked protests and strikes by both students and faculty which have closed some institutions for months and even years. Uganda's once-prestigious Makerere University, formerly known as the "Harvard of Africa," was near collapse in the mid-1990s after two decades of civil war, political chaos, and financial neglect, and it is not an isolated case. The World Bank has recommended downsizing African higher education and student subsidies and transferring the resultant savings to primary education, with the aim of reducing sub-Sahara's high illiteracy rates and providing education for the many rather than the few.

Study abroad is an objective of most students, and it is surprising how many "been-tos" (Africans who have been abroad for study and then returned home) will be encountered among professionals. Many Westerners have a story about being approached by friends or even accosted on the street by complete strangers seeking someone to sponsor them for study abroad.

Higher education also reflects dissimilar colonial heritages. In francophone countries, as in France, students attend lectures, take notes, and read; in anglophone countries, there is more interaction between students and professors.

The French objective was acculturation—to create black French people, it has been said—and in many ways they succeeded. Francophone universities produced African graduates who were as much at home in Paris as in their own capital cities, if not in their ancestral villages. France first granted citizenship to certain Senegalese traders in 1848, and from 1870 Senegalese sat in the French National Assembly and some became ministers in the French government. Léopold Sédar Senghor, a French poet in his own right, was elected to France's most prestigious *Académie Française* and married a French woman before he became an African nationalist and the first president of Senegal. In dealing with such highly educated Francophones, foreigners who do not speak good French may be at a disadvantage.

Older-generation Africans, educated in French and English schools in Africa, are well steeped in the history and culture of the former colonial powers. A Gambian professor has noted how much at home he felt on his first trip to London. England, he explained, and not The Gambia, was the country whose history he had studied as a child in school. For years, young Africans in francophone countries recited a history lesson that began with *"nos ancêtres, les Gaulois..."* (our ancestors, the Gauls...). Young Africans today are likely to know more about the histories of their own countries, but lessons in science and math will often draw on examples far beyond the experience of the majority of students.

Close-knit influence networks, based on old-school university ties, are a hallmark of Africa's educated elites. Secondary school networks are also important because many African countries have only a few secondary schools, and they are often boarding schools, which bind classmates together long after they have finished their schooling.

With the growth in education, the adult literacy rate doubled, on average, between 1970 and 1992 but was still only 54 percent. And there was wide disparity among countries, as high as 83 percent in Zimbabwe and as low as 12 percent in Niger. Everywhere, moreover, literacy was higher for men than for women.[91]

In cities as well as in villages, visitors should not assume that everyone can read a local or national language. Even functional literates, such as waiters in restaurants, may take what seems like an exceedingly long time to record your order, and your taxi driver may not be able to read written directions or road maps.

Hazardous Health

Health is the main thing.

—Swahili proverb

Africans have always appreciated the importance of health care because good health is seen as necessary for the continuation and growth of their lineage. Poor health, however, has always been and still is a major problem in all the African countries, and international donors and development foundations have now recognized that without major attention to health issues there will be little progress in economic and social development.

Life expectancy at birth in 1992 for all of sub-Saharan Africa was 51.3 years, but for many countries it was much lower, and for Sierra Leone it was only 39.[92] In 1993 the mortality rate for children under age five was 178 per thousand live births, but in Sierra Leone it was 284.[93] By comparison, in Hong Kong it was 7 per thousand and in Singapore only 6, comparable to the lowest figures in the industrial world.[94] In the United States in 1996 it was 9.[95] Most child deaths in Africa are due to just a few causes—diarrhea and dehydration, measles and other immunizable diseases, malaria, and malnutrition—all of which can be prevented or reduced in severity at a moderate cost. As mentioned previously, child survival from some of these common illnesses has been increasing in the last few decades, but further improvements are slowed by the lack of access by many urban and rural families to basic health services of adequate quality. An estimated one to two million African children die of malaria and malaria-caused anemia each year.[96]

Malaria remains a menace for adults as well as children, in part because the parasite has become increasingly resistant to drugs such as chloroquine, which were once a cheap and effective means of prophylaxis and treatment. This drug resistance has been increased by the tendency of many people to stop taking their medication when the symptoms have disappeared but before the parasite has been totally eliminated from the body.

In some areas where malaria is endemic, it is not uncommon for 60-75 percent of the population to be infected subclinically (i.e., without overt symptoms). Visitors to Africa can significantly reduce their chances of contracting the disease by taking the prophylactic drugs recommended for specific countries, and for the entire period recommended. (For more on malaria, see "Tips for Travelers," and for advice on countries to be visited, call the International Travelers' Hotline at the U.S. Centers for Disease Control and Prevention, tel. 404-332-4555.)

Maternal mortality is also high, and sub-Sahara has the world's highest rate. According to UNICEF, one in thirteen women in sub-Saharan Africa dies of causes related to pregnancy and childbirth, compared with 1 in 3,300 in the United States and 1 in 7,300 in Canada.[97]

Abortion is officially proscribed in almost all countries or permitted only in cases of rape or incest, or to save a woman's life. Abortions, however, both illegal and unsafe, occur all too often and result in infections, hemorrhaging, and death. Other factors contributing to high maternal morbidity include high pregnancy rates among teens, low levels of contraceptive availability and use, a lack of health care during pregnancy and childbirth, and female circumcision.

The rapid spread of Acquired Immune Deficiency Syndrome (AIDS, or *SIDA* in French and Spanish) is a tragedy of catastrophic proportions. Sub-Saharan Africa, with less than 10 percent of the world's population, has 70 percent of the world's people infected with the virus and more than two-thirds of the AIDS cases. Since the emergence of the disease in the region more than fifteen years ago, an estimated ten million adults and one million children have been infected, and as many as three million have died as a result of AIDS-related illnesses. Moreover, whereas the human immunodeficiency virus (HIV, which causes AIDS) is prevalent in the West mainly among homosexuals and drug users, in Africa heterosexual transmission is the leading cause of the infection, and more women than men have become infected.[98]

According to World Health Organization estimates, as of mid-1995 one-half to two-thirds of sub-Saharan adult HIV infections were in East and Central Africa although that area accounts for only one-sixth of the sub-Saharan population. In countries most affected by the pandemic, one-quarter or more of the adult urban population is infected.[99]

Infection levels are higher among female teenagers and younger women than males in the same age cohort, while older males have a higher infection rate than females of the same age. This is due, in part, to the biological fact that women are more easily infected than men but also because a polygynous culture condones mature men having sex with young girls, which they often do in the mistaken belief that younger women are free of the virus. In several countries, initial HIV infections were most frequent among educated professional men, who can afford to have girlfriends or patronize prostitutes.

In addition to the millions who have died or are presently infected, the AIDS pandemic in Africa is having other far-reaching consequences. Health services in many countries are swamped by the need to care for increasing numbers of infected and sick people. Ameliorative drugs are too expensive for most victims, except for a very small number who are affluent. And the increasing number of AIDS orphans is placing additional burdens on extended families and poorly developed social welfare systems.

[1] Ambrose Moyo, "Religion in Africa," in *Understanding Contemporary Africa*, edited by April A. Gordon and Donald L. Gordon (Boulder, CO and London: Lynne Rienner, 1992), 223.

[2] Akilagpa Sawyerr, in *Africa: Dispatches from a Fragile Continent*, edited by Blaine Harden (Boston: Houghton Mifflin, 1990), 67.

[3] Harden, *Africa*, 63.

[4] Ibid., 72.

[5] Mamadou Dia, "Cultural Dimensions of Institutional Development and Management in Sub-Saharan Africa (SSA)," unpublished paper, Capacity Building Division, Africa Technical Department, World Bank, 17 October 1990, 5.

[6] Ibid., 5.

[7] Mamadou Dia, *Africa's Management in the 1990s and Beyond: Reconciling Indigenous and Transplanted Institutions* (Washington, DC: World Bank, 1995), 54-56.

[8] *Christian Science Monitor*, 14 September 1994.

[9] Patrick Manning, *Francophone Sub-Saharan Africa, 1880-1985* (Cambridge, England, and New York: Cambridge University Press, 1988), 42.

[10] Colin M. Turnbull, *The Lonely African* (New York: Simon & Schuster, 1962), 248.

[11] Cited by James H. Vaughan in "Population and Social Organization," in *Africa*, 2d ed., edited by Phyllis M. Martin and Patrick O'Meara (Bloomington, IN: Indiana University Press, 1986), 170.

[12] Dia, *Africa's Management in the 1990s*, 109.

[13] *Financial Times*, 22 March 1996.

[14] Ali A. Mazrui, *Political Values and the Educated Class in Africa* (Berkeley: University of California Press, 1978), 155.

[15] Ibid.

[16] Ali A. Mazrui, *The Africans: A Triple Heritage* (Boston: Little, Brown, 1986), 199.

[17] Turnbull, *Lonely African*, 14-15.

[18] Roland Oliver and J. D. Fage, *A Short History of Africa*, 6th ed. (London and New York: Penguin Books, 1990), 261.

[19] Newton Leroy Gingrich, "Belgian Education Policy in the Congo 1945-1960," unpublished doctoral dissertation, Department of History, Tulane University, 6 May 1971.

[20] David Lamb, *The Africans* (New York: Vintage Books, 1987), 160.

[21] Ibid., 159.

[22] Mazrui, *Africans*, 246.

[23] Wole Soyinka, *The Open Sore of a Continent: A Personal Narrative of the Nigerian Crisis* (New York: Oxford University Press, 1996), 136.

[24] A. Adu Boahen, *African Perspectives on Colonialism* (Baltimore: Johns Hopkins University Press, 1987), 99.

[25] Paulin J. Hountondji, "Producing Knowledge in Africa Today," *African Studies Review* 38, no. 3 (December 1995): 6.

[26] Boahen, *African Perspectives*, 107-08.

[27] Ibid., 108.

[28] *New York Times*, 12 October 1995.

[29] *UNESCO Statistical Yearbook* (Paris: UNESCO, 1994), 3-411.

[30] Nelson Mandela, *Long Walk to Freedom: The Autobiography of Nelson Mandela* (Boston: Little, Brown, 1994), 263.

[31] Immanuel Wallerstein, *Africa: The Politics of Independence* (New York: Vintage Books, 1961), 75.

[32] Anton Andereggen, *France's Relationship with Subsaharan Africa* (Westport, CT: Praeger, 1994), 94.

[33] Jean-Pierre Cot, quoted in *New York Times*, 13 March 1995.

[34] *New York Times*, 22 May 1996.

[35] Ibid.

[36] Ibid.

[37] Manning, *Francophone Sub-Saharan Africa*, 181.

[38] Harden, *Africa*, 18.

[39] Herskovits, *Human Factor*, 426.

[40] Mazrui, *Africans*, 142.

[41] *New York Times*, 2 September 1996.

[42] Bohannan and Curtin, *Africa and Africans*, 206-07.

[43] Francis Cardinal Arinze, quoted by Paul Wilks in the *New York Times Magazine*, 11 December 1994.

[44] Moyo, "Religion in Africa," 249.

[45] John S. Mbiti, *Introduction to African Religion*, 2d ed. (Oxford, England: Heinemann Educational Publishers, 1991), 42-43.

[46] Herskovits, *Human Factor*, 19.

[47] *New York Times*, 28 July 1996.

[48] Chinua Achebe, *Things Fall Apart* (New York: Fawcett Crest, 1959), 18.

[49] Robert Coughlan, "Black Magic: Vital Force in Africa's New Nations," *Reader's Digest* vol. 79, no. 473 (September 1961): 157.

[50] *Washington Post*, 7 April 1996.

[51] Turnbull, *Lonely African*, 216.

[52] Camara Laye, "African Child," trans. James Kirkup, in *Coming of Age in Africa: Continuity and Change*, Unit 1 in *Through African Eyes: Cultures in Change*, edited by Leon E. Clark (New York: Praeger, 1971), 75.

[53] Herskovits, *Human Factor*, 295.

[54] *New York Times*, 1 May 1997.

[55] *Washington Post*, 22 May 1995.

[56] Robin Horton, "African Traditional Thought and Western Science," *Africa* 37 (1967): 53.

[57] Kae Graham, from an inscription in Museum Africa, Johannesburg.

[58] Ali A. Mazrui, "Development in a Multi-Cultural Context: Trends and Tensions," in *Culture and Development in Africa*, edited by Ismail Serageldin and June Tabaroff (Washington, DC: World Bank, 1994), 135-36.

[59] Mazrui, *Africans*, 234.

[60] Ibid., 128.

[61] Lawi Joel, in *Botswana Guardian*, 1 December 1995.

[62] *Washington Post*, 2 May 1996.

[63] *Better Health in Africa: Experience and Lessons Learned* (Washington, DC: World Bank, 1994), 18.

[64] Nahid Toubia, *Female Genital Mutilation: A Call for Global Action* (New York: Women, Ink, 1993), 5.

[65] *Washington Post*, 28 February 1995.

[66] Bohannan and Curtin, *Africa and Africans*, 122.

[67] James H. Vaughan, "Population and Social Organization," in *Africa*, edited by Martin and O'Meara, 166.

[68] Ibid., 165-66.

[69] April A. Gordon, "Women and Development," in *Understanding Contemporary Africa*, edited by Gordon and Gordon, 204.

[70] *Factors Affecting Contraceptive Use in Sub-Saharan Africa* (Washington, DC: National Academy Press, 1993), 92-95.

[71] Chenjerai Hove, *Shebeen Tales: Messages from Harare* (London: Serif; Harare, Baobab Books, 1994), 95.

[72] Ibid., 96.

[73] Florence Abena Dolphyne, *The Emancipation of Women: An African Perspective* (Accra: Ghana University Press, 1991), 20-21.

[74] Interview with Samu M. Samu in Malawi, November 1994.

[75] Bohannan and Curtin, *Africa and Africans*, 118.

[76] Turnbull, *Lonely African*, 171.

[77] Mbiti, *Introduction to African Religion*, 112.

[78] In Southern Africa, the prefix *Ba* indicates "people," as in Batswana (the Tswana people) and Basotho (the Sotho people).

[79] Harden, *Africa*, 15.

[80] James P. Grant, *The State of the World's Children* (Oxford and New York: Oxford University Press, published for UNICEF, 1994), 82.

[81] In discussing colonial education, the authors have drawn from Turnbull, *Lonely African*, 89-93.

82 Bohannan and Curtin, *Africa and Africans*, 207.

83 Wallerstein, *Africa*, 66.

84 Jacob Ngu, quoted in *New Scientist* (7 October 1995): 57.

85 Basil Davidson, *Africa in History* (New York: Macmillan, 1968), 318.

86 Ibid., 319.

87 Ibid., 318.

88 Bohannan and Curtin, *Africa and Africans*, 263.

89 Education enrollments used here are for 1992, in World Development Report 1995 (Washington, DC: World Bank, 1995), 216, 241.

90 In Uganda in 1991 primary school teachers were paid 8,000 shillings per month while the "living wage" was 70,000 per month.

91 *Human Development Report 1995* (New York: Oxford University Press, published for the United Nations Development Programme, 1995), 163.

92 Ibid., 159.

93 Ibid., 169.

94 Ibid., 168.

95 Thomas M. McDevitt, *World Population Profile: 1996*, U.S. Bureau of the Census Report WP/96 (Washington, DC: Government Printing Office, 1996), A-35.

96 J. G. Breman and C. C. Campbell, "Combatting Severe Malaria in African Children," *Bulletin of the World Health Organization* 66 (1988): 611-20.

97 *New York Times*, 11 June 1996.

98 *USAID Responds to HIV/AIDS: A Report on the Fiscal Year 1994 HIV/AIDS Prevention Programs of the United States Agency for International Development* (Washington, DC: USAID, 1995), 5-6.

99 *HIV/AIDS in Africa*, Health Studies Branch Research Note No. 20 (Washington, DC: U.S. Bureau of the Census, 1995), 2.

Face-to-Face with Africans

We join together to take wise decisions, not foolish ones.
— Yoruba proverb

Communicating with Africans

Talking with one another is loving one another.
— Kenyan proverb

Whether in West, East, Central, or Southern Africa, in francophone or anglophone countries, in Senegal, Kenya, Congo, or Zimbabwe, the spoken language rather than the written is the main means of communication. As Tanzania's founding father, Julius Nyerere, has written, "The very origins of African democracy lay in ordinary oral discussion— the elders sat under a tree and talked until they agreed."[1]

Written language, with few exceptions, came late to Africa, and the spoken word has remained the principal means of imparting information, both between and within generations. Somalia chose its alphabet only in the 1970s, and many African languages today remain unwritten. Most educated Africans, nevertheless, are at home in at least two or three languages—that of the former colonial power and one or more local languages.

Storytelling, it follows, is an African art, and many sub-Saharan writers have of late achieved prominence outside of Africa. The art of storytelling can tell us much about the African art of conversation. African stories follow a standard pattern to hold the attention of listeners, says Vusamazulu Credo Mutwa, the celebrated Zulu author and witch doctor:

> At no time must boredom set in. One must play with the listeners' emotions as one does with a toy doll. Make them laugh, make them cry, make them angry, thwart their expectations, puzzle them one moment, delight them, or repel them, the next. And always leave them with wide open mouths, begging for more.[2]

Among the Yoruba of West Africa, on the other side of the continent from the Zulus, storytelling is also a high art form. One Yoruba storyteller, Wole Soyinka, is a Nobel laureate in literature. The narrative line, writes one critic, "...incorporated elements of theater, music, mime, ritual, magic, dance, and the linguistic elements of proverb, poetry, riddle, parable, and song. They were not so much told as performed...."[3] The Uncle Remus stories and many other tales so familiar to Americans from childhood have their origins in West Africa.

Also celebrated in African cultures are the griots, a caste whose members we might call bards or troubadours—tellers of tales and singers of songs. In former times, each well-situated family had its hereditary griot who preserved family history and traditions by handing them down from generation to generation. Today, some griots still play the role of family historian, but now that family history is often written, they function more as entertainers, performing at family events like weddings, birthdays, and funerals, and on radio and television.

In conversation, as in storytelling, proverbs and parables which transmit the wisdom of past generations play an important role. "Nothing is closer to the heart of African society and thought than the proverb," writes Jan Knappert, a Dutch Africanist. "More than any other African tradition, it expresses the essence of African wisdom."[4] African proverbs, moreover, express universal truths which also have parallels in Western wisdom and experience. Westerners should embellish their speech with their own proverbs, which Africans will surely understand, appreciate, and in many cases, find similar to their own.

Because of their oral tradition, Africans enjoy debate and exchanges of views. Like storytellers, they seek to hold their audiences' attention, making prolific use of proverbs and epigrams which not only enrich their speech but also provide insights on how they feel about particular issues.

Repetition is a practice common to oral tradition, in song as well as in conversation, and Africans use it for emphasis as well as a reminder of what has been said before. Repetition makes it more likely that something will be remembered but it also adds to the time needed for presentation, as does embellishment with stories. When planning a meeting or workshop, it is prudent to allot more time than in the West for both small- and large-group discussions.

With the oral tradition come good memories, and it may not be necessary to put everything down on paper. When computers crashed at a women's conference held in Dakar in 1994, the African women were not at all fazed. True to their tradition as good storytellers, they re-created their agenda from memory and proceeded with their deliberations without the help of technology.

Whatever language they may speak, Africans seem to be born orators, and visitors may be expected to be equally gifted. You can count on being called on to give extemporaneous speeches, and it pays to be prepared with a few appropriate points illustrated with amusing stories.

The Languages of Africa

> African languages are highly developed and fine instruments;
> they are as expressive and as expandable as their speakers care
> to make them.
> —Paul Bohannan and Philip Curtin, *Africa and Africans*

The facial features of one ethnic group may be recognizable to members of another but their languages usually are not. Africa, as noted before, is a patchwork of dissimilar groups of people living within boundaries imposed by colonial powers without regard to ethnicity or language.

Prior to colonialism, several African languages were expanding along natural trade routes—Kiswahili in East and Central Africa, Hausa in West Africa, Arabic in the north—and, in time, they would have developed into major regional languages (as Hausa and Kiswahili already have) and facilitated cross-cultural communication. Today, however, Africans are forced by necessity to use European languages—mainly English or French—as lingua franca to communicate with each other and to support a sense of nationhood.

More than one thousand languages are spoken in sub-Sahara, as well as thousands of dialects, which is not so strange when we consider that North America once had about five hundred languages, of which some one hundred are still spoken. Moreover, if we add the languages brought by immigrants, more than three hundred languages are spoken in the United States today.

Congo, with forty-five million people, has more than two hundred fifty languages. Gabon, with only one million or so people, has forty-three dialects. Some of these languages and dialects are closely related, but others are very different from those spoken in adjacent areas.

Languages in Africa are classified according to five major groups. Niger-Congo, the largest group, is spoken in most of Western, Central, and Southern Africa and includes the closely related Bantu languages. Nilo-Saharan is spoken along the upper reaches of the Nile River, the middle Niger River, and in western Sudan. The Hamito-Semitic group is spoken across North Africa, the Sahara, the Horn, and in the area around Lake Chad; of this group, Hausa is the most important. The Khoisan languages are spoken in the highlands of Southern Africa. Malagasy, the final group, is spoken on the island of Madagascar and is similar to the languages of the Malayan archipelago from whence its settlers came to the previously uninhabited island some one thousand years ago.[5]

South Africa, an ethnically diverse country of some forty-two million, has eleven official languages including English and Afrikaans, the latter a creole spoken by descendants of the Dutch who settled in southern Africa more than three hundred years ago. Zulu is the most commonly spoken of South Africa's local languages, but many black South Africans without formal education are fluent in several languages which they need in order to communicate with other inhabitants of the multilingual black townships.

The language that South Africans choose to speak in mixed company is a matter of etiquette, reports Ann Cooper of National Public Radio. "A woman usually adopts her husband's home language if it's different from her own. Younger people address their elders in whatever language the elders prefer."[6]

In other situations the basic rule is to be hospitable, says Lebo Chanza, a South African woman. "When we have company at my house and we have people who speak various languages, we try to make them feel comfortable—all of them. So, my mother, when she summons them to eat…she might say 'Avon tu, lali zheng,' which is both Suthu and Zulu.… She calls *avon tu*, which is 'eight people' in Zulu. *Lali zheng* is Suthu for 'come and eat' so that way, everybody feels equally welcome and equally…taken care of and sort of equally paid attention to."[7]

In addition to their local languages, educated Africans, as noted earlier, are also at home in one or more European languages, a factor which facilitates communication with expatriates and other Africans. But the European languages are no longer considered foreign by many Africans. As Congolese writer Henri Lopes explains, "...they are African languages, and they belong to us. They have now become part of our culture. We can manipulate them, we can transform them."[8]

Africans, even those without formal education, are adept in learning languages. An American in Mali reports that her housekeeper, who never went to school, speaks the local Bambara language, is fluent in French, and understands English.

Most African languages are not too difficult to learn, despite their divergences from those of the West, and with a little diligence it is possible to acquire a basic working knowledge of one in a few months. Easily learned is Kiswahili, literally, the language of the Swahili people. A Bantu language with many Arabic and English loan words, Kiswahili is fast becoming the lingua franca of East and Central Africa. Along with English, it is also an official language in Kenya and Tanzania. Wherever they may be, foreigners who learn to greet in the local language will be assured a warm reception.

"The most important art in Africa," says Knappert, "is the art of language."[9] Learn a few words and key phrases of a local language and you will be accepted as a member of the community. When you speak the local language, Africans will feel that you are someone they can talk with and who will "understand" what they are saying. Colonialists who did not make an effort to learn the local language were viewed as outsiders although they may have lived in one place for many years.

In anglophone countries, people without formal education may speak a pidgin English or no English at all, and educated people may use British expressions which may sound strange to North Americans. In anglophone countries, for example, when you ask to speak with someone in an office and are told "He's not on seat," it means he's not there now. To make sure that you are understood, avoid using American idioms that Africans may not be familiar with. Instead, try to learn the local idioms, and use them.

Whatever language is spoken, visitors should expect, at times, to be misunderstood when conversing with Africans who have limited knowledge of English or French. But some foreigners may take it personally, suspecting that there is a hidden agenda for Africans who feign a "Yes, I understand," but then show that they do not. In such cases, give them the benefit of the doubt. Assume that they indeed do not understand and avoid thereby a confrontation.

Languages may be easily learned, but the spelling of African names is another matter, since there seem to be no generally accepted rules of orthography. In some countries the familiar Muslim name will be Mohammed, and in others Muhammad or Mamedou. As one Englishman expressed his frustration, "The problem of spelling African proper names has, over the years, substantially shortened my life."[10]

Whatever their spelling, names are very important in African cultures. They help to create a bond with the person you are addressing, and they should be remembered and used. If someone gives you his or her European name, ask if he or she has an African name, and use it.

Reaching Consensus

Wisdom comes from reasoning together.
—Yoruba proverb

Communication styles can vary considerably across the continent, depending on language, culture, and tradition. Some things are decided by men only, others by women only, and still others by men and women together. One thing is certain, however. No matter where you go in Africa, decisions are not made on the spot but rather take some time to reach through consensus.

Consensus is crucial in decision making. Africans must be consulted on almost everything, and within the clan everyone—which means all the men, in most cases—must be brought on board before a decision is made. The need to reach consensus helps to explain why it may appear so difficult to get things done. But, as Africans point out, reaching a decision through consensus has the advantage of taking into account all dissenting opinions, whereas majority rule does not. Reflecting all differences of opinion within a group is a key African value.

A Western trainer at a workshop relates how he once asked for a show of hands for and against a proposal he had just made. But such an approach was puzzling to the participants, who wanted first to thoroughly discuss the proposal and then reach a decision with which all could concur.

In another more graphic example, an expatriate relates how he once hired an artist to prepare a poster, having reached an agreement with him beforehand on job specifications. When the completed poster turned out to be different from what they had agreed on, the expat said that he would not pay, to which the artist retorted, "Since we reached consensus on what the job specs would be, we must also have consensus on whether or not you pay me!"

This need for consensus calls for prudence on the part of foreigners. Confrontation should be avoided, since it inhibits the achievement of consensus. If differences are openly aired, Africans may believe that you are trying to pick a fight with them. To dispel such suspicions, speak softly and slowly, repeat your talking points over and over, and take your time. Never say "That's not true." Rather, propose an alternative while recognizing the sincerity of your interlocutor's concerns and needs. "The best remedy for a dispute," a Chuana proverb says, "is to discuss it."

This is not to imply that Africans do not have disagreements among themselves. At work, people do indeed have quarrels, but heated argumentation and confrontation, especially in public, are rare except in Coastal West Africa, where people are more outspoken. Within the family or village, where they live in close proximity, there may well be disagreements, but confrontation is avoided by searching for common ground.

In the Dogon region of Mali, where people believe that true speech can only be expressed while seated, village meetings are held in huts with ceilings only three feet above the ground. People must crawl into the hut, and anyone who rises in anger will literally hit the roof. "Blowing your top" is physically impossible.

At village and tribal meetings, all men are allowed to speak (and in some societies, elder women as well), and meetings can last for several hours until a consensus is reached that is acceptable to all. As Nelson Mandela describes such meetings, "Democracy meant all men were to be heard, and a decision was taken together as a people. Majority rule was a foreign notion. A minority was not to be crushed by a majority."[11]

In Benin, for example, a group of education experts was once trying to rate the elements essential to quality schooling. Eight of the ten educators believed that trained teachers was the most important, but the meeting could not proceed to other items on the agenda until the group had thoroughly discussed why the two dissenters had a different opinion. Only when those two had changed their minds and formed a consensus with the majority could the meeting move on.

In the village, decisions are usually made by the chief or headman but only after all views have been fairly heard, including his own, which may be presented by another speaker, who will say, "The chief says...." Also taken into account by the chief are the history, culture, and beliefs of his people. In this sense, consensus indicates a joint decision acceptable to all.

Although seemingly democratic, consensus may at times mean that the group will agree to whatever they believe the most important person wants to hear. Africans at an early age learn to please teachers and elders by giving the "right" answer, and in later life they often tend to give the answer they believe will please a more senior person. Employees will assume that the boss knows best, and participants in meetings will freely exchange ideas and opinions until the "Big Man" arrives and takes charge, after which they will clam up.

An American health-care specialist reports that when she asks her African assistant for an opinion, the assistant, an experienced physician who has studied in the United States, tries to learn first what her American colleague wants to hear.

What to do? One simple solution is to ask Africans for their views before giving your own. But do not ask, "What do you think?" because some Africans will only tell you what they believe you want to hear. Do not put all your inquiries into a single question which requires a simple answer. Talk around the issues in a circular, indirect fashion, and then return to them. This is a characteristic African way of exploring an issue, as will be seen below. If you feel your question has not been answered initially, don't give up. Take your time, be patient, and wait for another opportunity. When trying to get a genuine opinion, listen for silence and look for blank faces. These will indicate areas of disagreement which Africans may be reluctant to express openly.

If you are lost in a city and ask an African for directions, he may summon several bystanders, whether he knows them or not, and a long discussion will ensue on how to direct you to your destination, but only after a consensus has been reached will you be given directions. Harden writes that the man you ask for directions is also likely to get into your car, ride with you to your destination, and insist on walking home.[12] Before asking for directions, remember to say "hello" and "how are you?" At least one such exchange of greetings is expected before you pose your question.

In recognition of the importance of consensus, do not ask

decision makers to decide in public. Sound them out in private and get their agreement in advance before formalizing it in the presence of their associates. Allow time for them to consult with others and to develop support for your proposal.

The foregoing helps to explain why it is often so difficult to get decisions from African high government officials. They may appear to be giving you the dodge and trying to avoid a straight answer, but, in fact, such officials rarely make decisions on their own. They will want to consult with advisers and staff before rendering a decision and after reaching a consensus.

Ambiguity and Imprecision

> Nobody tells all he knows.
>
> —Senegalese proverb

"[T]he principle of circumspection in dealing with all strangers and superiors...," wrote Herskovits, is another aspect of African behavior which is "...implicit in traditional narrative and reinforced by the experience of conquest, colonial or indigenous...." It is important

> ...to listen with passive deference, to disclose as little as possible when questioned, to reach decisions through discussion and consultation with one's own people, to manifest an outer docility while biding one's time for the moment of redress....[13]

Ambiguity is an art in Africa, and imprecision is its first cousin. Africans speak naturally, with eloquence, and without hesitation or stumbling over words, but their language is often imprecise and their numbers inexact. Every personal interaction becomes a discussion which establishes a basis for the relationship between the two parties. Westerners should probe gently for specificity and details until they are reasonably satisfied that they understand what is meant even if not stated.

To avoid giving offense, Africans will often nod and say yes when they really mean no, even though they may strongly disagree. If you ask someone, "How shall we do this," the response might be yes, strange as that may seem. But if the response from a high official should be *on verra* ("we shall see" in French), it likely means that the project you are proposing is questionable and you may have to go back to a lower level and restart the discussion. The challenge is to determine whether the true response is really affirmative or negative. As British businessman Peter Biddlecombe explains,

> You ask a question or make a proposal. The African disagrees or is uncertain, but doesn't want to offend you so he agrees. But it's a formality, he uses symbol words or codes. Like a diplomat saying yes when he means perhaps and perhaps when he means no. He has observed the rules of courtesy, but has conveyed his true feelings. The problem, of course, is interpreting the signals.[14]

Saying yes avoids a confrontation but may also indicate that an African has not quite understood what you have said. To find out if yes really means yes, rephrase your question. Another way to avoid the automatic affirmative is to refrain from asking questions that invite a simple yes or no response.

As a noncommittal sign of acknowledgment that a controversial subject has been raised, Africans will often take a deep breath, somewhat like a gasp with an "eh" or "uh" sound. This prepares the way for discussing difficult topics while maintaining cordial relations with their interlocutors.

Proverbs, parables, and moralizing myths which, to the American, may seem tangential or irrelevant should be listened to attentively. They usually relate to the subject under discussion and can serve to shed light on hidden meanings and agendas.

Here's a fairly typical example. You are unlikely to get the results anticipated by asking an African official directly whether he would like to have an American volunteer working on a project in his community. To gauge the level of interest and commitment among the Africans, the proposal must first be developed in a preliminary fashion with input from both Americans and Africans. After a degree of mutual respect has been established, specific questions may then be asked, such as "What would you like to have a volunteer do? How much time can the African staff devote to working with the volunteer? What kind of housing can you offer?" From such questions, the true level of commitment to the proposal can be assessed. Questions asked in a negative rather than positive way may also elicit better responses, such as "What do you *not* want in a volunteer?" or "What mistakes have volunteers here made in the past?"

Interpreters may often be necessary but cannot always be relied upon for accuracy. An American education adviser tells of her visit to a village in Mali, where she asked the chief about education for girls. Her government-provided interpreter told her that the chief was saying wonderful things in support of education for girls. But a second interpreter, a missionary, was reporting exactly the opposite to another member of the visiting party.

What a Westerner is asking or proposing may not be applicable to Africa nor even translatable into African languages. As Turnbull notes, "There is a very real problem of communication...when it comes to translating European concepts into an African language, particularly those that are relatively simple and limited."[15]

Also, it may take longer to say something in an African language, particularly when translating a Western idea or object. *Kibonyezo cha kuvuta choo*, a sign which travelers will encounter in rest rooms at Nairobi's airport, is simply Kiswahili for "toilet flush."

Body Language

The eye is an organ of aggression.

—Zulu proverb

Watch Africans' body language (*les gestes*, in French), but be aware that they will be watching yours just as carefully, if not more so. Movement of eyes, faces, hands, and other body parts can indicate acceptance or rejection, although such body language may vary from culture to culture. As the Zulu proverb above indicates, the eye can be an instrument of aggression, as "the evil eye" may be in the West.

Body language in Africa is rather similar to body language in the West. You can determine, for example, if Africans are enjoying a meeting or workshop by whether they are sitting forward and looking involved or are leaning back and not speaking up.

If Africans do not like what you are saying, they may purse their lips, furrow their foreheads, or look elsewhere. They will laugh when nervous or unsure of themselves and fidget when uncomfortable. To demonstrate subservience they may use honorifics, remain seated, or stand in a hunched position. In Bantu societies it is impolite to stand upright in the presence of a higher-ranking person. In the West we do the same when we bow, curtsy, or genuflect as a sign of respect. Be careful, however, in Muslim regions, where body language and gestures may differ. A "thumbs up," for example, a sign of success in the West, may be seen by Muslims as a very lewd gesture!

Making eye contact when communicating with a person who is older or of higher status is considered a sign of disrespect or even aggression in many parts of Africa where respect is shown by lowering the eyes. Occasional eye contact may be acceptable but not a stare, as a Peace Corps volunteer in Senegal discovered.

While serving as a teacher, he recalls how upset he became when speaking one-on-one with his students because they never looked directly at him. He would admonish them sternly, as he would a student in the States, "When I talk to you, I expect you to look at me!" But all they would do was whip their heads up, briefly glance at him, and then look down again. In the United States, this would be taken as a sign that they had something to hide. In Africa, however, they were showing respect for an elder.

This is changing in some countries. A Somali who returned home in 1993 after a fifteen-year absence remarked that he felt like a stranger in his own country. After civil war and twenty-two years of violence and repressive rule, it was no longer the quiet and peaceful country he had known as a young man. The attitudes of Somali youth had also changed, he noted with regret. They now looked their elders straight in the eye.

So what should a foreigner do when meeting an African? If the visitor and the African are of comparable station, eye contact is acceptable but not an extended gaze. Africans who are older or more senior will be understanding when Westerners look them straight in the eye, even in cultures where it still may not be acceptable. But to avoid such dilemmas, old Africa hands advise visitors to avoid a direct gaze during the start of a conversation or, alternatively, to look down or focus on an earlobe of the person being addressed rather than the eyes. Others advise turning the head slightly so that your ears, and not your eyes, face your interlocutor. Still others say just be yourself and don't be overly concerned about whether or not you make eye contact.

Deference for status and age can also be shown in other ways, how loudly you speak, for example. With those you respect, you speak quietly.

Body language is also expressed by how Africans queue up, or rather fail to queue up, a practice that most foreigners find very annoying. Waiting is a way of life in Africa—in airports, railroad stations, banks, and government offices. But in much of Africa (East and Southern Africa excepted), queue discipline is delinquent and the customary African courtesy gets lost in the long lines people have to wait in. In banks, when you reach the head of a line after waiting patiently for your turn, persons standing behind you may reach around you in an attempt to make their teller transactions before you do. At airports passengers will line up for flights but when a plane is being boarded they will break from the line and storm the flight gate or plane ramp. What to do? If it really bothers you, use your elbows and protect your place. If not, stand back and enjoy the scene.

Coping with Customs

Follow the customs or flee the country.

—Zulu proverb

Customs, conventions, rituals, and rites are of long standing in Africa and they play an important role in how Africans relate to each other and to foreigners. While Westerners are not expected to behave as Africans would in all situations, knowing what is culturally correct and what is not can often mean the difference between success and failure.

Interpersonal Relationships

A good deed is something one returns.

—Guinean proverb

Africans lead materially simple but socially complex lives. Within that complexity, interpersonal relations take precedence, in everything from working with government officials to making purchases from vegetable vendors.

In relating to Africans you must first connect with them on a human basis. Talk about family, theirs and yours. Go out of your way to develop a good relationship so that you don't seem like the usual businesslike, distant foreign visitor. Ask them to suggest a name for you in their local language that you can use with them.

Invite them to lunch at a restaurant or to dinner at your home but don't provide posh hospitality which may intimidate, because they will not be able to match it. Start with a modest restaurant or, depending on their rank or status, treat them to a sandwich and soft drink at a street kiosk. Call on them when there is sickness in the family or some other untoward event. They will then regard you as different from the typical short-term or even long-term foreign visitor, and you will find it easier to focus with them on the tasks at hand.

Greetings and Salutations

The Yoruba are sticklers for form, one of the forms most insisted upon being the courtesy of extending greetings to all people one meets in the course of one's day, be they family, friends, acquaintances, or even complete strangers. A person who asks a favor of another person without the courtesy of extending the proper greeting...would be considered ill-mannered.

—Oyekan Owomoyela,
A Ki i: Yoruba Proscriptive and Prescriptive Proverbs

Proper greetings open a relationship and prepare the way for a successful encounter, not only among the Yoruba of Nigeria but throughout Africa. They indicate respect and acknowledge the importance of the person being greeted. It is not necessary to speak the local language, but you will earn respect if you can use it when greeting people. Learning a few key words will suffice and be appreciated.

Like all other personal interactions, greetings in Africa are social events and if you try to shorten them, you will be considered rude. In francophone countries, a person who does not say hello will be regarded as *gonflé*, inflated or impressed with one's own importance. Greetings (*les salutations*, in French) thus become a long litany of inquiries about the health and well-being of one's entire family, and like the family, they are extended.

"How are you" is the usual opener, followed by "and your parents...and your wife...and your children?" Such greetings take time, and they continue with much nodding and many "eh, eh" sounds. They are also repetitious, in both English and French as well as in local languages.

In Malawi, reports an American woman who lives there, when her driver comes to her home each morning, he always asks about her young daughter. The mother at first thought he was inquiring because the daughter is so pretty and winsome, but she gradually learned the importance that Malawians attach to asking about every member of the family.

When greeted by an African and asked "How are you?" you *must* add to whatever response you may give, "...and you?" If not asked about their health, Africans will be offended. In the initial stages of greetings, however, everyone's health may appear to be "fine," and it is only after continued conversation that, as time permits, the true state of health and other problems may be revealed.

Peace Corps volunteers, when preparing for service in Africa, often ask facetiously, "When am I allowed to say that I am not feeling well, or I am dying?" The answer: "Pain or discomfort can be acknowledged but only after first saying that everything is fine."[16]

Hands play a key role in greetings. The remedy for man, say the Senegalese, is man and his hands—we are born into the hands of people, carried through life by the hands of people, buried by the hands of others, and are greeted by hands.

You *must* shake hands on greeting Africans, not with a perfunctory handshake but with an extended one, and always with the right hand. Between men, a handshake may extend for minutes and well into the conversation that follows.

Variations on the traditional handshake will be encountered across the continent. In some parts of West Africa the handshake is concluded with a light tap with a clenched fist or a snap of the fingers. In Southern Africa, a handshake may be completed by locking thumbs with the other person—wrapping your fingers around their thumb—and then resuming the conventional handshake. In some cultures, as a sign of respect when greeting older or more senior people, you greet with the right hand while grasping your right hand with your left. Muslims may hold their left hands over their hearts while shaking hands with their right. Everywhere, however, African handshakes are gentle, even limp. "Bone crushers" are not appreciated.

A woman's hand, as in Europe, should be shaken only if she extends it, but in Muslim lands she should wait for the man to extend his. Some Muslim men, however, will not shake hands with a woman, and if an American or European woman is so treated she should accept it as a local custom and not take it personally.

African society is inclusive. Westerners might call this networking, but Africans were doing it long before North Americans coined the expression. An African expression, "The world walks," indicates that we never know when roles might be reversed, and it is therefore in everyone's best interest to maintain a broad network of contacts. People can be included in your network by eye contact, physical contact, considering their needs and ideas in your plans, or simply by greeting them.

When entering a room you must shake the hand of each, even if you may have greeted them somewhere else on the same day. The most senior or eldest person is usually greeted first, and then the others, including women, moving around the room in a circular direction. The same procedure is followed on leaving. If you approach a table where you know only one person, greet your friend first and then continue around the table greeting each person, or greet the one you know and let that person introduce you to the others. If an African has a title—minister, professor, or doctor—use it. Close friends are embraced.

Typical American abruptness will appear discourteous. An American, for example, may enter his or her office in the morning without greeting an employee and abruptly ask, "Have you finished that task I gave you last night?" Africans will be offended by not being greeted first, and they may show it by replying sarcastically, "And how did you sleep last night?" When phoning, greet the secretary or other person who picks up the phone; do not just ask for the person you are calling.

Extended greetings become second nature to expatriates who have worked in Africa for some time. When one American returned to Washington for consultation, he greeted a colleague with "Hi, Barbara, it's great to see you. How are you, and how's your family?" Puzzled, Barbara replied, "Do you know my family?"

In work situations Africans tend to be more formal and will address each other with "Mr." or "Mrs." In a business meeting in Nairobi, for example, where participants included Africans and Westerners, the Africans referred to each other as "my colleague, Mr. or Mrs. So-and-So," although they were all working for the same firm and knew each other well.

In offices of American organizations, where informality is usually the rule, Africans will eventually interact on a first-name basis. But American informality may initially seem rude to them, and first names should not be used until initiated by Africans. Otherwise, address them as "Mrs.," "Miss," or "Mister." ("Ms." is not widely used in Africa.)

Americans make friends easily and use *friend* to refer to people they may have just met and hardly know. This can confuse Africans for whom friendship means participation in family life and helping out when someone shows up on your doorstep and needs assistance. Americans should be somewhat reserved when first meeting Africans so as not to mislead them.

Other greeting rituals may also seem strange, as expat advisers to a health clinic in Burkina Faso once found out. In training health workers, the expats emphasized that mothers arriving at the clinic with their sick children should be greeted with a smile and made to feel comfortable. No, the health workers said, in Burkina Faso the arriving person initiates the greeting, and for health workers to greet the mothers would run counter to their culture.

Africans are a very physical people. They tend to touch members of the same sex in public more than Westerners do, and they are surprised and offended when this is not appreciated by their Western colleagues. Between acquaintances, touching on the arm is considered a good sign, and touching a person during a conversation is quite normal and should be seen as a way of emphasizing a point. If a man puts his hand on another man's knee while seated and conversing with him, it's merely a gesture of conviviality.

In addition to touching, Africans also get physically close to complete strangers and stand even closer when conversing. They also stand close when queuing up and, as noted before, do not hesitate to make physical contact with people standing ahead of them in line.

But whom you can and cannot touch will vary from country to country and between genders. The Senegalese and Ivorians, for example, do not touch in public, nor do the Batswana unless they have known each other for a long time. African men, as noted above, may hold hands when walking in public, and women will walk arm in arm. Cross-gender touching, however, is not common, in public that is.

Rules exist not only for greeting but also for taking leave. Guests in francophone countries, when taking leave, will colloquially *demande la route* (ask for the road). But when the hosts implore them to stay a few minutes more, they will continue to sit and talk. After a while the guests will repeat their intent to leave while rising from their seats and continuing to talk. Finally, with the third or fourth repetition of this ritual, the guests actually leave after the hosts have given them "half the route," implying that they must come back again.

Another departure ritual and common courtesy, this one

for hosts, is to accompany their guests to the street and to their cars if they have them. In office buildings, departing guests are often accompanied to the elevator. This is a courtesy we Westerners can learn from Africans.

Home and Hospitality

> The house that welcomes a guest does not die.
>
> —Luganda proverb

Hospitality in Africa is traditional, and it is impolite to refuse. If you visit a village where there is only one chicken and it is offered to you, accept it. You may feel embarrassed about taking the last chicken, but once it is offered, you cannot refuse. When offered a drink in a village, you should appear to drink, even if you only place the cup to your lips. Alternatively, you may pass up the drink, but in some regions you may be expected to sprinkle a few drops on the ground for the ancestors.

One Western consultant tells of his arrival in a village in Côte d'Ivoire, where the headman welcomed him with a tall glass of whiskey. Since it is impolite to refuse, he was soon one very inebriated consultant. In most environments, however, you are more likely to be offered something more refreshing—beer, soda, tea, or coffee.

Africans will go out of their way to be hospitable to foreigners, and visitors should be prepared for regal treatment. In Congo once, a party of three foreign health officials traveled to Idjwi Island on Lake Kivu to visit a hospital. Since local phones were not working, it was not possible to call the hospital head doctor in advance, and the party took the ferry to the island on the chance that he would be there. But as luck would have it, the doctor had taken an earlier ferry to the mainland and the next one would not be leaving for several hours. The hospital staff, however, quickly organized a boat and crew to row the foreign visitors back to the mainland. After serving soda, the staff took them down to the shore, where a pirogue had been outfitted with comfortable, upholstered armchairs. And thus they rode in regal style, as African royalty might have, but feeling somewhat embarrassed as the crew labored at their oars on the ninety-minute return trip. Such courtesies are not unusual in Africa.

Despite such courtesies many Africans will be reluctant to invite foreigners to their homes for fear of embarrassment over differences in living standards and their inability to provide the level of comfort to which expats may be accustomed. Africans apologize for not inviting expat colleagues to their homes, explaining "Your house is so much nicer than mine." Everywhere, however, an invitation to accompany an African on a visit to the family village is an honor and means that the expat has been accepted as a friend.

Some Africans may hesitate to invite foreigners, fearing that they will appear too forward, and guests might presume that the host has an ulterior motive. One Batswana suggested that foreigners take the initiative by asking "Where do you live, and what is your house number?" and then dropping by for an informal visit, as an African might do. Among friends, people drop in unannounced, even at mealtime, and are welcomed to the table. An unexpected visit by an expat would indicate that the guest is willing to pay a visit no matter what the housing conditions may be. A brief visit, however, is just not possible. Expect to stay a while. A caller is never turned away, and a home visit is always returned, as an American ambassador learned.

The ambassador had asked one of his senior African employees, who had been a guest in his home many times, why she never invited him to her home. "If I have been to your home," the African woman replied, "you do not need an invitation to come to mine." And indeed the ambassador did so, arriving unexpectedly one weekend afternoon in his big chauffeur-driven car, much to the surprise of the woman and her neighbors.

When Africans do invite foreigners to their homes, they will go to great lengths to please their guests and will buy things not normally eaten or which are special for the occasion such as new dishes, a pretty tablecloth, or butter for the table. But once in an African home, you should be careful about expressing admiration for something you see and like, lest it be presented to you as a gift. When invited for dinner, be punctual, although the meal may not be served until quite some time after your arrival. In the meantime, remove your shoes. Many Africans remove shoes in their homes, and so should their visitors. And when you leave, you may be given some small gift to express the family's pleasure in having had you as a visitor in their home.

In villages, the big meal of the day is in the evening before dark. In cities, residents formerly followed the old European custom of going home at midday for their big meal and then taking a siesta. But this practice has changed in many countries as cities have grown and commuting distances have increased. With the pace of life quickening, the big meal in the city is now more likely to be taken at home in the evening.

When in an African home, however, be prepared to eat at any time of the day, and if you are not fed, then something is surely wrong. "Eating together," an Ila proverb says, "means union in close relationship between equals."

Men are fed first in many cultures—and get the preferred portions—then women, and leftovers go to the children. This will seem strange to Westerners, but, as a Kenyan proverb tells us, "It is the duty of children to wait on elders, and not the elders on children." Westerners, women as well as men, will be treated as honored guests and fed first.

Africans may prepare a Western dish on the assumption that foreigners do not enjoy African food. But if an African dish is served, show your appreciation by asking for a second helping. Refusing courses that you may not find particularly appetizing is considered impolite. Vegetarians, for example, may have difficulty in avoiding meat, and dealing with such basic cross-cultural problems may call for some quick thinking. One American vegetarian broke her own rules and partook of the beef but drew the line at monkey, explaining to her hosts that monkey was her totem animal, an excuse they accepted. If eating insects turns you off, you may wish to recall that they are a good source of protein and are standard fare in many parts of the world.

An experienced American diplomat and his wife, principal guests once at a dinner in Zululand where an entire roasted lamb was the main course, were honored by being served the eyes of the lamb. While the other guests watched with approval, they dined on this local delicacy, which, they later confided, was like eating a firm grape. Fortunately, they did not have to ask for seconds.

While a meal of lamb's eyes, monkey meat, snake, flying ants, and caterpillars may indeed be a bit unusual, there are many other dishes considered delicacies by Africans that may also seem strange. In Nigeria the delicacy from cattle is not steak but other parts of the bovine body such as tail, tongue, shank, stomach, intestines, and other select cuts, all of them blended in a stew pot and served over rice or with cassava or boiled yam. The greatest delicacy of all in Nigeria is goat's head, prepared by women but served only to men.

In some parts of Africa certain dinner items may be considered unappetizing and are not eaten—shellfish, for example, or uncooked salad greens, which may be considered fit only for animal fodder. When hosting a dinner for Africans, it is prudent to check with a local friend as to what should be served and not served. Observant Muslims, for example, do not eat pork or drink alcohol. Be sure to have enough food— Africans invited to your home for dinner may bring along family members or friends.

Western guests will be urged to eat more but should be considerate and leave enough for those not seated at the table or around the communal bowl. Also, when eating from a plate, do not completely clean it or the hosts will assume that you are still hungry and will insist on serving another helping. In even the most modest of homes, food is shared unstintingly.

Whatever is served, you must never eat with your left hand. Similarly, you never offer or receive anything with your left hand. As in many other parts of the world, the left hand is considered unclean, since it is used for functions performed in another room of the house (or outside the house).

The stand-up Western cocktail party may seem strange to Africans, who would never invite guests to their homes for just snacks and drinks or wine and cheese. Even at an office party, guests should expect to be seated and not have to stand while juggling a plate, fork, and glass. Nothing less than a full meal is likely to be offered.

Privacy has no meaning in Africa, where the concepts of "private time" and "private space" do not exist for most people. Whereas a Westerner may wish to be alone when seeking to resolve a problem, an African in the same situation will seek interaction with others, in a kind of informal group therapy.

On the absence of privacy, Nelson Mandela writes that the three huts over which his mother presided in his home village were always filled with the babies and children of his relatives, and he can hardly recall an occasion as a child when he was alone.[17] Africans, accordingly, cannot understand why a single foreigner would want to live alone without a family. Westerners who prefer to be alone will repeatedly be asked, "Aren't you lonely?"

Africans will be concerned about your "loneliness," and when a close working relationship has been established, they may come by to see you in the evening even though you may have been with them all day at work. You may prefer to settle into an easy chair with a book or write a letter home to your family, but African colleagues will still believe that you may be lonely and need company.

Such a privacy problem was solved by one Peace Corps volunteer in Cameroon by instituting an "open door" policy. When the door to her hut was left open, she explained to the villagers, they were free to enter. When it was closed, she wanted to preserve her privacy.

Giving Gifts

> Mutual gifts cement friendship.
>
> —Côte d'Ivoire proverb

Gift giving is traditional in Africa, a sign of friendship between people who know each other and a sign of respect for people of higher status. Also traditional is sharing what you have, a custom of the extended family and a still-common communal way of life.

But there are times to give and times to receive. When visiting an African home, it is not necessary to bring a gift because the visit itself is considered a gift. But if you do bring one, be careful not to bring commonly available food items, which Africans may see as implying that they cannot feed you adequately. Alcoholic drinks will be appreciated (unless the family is Muslim), as will candy, pastries, flowers, or fruit in season. T-shirts and baseball caps with logos are welcome everywhere.

Be careful about giving expensive gifts, since Africans may feel obligated to give something more valuable in return, which may be difficult for them to do. If you are given a gift, you cannot refuse to accept. Bear in mind, though, that if someone gives you a valuable gift, you will be beholden to that person in the future.

On a village visit, bring sugar, fruit, vegetables, tea, or other food items which may not be available. Ask in advance what kind of gift will be best for the village you are visiting; it will vary from region to region, and you will be appreciated for showing concern. A gift for the chief or headman is also appropriate as a sign of respect and tribute.

The way to an African's heart is through children, and by
all means bring gifts for them—inexpensive toys, pencils or
crayons, balls, and balloons. When in doubt, ask what to
bring.

When arriving from the United States or Europe or going
up-country from a capital city, bring recent reports on subjects of interest to the professional people you will be visiting. These will be much appreciated because in most countries rural Africans have little access to printed material,
especially from abroad.

Africans may ask you to bring them something from home.
Take care, for they may be expecting you to present it as a
gift. If you do ask to be reimbursed, you will be paid, but the
recipients may show their disappointment by avoiding you in
the future.

Dash, Bribery, and Goodwill

> As in many places in Africa, everyone from the traffic cop to
> the Cabinet minister here is suspected of being subject to
> persuasion through the well-placed "gift" or bribe.
> —Howard W. French,
> *New York Times* (15 May 1995)

Gift giving, as noted above, is an old custom in Africa—and
in many other parts of the world—where you give something
in anticipation of or to return a favor. In the village, as we
have seen, the gift might be a chicken or a few kola nuts. In
government and business offices the custom continues but
the value of the gift increases, and the kola may become
"moola."

Dash, as the practice is known in anglophone West Africa,
is a time-honored tradition in most countries of the continent where officials are poorly paid and seek to supplement
their meager salaries or, in some cases, to substitute for salaries that have not been paid. It is thus more related to survival than to self-aggrandizement. While the term *dash* is not

as derogatory as *bribe*, the difference, for Westerners, may be difficult to discern.

Dash is something you give to grease the gears of the bureaucracy and get things going. It is a way of life, an annoyance you face almost everywhere in Africa.

Shakedowns can start with your airport arrival when a customs official asks for a little something to quicken your clearance. Or an immigration official checks your International Vaccination Certificate and tells you that you need a particular immunization for that country, one that you know is not needed. It continues when a taxi driver from the airport to your hotel charges you more than he would charge an African. And so it goes until the new arrival becomes "dash wise" and learns when to pay and when not to.

Police and the military—or those dressed in their uniforms—may also solicit bribes when they check cars at roadblocks or stop drivers for minor infractions and assess on-the-spot penalties. Have something in your car to give—a baseball cap, T-shirt, or souvenir with a logo. If you have nothing to give, say so. Africans have a good sense of knowing when foreigners are fibbing and when they are leveling with them.

Officials at government offices may also ask for something to "facilitate" a request. In such attempted rip-offs you don't have to pay, and most experienced Africa hands recommend you do not, even if you are intimidated when refusing to cough up some cash. If you do not pay, the threat will likely turn out to have been a bluff. If you do pay, it will only make things more difficult for others who come after you, and in the long run everyone will know about it and you will lose respect. NGOs (nongovernmental organizations), in particular, should not pay or they may have trouble with local tax inspectors later on. While bribes are out, lunches and Christmas gifts are in, and will be appreciated.

Tipping for services rendered is another matter. There is no hard-and-fast rule, but most Africans—the wealthy few excepted—do not tip. "Wealthy" foreigners—and this will include all Americans and most other expats—may be expected to give a little extra in taxis and upscale restaurants by rounding off the amount due.

Tipping, however, is often done differently in Africa. In America and Europe you tip after receiving a service. In Africa you give something beforehand to show your appreciation for the service you are about to receive, as an American in Kenya came to understand. The American, who shopped regularly at her neighborhood grocery, had established a good relationship with the owner to whom she occasionally gave a little extra money, and for good reason. Milk, at times, was in short supply, but our shopper knew that she could always get some for her children by going to her friend, the grocer. For his special customers, the proprietor kept milk and other hard-to-find items stashed away in the rear of his store.

Such "tipping in advance" is no different from the Western practice of giving a Christmas gift to the postman and others who provide regular services, in appreciation for the past year's service but also in anticipation of the next year's.

Some expats might regard this as bribery. Others may say it's expected of them because they are foreigners and presumed to be rich. Africans, however, do not see it as bribery, for this is how they deal with each other, and they will be treating expats no differently.

In business deals and transactions with government officials the difference between a bribe and a gift becomes more problematical. Reflecting local custom, Africans may expect a gift—cash or material—as a token of appreciation for the successful conclusion of a negotiation or the signing of a contract. U.S. law prohibits payment of bribes abroad (see the section, "Crime and Corruption"), and U.S. government regulations forbid federal employees to accept gifts. One U.S. official reports that he is constantly being offered lambs and other gifts that he must refuse, which puzzles his gift givers.

As Mazrui puts it, "...one culture's bribery is another's mutual goodwill."[18]

Money Problems

> Money is a kind of language here that nobody teaches you but you need to know. If you hang onto it too tightly you're stingy, and if you part with it too easily, you're a sucker.
> —Susan Blake, *Letters from Togo*

Money matters can cause needless friction between Africans and Westerners, and they are often cited by foreigners as the cause of their first mistakes in Africa. Unless an African is wealthy—and most are not—they must do many things for the sake of money, and expats who do not understand this will lose the trust of their African colleagues.

One American health-care professional describes her first money mistake, made on a trip up-country in Nigeria with a nurse and a midwife. To save funds for their health-care project, the American suggested that any money remaining after all travel costs had been paid should be returned to the project. This upset her African colleagues because per diem meant money for their families, and they did not want to return the excess funds.

With their large extended families, Africans have more people to care for than have most expats. At workshops, Africans will skip meals and drink only a cheap soda in order to bring home part of their per diem to their families, and they will consequently be disappointed if hotel rooms and food have been paid in advance by the organizers rather than through per diem paid to the participants. Unspent per diem can serve to supplement a needy family's income.

If a mixed group goes out for lunch, expats should offer to pick up the tab, since the cost of a lunch may be equal to an African's salary for the entire day. In one West African country, an African on the professional staff of a Western aid mission earned only the equivalent of six thousand dollars a year, although he previously had been a regional medical officer for his government, one of the more prestigious positions for an experienced physician.

Repayment of loans can also cause problems and may be perceived by some Africans in wildly unrealistic terms, as one Westerner learned. One of his employees asked him for a loan of ten thousand dollars and offered to pay it back at the rate of five dollars per month, failing to realize that he would not live long enough to liquidate the loan.

An obligation or agreement, moreover, is not absolute in Africa (as we were told by an African cross-cultural trainer), particularly when it concerns money. Rather, an obligation or agreement may depend upon relative need and personal relationship. A Malawian, for example, may ask an American friend or colleague for a loan but not say anything about repayment or even think much about it. Although he knows that payment is expected, he may reason that the American does not need the money, and it can be repaid if and when it is needed. The American, by contrast, sees the lending of money as an absolute principle—you borrow and you must repay. And if the American should insist on payment, the Malawian might have to borrow from someone else to repay the loan, and thereby go deeper into debt.[19]

To avoid such conflicts, caution should be exercised in lending funds to friends. Old Africa hands advise never to lend unless the borrowers are your own employees and you can deduct the repayment from their salaries. Others counsel that if friends ask to borrow money, offer instead to lend something, but less than the amount requested. Since they may be unable to repay a loan, the best course, if you hope to remain friends, is to make a small gift. If you do actually lend money, the recipient may become embarrassed when unable to repay and will avoid you. To resolve such a dilemma, meet them partway by saying that you prefer to give something outright but can afford only an amount smaller than requested. As a final resort to avoid lending money, you might quote a proverb that is common to many African cultures, "Lend money and buy an enemy."

The needs of the extended family can place demands on

their employed relatives. An American in Somalia and her Somali counterpart managed funds that were used to conduct health programs in refugee camps. So that he would not have to refuse to lend office funds to his many relatives, the Somali, at the outset, asked his American colleague to maintain full control of the funds. For the same reason, many Africans choose to work in African countries other than their own, and distant from their extended families.

Similarly, some expats will not entrust their African employees with an office checkbook, which in effect establishes a job ceiling above which Africans cannot rise. But as one foreign management consultant with many years of African experience points out, we all learn by doing, and expats seldom give Africans that opportunity. This consultant, who makes loans to small businesses, believes it is possible to set up financial controls which give employees the opportunity to learn how to manage money. Use accepted accounting procedures, he suggests, with a paper trail for each time money changes hands. Separate office functions—one person to approve expenses, another to keep the checkbook and write checks, a third to sign, and a fourth to reconcile bank accounts. Use checks instead of cash, require double signatures, and hire the best possible people to handle your finances. These, of course, are all things you would do in the States; in Africa do them more carefully.

Between friends and close acquaintances, however, business transactions can be conducted on a basis of trust. An African businessman once sold a car to an acquaintance on a handshake although the price was no small sum. When a friend later asked the businessman if he had been paid, he replied, "No, but I know him. He will pay."

Are there exceptions to these caveats? Yes, there are, and they are mostly women. African women have a well-earned reputation for being better money managers than men. Studies of West African community banks—the *tontines* whose members make regular payments to the bank and can borrow from the accumulated capital—show that women have achieved phenomenal repayment records, often exceeding 90 percent.[20] In Burkina Faso cooperatives which manage village health clinics, 33 percent of the members of the community committees that run the co-ops are women, but women hold 97 percent of the treasurer positions.[21] And in a management study of the Côte d'Ivoire Electric Company, the company "...capitalized on women's strong performance in financial management by reserving for females the top managerial jobs related to ensuring operational reliability and greater accountability."[22]

African Time

C'est l'Afrique; on a le temps. (This is Africa; we have time.)
—francophone saying

Africans usually show up late for appointments, meetings, and social engagements, a practice known as "African time." One Westerner recalls being kept waiting ninety minutes for an appointment he had earlier confirmed before being informed by a receptionist that her boss would be "a little late." Another ninety minutes elapsed before the boss finally showed up for the scheduled appointment. This too is traditional—in the village the headman shows up late and is the last to arrive for a meeting.

Among expats, various acronyms are used to denote African time. "WAIT" stands for West African International Time, and in Ghana, "GMT" indicates "Ghana Maybe Time." But foreigners who satirize the African tendency to tardiness should consider that Western punctuality is a relatively recent phenomenon, a product of the industrial age. Those of our ancestors who led an agrarian life also had a more relaxed attitude toward time.

In Africa, time is not money. If a task is not finished today, it can be completed tomorrow, and forty-eight hours can be the same as twenty-four. Good management of time is not a virtue, and waiting is a way of life, as two Hausa proverbs illustrate: "Going slowly does not prevent arriving" and "Hurry is not strength." People in a hurry, moreover, are viewed with suspicion and distrust.

Time for Africans is defined by events rather than the clock or calendar. A South African relates how he once gave a lift to an old farmer who said he was going to visit his daughter. "How far away does she live?" the driver asked. "Three days' travel," answered the farmer. "When did you leave home?" "When I left," answered the old man. "And when will you get there?" "When I get there." "Does your daughter know you are coming?" "No." "And what will she say when she sees you?" "Oh, you are here."

Most of the Africans with whom foreigners work are only one generation removed from the village and an agricultural way of life, where time is measured not by hours and minutes but by the sun and by the seasons which regulate the villagers' activities. Ugandan writer Okot p'Bitek, in his "Song of Lawino," describes the two seasons in the agricultural village where he was born: "Wet Season means hard work in the fields, sowing, weeding, harvesting. It means waking up before dawn.... Dry Season means pleasure, it means dancing, it means hunting.... Wooing and eloping with girls...."[23]

If you invite an African for dinner at 8:00 P.M., your guest may not arrive until 9:30, unless you make it clear that you are *not* on African time. And the dinner guest who does not show up at all and does not call to express regrets should not be seen as insulting, as in the West. Something may have come up to prevent his or her arrival, and since few Africans have telephones, it may not have been possible to call and let you know.

Meetings begin, therefore, not at the appointed hour but somewhat later, after enough people have shown up. More punctuality can be expected in cities than in the countryside, in private firms than in government offices, and with higher-rather than lower-level officials. But even in South African business circles, punctuality is not an issue. In Johannesburg, top-echelon officials will be on time, but for most other people ten o'clock can mean eleven, and no one is upset if someone shows up late, unless that someone is an expat, to whom stricter standards pertain.

For Africans, the person they are with is more important than the one who is out of sight and to whom a commitment of time, money, or other resources may have been made. If a meeting is running so over schedule that an African will be late for his next appointment, he may elect to stay and finish his present business, reasoning that the "uncle" waiting for him elsewhere will understand his tardiness. Or, he may reason that this "uncle" may not be able to come to the appointment on time anyway, so he might as well finish this business here and now. To excuse himself by saying that he has another appointment to keep or something else to attend to, as an American might do, is totally unacceptable.

American attention to being on time makes sense because we have control over most aspects of our lives and expect that those with whom we interact will have similar control. We have support systems, such as our own cars and dependable taxis, that make it easy for us to be on time for appointments, and if not, to call from a telephone which works to explain that we will be a little late. (Although, we might ask, when did your plumber last show up on time for a house call?) Indeed, the value of punctuality is reinforced by any number of American customs and is an intrinsic part of our fundamental value system.

In offices, Africans may be late but an American must show up as scheduled, because the one time when you are late, they might be on time. Indeed, Africans may be late, but they expect Americans to be on time. On social occasions, however, Westerners need not arrive on time unless the occasion is official, as some expats discovered when invited to a reception at the president's palace in a francophone

West African country. Invited for 9:00 P.M., the foreigners all showed up promptly at nine, after which the gates to the palace were locked. The president, however, did not show up until 11:00 P.M. In the interim two hours the guests were served champagne nonstop and were thoroughly sloshed when the Big Man finally made his entrance.

Even when an important official is to open a meeting at 8:00 A.M., the other participants may not show up until 8:30, and the VIP not until 9:00 or later. Protocol demands that the meeting not start until the VIP arrives, so people will sit and chat until the very important person appears. Westerners may suggest that the meeting begin without the official and that the proceedings be interrupted for the opening remarks when the VIP arrives. Such a tactic, however, is usually not possible; the meeting cannot begin without the VIP.

In restaurants you will have to ask for your bill. Diners can sit at their tables until closing time and the waiter will not bring the check unless asked. In contrast to the United States, restaurants in Africa are in no hurry to have you vacate your table for other diners.

What about Muslim punctuality? one might ask. Muslims pray five times a day and at certain specified times when they are called to prayer by muezzins from their minarets. But, as Mazrui explains, Islam brought punctuality to Africa only in the religious sphere, not in the secular domain.[24]

Africans are accustomed to waiting, and the advice given most often to Westerners is "Be patient." Things do not always go as planned in Africa, and sometimes they do not go at all. The means are often missing, and the lack of where-withal can cause delay or inaction. More time is needed to do almost everything, partly because the pool of human resources, especially trained manpower, is so small, and those with experience or training have many responsibilities and can be easily diverted from an assigned task. No matter what has been promised, another task may appear to have higher priority.

Despite the general advice to be patient, there may be times when you will want to explain firmly, clearly, and up front that your time is limited and you have a schedule to adhere to. If you set up your trip from the United States by fax or e-mail, ask for confirmation of your meetings and the scheduled starting times. You may also want to indicate how much time you have budgeted for each meeting. Africans can be punctual if they understand the importance a Westerner attaches to time.

One final caveat regarding time. Do not schedule back-to-back meetings or two meetings on the same morning or afternoon—you may be late for one of them.

Household Help

In Africa a servant expects to be treated like a servant. He might be a cousin or a niece, but he or she is there to fetch and carry. None of this: "We're all the same really, all one happy family."

—Peter Biddlecombe, *French Lessons in Africa*

"Africans have servants," explains Peter Biddlecombe, a British businessman who has traveled throughout francophone Africa for many years, "because they have always had servants. Throughout history African chiefs have been surrounded by advisers and retainers and slaves, sub-chiefs have had sub-servants, and so on."[25] Today, African officials, business executives, and professionals also have servants, and Westerners are expected to have them as well.

Americans who are unaccustomed to full-time household helpers may balk at employing them in Africa. Most Americans today, including many who are well-off, have never experienced having a servant in their homes and may want to maintain their privacy. Single women, in particular, may feel uncomfortable having a man around the house in countries where hired cooks are usually men. But new arrivals will soon find that they really need the help that a *domestique* can provide. There are, however, a few basic rules to bear in mind.

Some Americans, unfamiliar with full-time household help, may believe that employees should be treated as friends and equals, and not as servants. Egalitarianism is embedded deeply in the American psyche and informs and determines much of our behavior and the values we hold dear. But Africans, who keep their own help at a distance, believe that Americans get too familiar with their workers. Egalitarian treatment, moreover, will be seen by African employees as a sign of weakness and a lack of leadership, which they may take advantage of. In the same vein, in francophone countries you should *tutoyer* (use the familiar "you") your household employees but they do not tutoyer you in return.

It's not so much that you will be taken advantage of but that if you regard servants as friends, they will relate to you as they would to their African friends. They may use anything in the house they wish, take food from your kitchen to consume in their own homes, ask you to lend them money, and keep irregular hours. Those are some of the liberties they would take with their other friends.

Lay down the law from the first day. Tell your help what is expected of them—these are the rules of the house, your way of doing things, and they either adopt them or find another job. You can always ease up on the rules later, but once you have been permissive, you will not be able to tighten up.

When deciding how much to pay household employees, ask around among other foreigners to see what they are paying. But don't just look at the going rate for work of the same type. Try to figure out what an African needs to live, and go through the actual calculations. See how they live—do they have a bed, do they cook with gas on a stove or over three stones around an open fire?

How do you keep your household help honest when they are so poor? One expat solves this problem by asking his house guard to do extra tasks on a regular basis as an excuse to give him some additional money. Good attendance can be rewarded by giving a bag of rice or maize for not missing any workdays during a month. A large bag of grain may feed an entire family for a month. For the weekend, give an occasional kilo of meat, a luxury for lower-paid workers.

Many expats prefer to do their own grocery shopping, even for perishables, so they won't have to worry about how their money is being spent. Bear in mind, though, that your household help may get a much better price at the marketplace than you will. The downside is that they may skim something from the shopping money you give them.

Letters of recommendation from other Americans about prospective employees should be taken with a grain of salt. Americans usually do not like to be critical about former employees, not wanting to be responsible for their failure to find a new job because of an American's lack of endorsement. Instead, they may opt to write vague or inaccurate letters of recommendation. Old Africa hands advise hiring only persons with a record of uninterrupted employment with a series of employers of two- to five-years' duration each, and with written references for all periods.

To avoid disappointment, hire new employees for a short trial period—two weeks or so—and if they don't work out, release them. If kept beyond the trial period, labor laws in many countries may make it difficult for you to fire them. Employers should be familiar with the local laws on hiring and firing because their employees will certainly know them and may take legal action if fired.

Firing, moreover, may have consequences reaching out to many people in an extended family, far beyond the employee in question. An Ethiopian once gave vivid testimony to the significance of those consequences when explaining why his people preferred Americans to Russians.

"Russian families don't hire anyone," the Ethiopian explained. "Americans have a cook, a maid, a nanny, a driver, night watchmen. Each family has ten servants, maybe. And each one has ten people dependent on him. So every American feeds 100 Ethiopians. We love you."[26]

Rivalry within a household staff can cause dissension, especially if employees are from different ethnic groups. One sure way to avoid domestic dissension is to hire all your staff from the same extended family or clan, a tactic that has found its way to Washington, D.C., where all the African employees of the authors' local supermarket are Wolofs.

Household employees will turn to you for favors, as their *patron* (boss) or *patronne* (in the feminine), requesting a day off or the loan of your car. There is a give-and-take to favors—you give one and you get one in return, not immediately but sometime later when you may really need it. Africans ask favors easily, especially from a Big Man or person of authority who is expected to approve the request. To broaden your relationship, you may wish to grant some of the requests. But, as noted earlier, make no loans unless you can take the repayment out of their salaries.

If a long-time employee should die, certain obligations to the family must be met. One expat whose cook died found that the cook's several wives and children came to stay in his small room in her house because, according to local custom, the family must reside a while in the last residence of the deceased. The employer was also expected to pay for the funeral and coffin, and she had to make inquiries to learn how much to spend. She did not want to appear miserly but also wanted to provide only what local custom required.

Addictions and Stimulants

> He who brings kola brings life.
>
> —Igbo proverb

Alcohol and other stimulants have long been a component of many traditional African cultures, and today they may be used in doing business, much as tobacco, coffee, and tea are.

To do business in Somalia and Djibouti, as well as in adjacent parts of Kenya and Ethiopia, you may have to chew *khat* (also spelled *qat*). Serious business is not discussed at the office, reports one expatriate. Rather, he and his Somali colleagues, after lunch at the end of their normal 7:00 A.M. to 2:00 P.M. workday, would retire to a friend's home and don sarongs. There, they would sit on the floor, reclining on pillows propped up against a wall, and listen to Somali music, drink tea, and chew khat for a long and leisurely five or six hours during which they would discuss business and anything else that came to mind.

The bark or leaves of the amphetamine-containing khat plant is chewed and the resulting wad retained in the cheek. The trick is to chew the wad without swallowing it. While not habituating, khat can produce a psychic dependence, and it does have side effects. As a cousin to the coffee plant, it can so energize users that they may have difficulty sleeping at night. To get off a khat "high," Somalis advise taking a cold shower or a long walk.

Chewing khat is a male activity, and Somali women do not normally participate. Western women, however, may be invited to join in, another example of how they can have the best of two African worlds—socializing with both men and women.

In West Africa, the kola nut, another of the few stimulants tolerated by Islam, is widely used. Kola, which contains caffeine, is a coffee substitute, and watchmen will chew it to stay awake at night. Kola is also a sign of friendship and is used in ceremonial greetings and in consecrating contracts. Visitors to villages may be offered a nut to chew, and it is impolite to refuse. In some Muslim lands, kola replaces beer in rituals.

In East Africa, the substance offered in villages may be a few coffee beans. In other parts of Africa, it may be the betel nut, which produces a mild sense of euphoria. In Kenya, the leaves and shoots of the amphetamine-containing miraa bush, a variety of khat, are chewed.

In Southern Africa, where marijuana is widely grown, it is the stimulant of choice and, although illegal, can be found for sale in many countries. A powerful South African variety, called *dagga*, has been grown for centuries and is used in local tribal customs. In Congo, marijuana is called *bangi* (in Lingala) and *l'herbe Zairoise* (in French) and is big business.

Also illegal are hard drugs, mainly cocaine and heroin, which are new to Africa but becoming prevalent in some countries, where their use is increasing among more affluent middle-class white youngsters. Laws are strict, however, and users can be expelled from the country or given a stiff sentence.

In West Africa you may be offered palm wine, the fermented sap of the palm tree, which can be very potent. Some say it tastes like gin, and others like warm beer sweetened with liqueur. Whatever the taste, beware of the kick. Also beware of other home brews which may have traces of methyl alcohol if not prepared properly. Imported wines are expensive, but wines made from South and East African grapes are inexpensive, and some are very good indeed.

If there is a national drink of Africans, it is beer, brewed for centuries in the villages. "Drink beer, think beer," says a Congo proverb.

Bush beer, made from sorghum, millet, maize, bananas, or other grains and fruits, is mild, keeps only a few days, and may not be to every expat's taste. (The banana that is a food staple in equatorial Africa is actually a plantain and not the sweet banana that Americans know.)

But the European type of beer brewed in modern African breweries today is very good, although imbibers should be aware that it has a higher alcohol content than American beer and the standard bottle size is usually a half liter. The distribution system is efficient—by truck, plane, or pirogue—and good beer is available almost everywhere in Africa. Many a commercial or development project has fantasized how it might use this most efficient of distribution systems to get its product or message out to rural areas.

Beer drinking is prodigious in sub-Saharan Africa. For an office party in Lesotho, to estimate the number of twelve-ounce cans of beer to order, count the number of people and multiply by six. For the same party in Togo or Benin, order only one-third that amount. Harden recalls his visit to a Nigerian brewery, where a customer phoned in an order of 620 gallons (100 cases) for a party he was giving. That same morning the brewery also received orders of 204 gallons for a naming ceremony for a new baby and another of 510 gallons for a gathering commemorating the death of a parent.[27]

"Everything is centered on beer-drinking," writes Chenjerai Hove, Zimbabwe's leading novelist. "After the soccer match, the place to go is the bar. After work, it is the bar.... A party without enough alcohol is a disaster from the outset."[28]

Drinking early in the morning is socially acceptable in many countries, so don't be surprised if you are invited to have a beer before an early morning meeting. In Burkina Faso, after a coup in 1980, one of the first actions taken by the new government was to decree that bars must close during working hours and open in the daytime only during the lunch hour.

While beer drinking may be prodigious, getting drunk is seen as an aberration and a sign that something is wrong. Moreover, persons who become inebriated are not respected. Alcoholism is more of an issue in Southern Africa, however, where miners return home for month-long vacations during which many drink heavily. Elsewhere, alcoholism varies from country to country, and is, of course, less prevalent in Muslim regions.

Alcohol can also lead to domestic violence, which is as common in Africa as elsewhere. The AIDS pandemic has also led to misgivings about the role played by alcohol in forced sex and the failure to follow safe-sex practices.

African Humor

Laughter gives confidence; its absence causes dispute.
—Tuareg proverb

Africans will laugh about almost anything—their weaknesses, the hardships of their lives, the loss of a job. Even the Tuareg, a nomadic people of the Sahel who live in a very harsh environment, recognize the importance of laughter in their lives.

"Life is hard in Africa," writes Knappert, "so it can only be lived by those who are endowed with a grim determination to survive and a boundless energy to enjoy every day. This makes African people more cheerful than gloomy northerners, more inclined to dance, feast, and make merry."[29]

Africans use laughter to ease life's trials and tribulations. They laugh over sickness in their families and invite jokesters to funerals to help the bereaved ease their sorrows. Uptight they are not, and expatriates who deal with Africans should learn to lighten up.

Jokes are made about other ethnic groups, their speech and their customs. Such humor is fashioned around the differences among ethnic groups, not in a negative way but rather to say, look how funny people are in their differences. Conformity, however, is important, and if persons are different, they are likely to be made fun of. Slapstick—falling down, for example—or committing a faux pas is very much a part of African humor.

The humor is situational, and expatriates sometimes have trouble figuring out what is really so funny. At the movies Westerners will wonder why Africans in the audience are laughing at scenes that to them seem so serious. African humor is also gentle, with much playful teasing to establish contact and to bond with another person. Courtship between men and women often begins with such teasing.

Africans can be completely disarmed by a joke, and humor can be used to resolve potentially difficult situations, as an American in Malawi found out when she needed to have her visa extended. At the local visa office, she asked to see the supervisor. Expecting that she would have to wait, she came well supplied with reading material. After a wait of more than two hours she was ushered into the supervisor's office, where an enormous man rose from behind an equally large desk. The American, after making the appropriate bow and greeting the official in the local language, alluded to his size as well as his importance by saying, "Oh, you really are the big *bwana* (mister or sir, in Kiswahili). The official smiled and immediately granted her request for a visa extension.

Such gentle teasing, however, can sometimes lead to misunderstandings with foreigners. Peace Corps volunteers have misinterpreted as harassment what their African colleagues have intended as jokes or compliments. An African man, for example, might say "I'd like to have a woman like you." The man means it as a compliment or flattery, but the volunteer may believe she is being propositioned or harassed.

Comic theater is one of the most popular forms of entertainment, and much of the performance is improvised. Audiences are invited to participate, and it is not unusual for spectators to mount the stage and join the actors. The double entendre is popular, especially in sexual situations. A typical joke might concern a wife who is having an affair with another man. Her husband returns home unexpectedly, and the humor lies in where she finds a hiding place for her lover.

In West Africa members of ethnic groups and extended families have a *cousinage* relationship which permits them to criticize and tease each other by poking fun.

"The tradition is as old as time," explains Burkina Faso sociologist Moussa Ouedraogo, "...cousins can say anything to each other...and the stream of jokes, scorn, blasphemy, and bawdy remarks is no respecter of title or position."[30] Even the president of the country is not immune from such scorn and is entitled to reply in the same vein. "[T]his unwritten law," adds Ouedraogo, "plays havoc with social hierarchy and the respect due to age. It allows the humble to blast those in power with their invective and deliver some much needed home truths with impunity."[31]

In an example of cousinage, an American tells of the initial call he made on a cabinet-level official, accompanied by his African assistant. On greeting his visitors, the minister asked the American's assistant, "Why aren't you selling pieces of cloth on the street?" Replying in the same vein, the assistant asked, "Why aren't you watching your cows today?" When two Africans do not tease each other like that, you should wonder why not.

Persons not related by cousinage may also joke if they know each other well. One man might say to another, "How is *our* wife today?" as if his friend's wife were also his own.

Does the expat have a place in African humor? The answer is an emphatic yes. Expat humor is appreciated, and your old high school jokes will go over well, even when translated into French. The ability to laugh at yourself is also appreciated, and expats should joke about themselves and their foibles. Laugh at your own jokes and Africans will laugh with you. Telling jokes establishes you as a human being they can relate to.

If you are the butt of African humor, don't take it personally. If you are being hassled, make a joke of it and avoid a confrontation. If you meet with rejection, make light of it, back off, and try another approach.

"Be prepared to be 'taken,'" counsels a veteran U.S. expat, "and to laugh when it happens. And don't go to Africa if you are uptight and do not have a sense of humor."

---

[1] Julius Nyerere, cited by Mazrui, in *Africans*, 75.

[2] Vusamazulu Credo Mutwa, *Indaba, My Children* (London: Kahn and Averill, 1966), 353.

[3] Michael Thelwell, in Amos Tutuola, *The Palm-wine Drinkard and My Life in the Bush of Ghosts* (New York: Grove Press, 1994), 183.

[4] Jan Knappert, *The A-Z of African Proverbs* (London: Karmak House, 1989), 3.

122

5 The language classification generally accepted and used here is from Joseph H. Greenberg, *The Languages of Africa*, 3d ed. (Bloomington: Indiana University Research Center, 1970).

6 National Public Radio, *Morning Edition*, 7 March 1995.

7 Ibid.

8 Henri Lopes, in *Culture and Development*, edited by Serageldin and Tabaroff, 537.

9 Jan Knappert, *Kings, Gods and Spirits from African Mythology* (New York: Peter Bedrick Books, 1986), 14.

10 H. B. Thomas, quoted in *The White Nile* by Alan Moorehead (New York: Dell Publishing, 1960), 391.

11 Mandela, *Long Walk to Freedom*, 18.

12 Harden, *Africa*, 18.

13 Herskovits, *Human Factor*, 466.

14 Peter Biddlecombe, *French Lessons in Africa: Travels with My Briefcase through French Africa* (Boston: Little, Brown, 1993), 45.

15 Turnbull, *Lonely African*, 215.

16 Gérémie Sawadogo, "Training for the African Mind," in *International Journal of Intercultural Relations* 19, no. 2 (Spring 1995): 288.

17 Mandela, *Long Walk to Freedom*, 8.

18 Mazrui, *Africans*, 241.

19 Interview with Samu, November 1994.

20 Michael E. M. Sudarkasa, *The African Business Handbook*, no. 2 (Washington, DC: 21st Century Africa, 1993), 13.

21 "Community Health and Village Empowerment," a report of the National Cooperative Business Center, Washington, DC, of a USAID-funded project in Burkina Faso completed in September 1995.

22 Dia, *Africa's Management*, 263.

23 Okot p'Bitek, "Song of Lawino," in *Coming of Age in Africa: Continuity and Change*, edited by Leon E. Clark (New York: Praeger, 1971), 68-69.

24 Mazrui, *Africans*, 14.

25 Biddlecombe, *French Lessons in Africa*, 63-64.

26 Mort Rosenblum and Doug Williamson, *Squandering Eden: Africa at the Edge* (New York: Harcourt Brace Jovanovich, 1987), 94.

27 Harden, *Africa*, 302.

28 Hove, *Shebeen Tales*, 94.

29 Jan Knappert, *African Mythology* (London: Diamond Books, 1995), 10.

30 Moussa Ouedraogo, in *Index on Censorship*, no. 10, 1992, 35.

31 Ibid.

Doing Business

No profit without traveling.

—Congo proverb

Much of the U.S. business community once regarded sub-Saharan Africa as a preserve of the former European colonial powers, but that has been corrected in recent years as the region has seen unprecedented political and economic change. American exporters and investors have come to realize its vast potential as they travel to Africa in increasing numbers.

The United States today is sub-Saharan Africa's leading market, purchasing (in 1996) $15.2 billion of the region's total exports, 70 percent of which was crude oil from Nigeria, Angola, Gabon, and Congo (Brazzaville). In the same year, the United States was sub-Sahara's fifth supplier, with a market share of just under $6.1 billion, trailing France, Germany, the United Kingdom, and Japan. Heading the list of U.S. exports were manufactured items—drilling equipment, aircraft and parts, motor vehicle parts, construction machinery, computers and peripherals, telecommunication products, and agricultural machinery—accounting for 86 percent of total U.S. exports to the region. Agricultural exports—mainly wheat, corn, and rice—were second with 14 percent of the total. To put this into perspective, U.S. sales to sub-Sahara in 1995 were 54 percent greater than its exports to the Newly Independent States of the former Soviet Union, and U.S. exports to South Africa alone were nearly equal to its sales to Russia, and greater than those to all the countries of Eastern Europe.[1]

Trade and investment in Africa is increasing as political and economic reforms proceed. To be sure, the reforms are not in place everywhere, but many countries have been lifting foreign exchange controls, phasing out import restrictions and price controls, dismantling monopolies, and privatizing state-owned industries. Moreover, legislation introduced in the U.S. Congress in 1997 with strong bipartisan support would encourage free trade agreements, eliminate trade barriers, and assist in creating new businesses and building infrastructure in Africa.

But as Africa brings its bureaucracies closer to internationally established trade policies and practices, and as opportunities for foreign trade and investment increase, so too in some countries do frauds and scams targeted at foreign business. Caution is advised.

Confirm the bona fides of prospective business partners. Beware of schemes involving the transfer of U.S. dollars to an overseas bank account of a foreign firm for a "fee" or "commission." Do not provide blank letterhead stationery to persons you do not know, or details of your bank account which could be used to filch funds. Question requests for payment of advance fees and for sample shipments of your products for which the requester does not intend to pay. Many other such scams have been reported, and their victims include charities, nonprofits, and religious groups, as well as businesses. (To check out possible scams and for other advice on a particular country, telephone the Office of Africa at the U.S. Department of Commerce, tel. (202) 482-4927, or contact a Commercial Officer at the U.S. embassy in the country concerned.)

As the prospects for business transactions increase, so too does the potential for cross-cultural misunderstandings, as the following sections will illustrate.

Building Trust

Chicanery is not business.

—Chuana proverb

The key to doing business and developing professional relationships in Africa is socializing. In the village Africans sit under a tree and chat before deliberating or doing business. In the city they also sit and chat prior to doing deals, not under a tree but at their offices or over food and drink.

Socializing builds the personal trust that is prerequisite to doing business, and in Africa it is difficult to determine where social interaction ceases and business begins, since the dividing line is very thin and often nonexistent. Some foreigners say they never discuss business during their first call on an African official and sometimes not even on the second. They just chat and get acquainted in a leisurely way in a *visite de courtoisie*. Leisure activities provide opportunities for socializing that can serve as a prelude to doing business. A backyard barbecue in East Africa or a golf course foursome in South Africa can put you foursquare on the path to business success.

This emphasis on leisure, however, has been misconstrued by some outsiders as a sign of African "laziness." In reality leisure and social interaction strengthen the group solidarity which is so important to Africans.

Africans seek equilibrium, a harmonious balance between the contending forces that surround them. Living in a harsh environment, they attempt to find a modus vivendi with the forces of nature rather than trying to tame them. Equilibrium is also sought in interpersonal relations through the time-honored tradition of consensus.

In the quest for equilibrium in business, socializing also provides an opportunity to create reciprocal obligations which must be accepted by each party to a deal. If a business relationship is strong enough, the obligations between the parties will be enforced and an equilibrium achieved. If not, the obligations may be ignored.

Other interpersonal considerations important to Africans may also be explored during the prebusiness social process—who you are, who the other parties are, how the parties relate to each other, and whose pride is at stake.

But the biggest difficulty in doing business is in recognizing the moment when you can easily shift from socializing to the business of the day. Europeans, who have been doing business in Africa for a long time, know exactly when to make the shift. Americans and other newcomers will need the advice of an intermediary or cross-cultural adviser.

The Intermediary as Mediator

The friends of our friends are our friends.

—Congo proverb

An intermediary can open doors, ensure a warm reception for your upcoming visit, and assess the prospects for the proposal you plan to present. If there is a major matter to be resolved, an intermediary can prepare the way by letting the other party know what some of the potential problems and solutions are from your point of view. An intermediary can float trial balloons to get the other party's reaction to your proposed plans as well as help you to formulate a plan, since asking direct questions of your African counterpart may result in responses you may not understand. And if something goes wrong, you can always blame the intermediary and avoid a confrontation.

Foreign business representatives will find that an intermediary is an absolute must in Africa when approaching someone of higher status. The intermediary should be someone close to you or a confidant of the person you are trying to reach and should, of course, be an African, since an African will know how to ask questions in a culturally appropriate manner and how to use humor to set the proper climate for the serious talks that will follow. Before hiring one, make sure that he or she has the access you are seeking.

An intermediary can also make apologies for missteps if making them directly might cause you to lose face. As noted earlier, saving face is a serious matter in Africa. In the Western world, if you have done something wrong, you are likely to be chastised publicly and expected to apologize and admit to your error. An African, however, would lose face by apologizing publicly. Instead, an intermediary will approach the wronged person in private and make a personal apology. "The desired corporate culture," writes Mamadou Dia, "should emphasize 'saving face' more than 'in your face' approaches to decision making."[2]

Westerners should be watchful for such roundabout approaches by Africans they meet or work with. An expatriate, for example, was once puzzled when an African with whom he was working complained to him at length about the behavior of someone from outside the office. The expat could not understand why his African counterpart should complain so much about an outsider's behavior. The African, however, was trying to explain indirectly what the expat himself should not be doing.

An intermediary, sometimes known as an "expediter," can also be useful in greasing the wheels of a sluggish bureaucracy, such as facilitating passage through customs of some equipment or goods you have ordered from abroad. You ask your expediter to remove the roadblock and he does, but you may not want to ask for details about how he did it.

Be aware, though, that your competitors will also have intermediaries, and they can mediate in ways that are not to your advantage. Meetings with high government officials, arranged well in advance and reconfirmed several times, can be canceled with only twenty-four hours' notice. Charter flights with local airlines to inspect prospective up-country business sites can be suddenly canceled without explanation. Previous agreements can be unexpectedly altered.

In such cases, keep your cool and don't give up. Reestablish contact with some official with whom you have established a good personal relationship, and start all over again.

First Meetings, First Impressions

The slow climber does not fall.

—Somali proverb

The initial visit, as noted above, is used to establish trust, and more than one call may be needed to create a framework for further discussion. Do not expect "done deals" during a first visit. Take your time.

What should be discussed during an initial visit? Personal affairs should not be mentioned. Never ask about marital status, how many children someone has, and other private matters until you have established a closer and more personal rapport.

One U.S. business executive recalls his first meeting with a government minister in a country where he was newly stationed. After the initial greetings, he mentioned how pleased he was to be in that country. Next, he talked about his past work in another African country which the minister knew well. And so it went, with the two of them talking about their past experiences but with the visitor being careful to show due respect to the minister. You may be able to get some feedback after such a meeting, since word gets around.

Even people you know well may not come to the point immediately. If there is something important to discuss they may drop by your office or come to your home for a visit and in the course of discussing unimportant and unrelated issues get to the point with an "Oh, by the way...."

The short-term visitor, however, might not have time for a second visit and may have to make proposals during the initial call. If so, do not come immediately to the point, particularly on important issues. Even in South Africa, where business practices approximate those of the West, ten to fifteen minutes of pleasantries is still the rule, and to be abrupt is considered impolite. With high-ranking and busy officials you will have to get to the point sooner.

Be honest and straightforward, advise veterans who have done business in Africa. Africans seem to have a sixth sense for discerning when someone is trying to slip something over on them. On a first meeting, as well as on subsequent visits, they will be regarding you with some skepticism, watching you closely, and trying to figure out what you really want from them. Africa's intellectuals are suspicious, warns Robert Klitgaard, a U.S. business and development consultant, for they have been doubly deceived in the past,

> ...first, by colonial powers that sold them on a certain view of religion and state as absolutely true; then, by their own governments after independence, by one or another ideology or cult figure. They have been tricked; above all, they do not want to be tricked again.[3]

This calls for caution when Africans are presented with a new idea by a Westerner, continues Klitgaard.

> When they receive a new idea, they don't ponder it, play with it, or investigate its applicability and utility. They wonder instead why this idea is presented to them by this person at this time.[4]

When Africans come to your office, particularly people with some status, they should be offered something to drink—coffee, tea, or a soda—or you are likely to be considered rude. Also rude or miserly is the pouring of drinks in another room out of sight of the guests, as Americans are likely to do. Even where beer comes in sixteen-ounce bottles, each guest should be given his or her bottle, poured before the guest, not in the kitchen.

Business cards with titles and degrees are essential, and the more elaborate the better. They indicate to Africans that you want to stay in touch. Be sure to have an adequate supply, since more cards than anticipated are always needed. At small meetings, hand them out to everyone at the table but don't ask for cards in return, since business cards are too expensive for many Africans. If you want someone's name and address, ask him or her to write it in your notebook.

While business cards should be passed out liberally, be careful about passing out information too freely; think carefully about to whom you tell what. Interpersonal relations are complex in Africa, and you never know who is related to whom. Do not make casual remarks about sensitive issues to a secretary, for you never know in whose ear it will end up. The best policy is no secrets and no confidences. As a Congo proverb cautions, "Watch your word; it will travel round like a fly from mouth to mouth."

First impressions are lasting, in Africa as elsewhere. People make quick judgments about newcomers, and the way you walk, dress, sit, and talk are important. Also meaningful is personal grooming. Africans put a high premium on cleanliness, neatness, and appearance.

Rules of dress in business and the workplace vary from region to region and country to country, but clothing and appearance are important to Africans everywhere and consume a considerable portion of their budgets. In the village the chief comes to an important meeting wearing his best clothes. To be respected, one must appear presentable.

In East and Southern Africa, office dress, as well as general demeanor, tends to be more formal, for both women and men. Men will wear a tie and jacket, and in some countries professional women and secretaries will wear stockings and dressy shoes.

In West Africa and the Horn, dress is more casual for both Africans and foreigners, and visitors there may even wear safari outfits. West African women wear colorful prints in both African and Western styles. Muslim men, who visit the mosque on Friday, may wear their boubous, the intricately embroidered long gowns, to the office on that day.

When choice of dress is in doubt, conservative is better than casual, for both men and women. Men, as is the case in East and Southern Africa, will wear a jacket and tie, and women, a dress or blouse and a skirt of midcalf length.

For women, dress is especially important, particularly in the Sahel and other Muslim regions. Muslims are not accustomed to seeing women dressed in shorts, skimpy tank tops, and see-through clothing. Such attire can also lead to harassment, since it may indicate to an African man that a woman is available, particularly if she is unescorted. A woman's potential for success can be limited by a first meeting that goes poorly, and professional women should make a special effort to make a good impression and do everything to avoid being seen solely as a female.

Protocol and Propriety

> The African generally is at his best when surrounded by solemnity. This is epitomized by the protocol and ceremonial surrounding modern politicians and Government officials....
> —Mamadou Dia, "Cultural Dimensions of Institutional Development and Management in Sub-Saharan Africa"

High-level African officials and business executives expect to be treated with the solemnity and respect due their positions. This calls for protocol to be observed and excess familiarity avoided, at least in initial meetings. Rank should also be respected. When calling on an African of high rank—a minister or senior official—bring along a ranking officer of your company or organization in recognition of the African's senior status.

Rank has its privileges, as elsewhere in the world. At official dinners, no one eats or drinks until the higher-ranking people partake, and no one leaves until the highest-ranking guests have left.

In Somalia once, to celebrate Revolution Day, officials in Hargeisa arranged an evening program of entertainment at the National Theater, the city's main auditorium. The program was scheduled to start at 7:00 P.M. but did not begin until 9:00 P.M., when the regional governor arrived. By 11:00 P.M. the foreigners in the audience were dead tired, but no one could leave. The governor, fresher than the rest of the audience, was still in his seat enjoying the performance.

Some mannerisms common to Americans may be considered crude by Africans, as they are by Europeans—draping an arm over a chair back, putting feet up on a desk or table, crossing the legs so as to show the sole of a shoe, or "lounging" in general. Observe carefully what is appropriate and what is not.

Presentations in francophone Africa, both oral and written, are more formal, language is more flowery, and adherence to protocol more strict. Know your honorifics and use them. Titles, such as Monsieur Ministre or Conseiller, are important and should be used when addressing officials. Businesspeople may be called Monsieur, le Directeur, and moderators of meetings will be addressed as Monsieur, le Président or Monsieur, le Facilitateur. In Congo, for example, you cannot refer to an official by name without using his title. You must say "Dr. Duale" or even "Dr. Duale, the Honorable Director of Medical Services." Someone who wishes to speak at a meeting might say (in French) "If you will pass me the word, I would like to ask..." (which sounds much more elegant than asking for the floor).

Such propriety and politesse can appear ponderous to Americans, who may be tempted to interrupt and speak out of turn without the diplomatic delicacies. But Africans, who are very patient and rarely break in, see such interruptions as uncultured. If you must interrupt, do so politely. Preface your interruption with such remarks as "With due respect..." or "You know more about this than I do..." or "I respect your views although I have a very important point to make before we proceed further."

Get your niceties down. Rather than being confrontational when you disagree, say something like "My distinguished colleague, I really appreciate what you are saying." Find a way to express your opinion without saying "I disagree" or using the word *but* as in "What you are saying is true, but...." Rather, you might say "I really appreciate how you said that night is day, and I feel that night is indeed day, however...."

French and many other languages have formal and familiar forms. The formal *vous* is both singular and plural and is used in addressing persons of higher status or those with whom one is not on familiar terms. The familiar form, *tu* (singular only), akin to the German *du* or the old English *thou*, is used for speaking with friends, family, children, and animals, and for talking down to people. Readers will appreciate the need to use the correct form. In any event, do not initiate use of the familiar *tu* form; let the Africans tutoyer first, and then return it.

In francophone countries, expatriates who do not speak good French may sound abrupt and curt and have problems communicating. How something is said is often more important than what is said.

French is a warmer language than English, which is more suited to business and brass tacks. Former U.N. Secretary General Boutros Boutros-Ghali, who, like his wife, is Egyptian and multilingual, was once asked which language they speak at home. "When I have tense relations with my wife," he replied, "we speak in Arabic. When we talk business, then we speak English. When our relationship is better, *then* we talk French."[5]

In anglophone countries, protocol and propriety can also

be important, although somewhat less formal than in francophone countries. In Kenya, for example, an American had set up a new development project to which employees of various Kenyan professional institutions would be seconded. In preparing for the project, agreements were signed with the Kenyan institutions, and each of the Kenyans selected for the project met in advance with the U.S. supervisor and agreed to participate. But when the American arrived to start the project, the employees were gathered together in protest. They would not begin work until each of them had been given a personal letter of invitation.

Besting the Bureaucracy

> This is a country where there is very little resort against the bureaucracy. The bureaucracy here can be spiteful, malicious, inefficient, crooked. People don't really have anywhere to go.
>
> —The Watchman, a Nairobi columnist

Bureaucratic red tape in Africa can tie you up and test your tolerance. A legacy of the colonial period, it comes in thick and numerous layers, and at each level there is a tendency to avoid responsibility, refer decisions to higher-ups, and observe slow and long-established procedures. When a newly hired finance director of Kenya Airways asked for a file, he found that his request had to be passed down through a chain of six people before it got to him.

Everything takes longer to do in Africa (three to five times longer, say some old Africa hands) than in Western countries. And target dates are not always observed, as one of the authors learned when applying for a visa to visit an African country.

The application form promised the visa within three working days. But when the author called the country's embassy in Washington, D.C., to confirm the visa requirements, he was told four working days. When he personally delivered his application to the consul, he was told it would be ready in five working days. Most documents, moreover, need a government stamp to become official, and rubber stamps take on a mystical significance, somewhat like fetishes. In some countries you may be required to submit a written request to obtain a copy of a public document.

Sufficient time should be budgeted for the simplest of actions, as Susan Blake, a Fulbright lecturer in Togo, discovered when she had to make many visits to the *Securité Nationale* over a two-month period before getting her *carte de sejour* (identity card). After submitting her application, Ms. Blake returned a week later and learned that she needed *timbres fiscales* (tax stamps) for the documents. On the next visit, she was asked to submit a letter from her school *directeur* explaining what she was doing in Togo. Then came a request for *sept* (seven) photos. Summoned again for "some inquiries," she was informed that her papers were now in order but she would have to pay a fee, although the American Embassy had told her that foreigners working for the Togolese government were exempt from the charge. One more visit was needed, this time with an embassy employee as intermediary, before her identity card was issued. Most of the added requirements, she believes, were really hints for "dash."[6]

What should you do? Just be patient and smile. The more annoyed you look, the longer you will probably have to wait. It does not pay to get angry and antagonize people who months or years later are likely to still be there to handle whatever business you may bring to them.

A former U.S. ambassador who returned to Sierra Leone many years after his tenure there found that the political leaders he had dealt with no longer held office but all the bureaucrats he had known still performed the same tasks in the same offices, and everything still took time.

Requirements for entrance to the bureaucracy—what Americans would call the civil service—vary from country to country but often involve an examination. In some countries, reflecting British tradition, the examination assesses general achievement and intelligence. In others, reflecting French influence, the examination is more legalistic and academic. In still others, reflecting American practice, the focus is on professional proficiency.

"Once hired," however, as Dia points out, "an employee is generally promoted on the basis of seniority or political or ethnic consideration," and while tenure is theoretically for life, "...in actuality the level of responsibility and pay may change whenever another political faction or minister takes over." Moreover, adds Dia, employees are usually not fired, and "...loyalty to tribe and extended family still rules most personnel decisions."[7]

In South Africa, where the bureaucracy is less burdensome than elsewhere in Africa, red tape can still tie you up. South Africa has four levels of government—national, provincial (state), local, and traditional (tribal)—and you need networks to navigate your way through the shoals of all four.

But the bureaucracy can be bested, at times, by using reciprocal leverage, as a Western trainer found out when conducting a workshop on water resources in Ethiopia, where interruptions in electric service were common. To make sure that she had electricity for her workshop, the trainer used "water power." She had someone from the water resources ministry make a deal with the electricity people—if you want water in your offices, make sure that we have electricity at the workshop site.

The Telephone

> Telephone service can be very good or very bad in Africa.
> —Sylvia Ardyn Boone, *West African Travels*

Business in Africa may be conducted orally, but not by telephone. The interpersonal relationship is paramount, and Africans will want to sit face-to-face, sizing you up and getting to know you before getting down to business. If you are able to make an appointment by phone, you will have done well.

Whether you speak English or French, telephoning in Africa can be an ordeal, unless you are calling to the Western world. Calls to the Americas and Western Europe usually go through immediately, and the quality of the connection can be as good as anywhere in the West. Calls within a country or to another African country are another story. From Nairobi, the capital of Kenya, for example, it was not possible in 1997 to telephone directly to Angola or Congo. Such calls may have to go through London, Paris, or the United States.

Equipment, moreover, is outmoded and poorly maintained, tone quality is substandard—you must often shout to be heard—and there never seem to be enough telephone lines. In many countries it can take years to get a phone line installed. Public phones on the street are often broken, and phone calls are best made from the post office (PTT in francophone countries). Fax and e-mail are possible, but the quality of transmission will depend on the local telephone lines and can vary considerably among countries. E-mail is usually more dependable, although not all African countries have a node, and you may have to go through another country to reach your destination.

Making a phone call from an office is not always a simple matter either, because phone calls will be limited by the number of outside lines. In one institute where a foreign visitor was conducting research, there were only three outside lines and one receptionist to serve twenty full-time staff and as many consultants. To place an outside call one had to first telephone the receptionist and request that he put through a call. Many of the foreign consultants would become impatient and shout at the busy receptionist when their calls were not put through in a timely fashion. But making friends with the receptionist or just sitting patiently in his office, as the researcher learned, would speed her calls enormously.

Help is on the way, however, if you can wait a few years. Western communications corporations have begun work to upgrade the technology and make possible the wide range of telecommunication services now available in the West. In the meantime, the telephone in many countries may still be better than the mail, which is delivered mostly to post office boxes. In many countries, moreover, mailing anything of value can be chancy. A safer alternative, although more expensive, is air express.

Crime and Corruption

> It became almost a patriotic duty to misappropriate the re-
> sources of the colonial government when this was possible
> without risk of punishment or exposure. After all, to steal
> from a foreign thief could be an act of heroic restoration.
> Post-colonial Africa still suffers from the cynical attitudes to
> government property generated by the colonial experience.
> —Ali A. Mazrui, The Africans

Bribery and other corrupt practices are endemic in Africa—as they are in many other parts of the world—where they are considered a normal cost of doing business. In such countries there is often no free media to expose illegal actions by government officials, no legal system to enforce laws outlaw-ing such practices, and no freely elected officials to be held responsible for their indiscretions. "In the worst cases," writes Chester A. Crocker, a former U.S. Assistant Secretary of State for Africa, "the sad result is gross mismanagement or outright theft of everything that is not nailed down."[8]

But it was not always so in Africa. In traditional societies the chief held the wealth of his tribe in trust for all its members and he did not have the right to use common resources as he wished. "Rare were cases of embezzlement," says Ghanaian economist George B. N. Ayittey. "In fact, within that traditional system of values and beliefs, embezzlement would be a sacrilegious act that would assail not only the ingrained sense of kinship but also the ancestral will. It would be un-African."[9]

Traditional values and beliefs, however, including those related to crime and corruption, did not apply to the new systems of government introduced by the colonialists but never fully accepted by Africans. Most of the one-party states and dictatorships of postcolonial Africa have continued the corrupt practices that evolved under colonialism but without effective controls to limit them or punish their perpetrators.

Those caught stealing money from the government may be transferred to new positions but are seldom punished. Pilferage in the private sector is considered a normal cost of doing business, and its costs are included in annual company budgets. Such practices are condemned by Westerners, but Africans are more likely to say "Isn't he clever, he got away with it."

Corruption may also be a consequence of the African penchant for the present—take what you can when you can get it—as an African parable illustrates. The parable tells of three brothers who went through school together, moved from their village to the city, and went to work for the same public agency. But from then on their paths differed.

One brother enjoyed his job, worked hard, resisted all temptations to enrich himself, and rose to be a department head in his government ministry.

The second brother also enjoyed his work but used his job to enrich himself and benefit his family. With proceeds from his workplace he built a large house in his home village for his parents to live in and rent out rooms. When in charge of automobile procurement, he ordered one for himself and sold another to buy land near his village. On that land he used government seed to plant crops, appointed a cousin to manage the farm, and hired people from his village to work it. He brought brothers, sisters, and cousins to live with him in the city and got them government scholarships to attend college at home and do postgraduate study abroad.

The third brother also used his job to enrich himself but spent his money on partying, drinking, and womanizing. After many years, the three sons visited their home village together. The first son was greeted cordially but sadly, for he was thought a fool for not taking advantage of his position to help himself and his family. The third son was greeted coldly, ridiculed for embarrassing his family and friends, and driven from the village. The second son was greeted warmly, and a cow was sacrificed in his honor. Merit had been rewarded.[10]

Between a bribe and a gift there is a blur, as mentioned earlier, but that blur can come into sharp focus when a government official makes clear that a substantial payment under the table will ensure favorable treatment in the award of a contract or license. To pay or not to pay is a question for each businessperson to decide, though both foreigners and locals should be aware that such practices discourage investment, increase the price paid for goods and services, and enrich only a few. Those who pay, moreover, will have to pay again and will only make it more difficult for those who come after them. They will also have to enter the payment somewhere in their company's books.

One American who has been doing business in Africa for many years says that he has never once paid a bribe. He adds, however, that it is quite acceptable, at times, to make a donation that will in some way benefit all of the people in a particular locality where his business activity may take him, much as a U.S. company would do at home.

Bribery is not normally a part of U.S. corporate culture, and American business representatives abroad enjoy a reputation for honesty and integrity. Moreover, the United States is the only major country to have legislation barring bribery abroad by its businesses—the Foreign Corrupt Practices Act of 1977. But those executives who observe the law often find themselves at a disadvantage. Their competitors, including most of the Europeans, regard such payments as a normal cost of doing business and deduct them from their taxes as legitimate business expenses, euphemistically called commissions or fees. As one representative of a major U.S. corporation in Africa has described it, he was passing out ballpoint pens with his company logo while his competitors were offering vacations on the Riviera. This may be changing, however. In 1997, after years of lobbying by the United States, twenty-nine of the world's industrial countries formally agreed to a treaty that would outlaw the practice of bribing foreign government officials.

Beware also of scams. Proposals written on official-looking stationery and promising huge rates of return can turn out to be bogus. Before investing, check and double-check. Even banks can be victimized. In the mid-1980s, many foreigners in Zaire lost funds they held in European bank accounts when phony telegrams, purportedly from the account owners, requested the bank to transfer large sums to other accounts.

Passengers departing from Africa will encounter an unavoidable airport obstacle. Most countries require payment of an exit tax, or service fee as it is sometimes called, as much as $20 U.S.—greenbacks only—payable on departure. Signs at airport collection booths may read, "Please have exact amount, no change given." In a rip-off witnessed by the authors, a departing passenger presented a $50 bill, pleading that he had nothing smaller, and the airport currency exchange bank would not change it for him. "Sorry," said the clerk, "you'll have to give me the fifty, and I cannot give you change," although the wads of $10 and $20 bills he held in his hands were clearly visible. The experienced traveler refused to be intimidated, stood his ground, and eventually got his change.

The Big Man

> An important man may be wrong, but he is always right.
> —Bambara proverb

The Big Man is omnipresent across Africa. He dominates the evening TV news and his framed photos and painted portraits are found everywhere, hanging on the walls of shops and offices and hawked in marketplaces and at stoplights in downtown traffic. Rather than follow written rules and regulations, Africans will observe the wishes of the Big Man. Omniscient and omnipotent, he is the law.

But the workplace in Africa will also have its Big Man. Like the father of the family, he too can solve everything, provided you can find out who he is and get in to see him. His deputy does not make decisions, and one should not assume that he can. The Big Man himself decides, though, as discussed earlier, only after consultation with all the relevant people—higher-ups as well as lower-downs—has produced a consensus. The wheels of the bureaucracy, however, turn slowly, and delayed decisions are likely. As a Nupe (Nigeria) proverb puts it, "Delay does not spoil things; it makes them better."

Africa has far too many people employed in its bureaucracies, but competent officials with decision-making responsibilities are often spread thin in ministries, especially those which may have a lower priority, such as health and human services. If the Big Man you want to see is away on business, you may have to settle for a somewhat smaller man, one who may be less versed in the subject or who cannot make decisions. The challenge is to see the real power wielders, and to do this you must somehow get by the low-level clerks and secretaries who guard the gateways to the inner sanctums.

You arrive at an office early in the morning, on time for your appointment with a high-ranking official, a Big Man. You knock on the door but there is no answer. You knock again, several times, until someone has found the key and lets you in. You next encounter a clerk who enters your name in the official register for visitors and ushers you into an inner office to see the Big Man's secretary, who has not yet arrived. When she does arrive, after having run her morning personal errands, you wait another hour or two until the Big Man himself enters, followed by his entourage and hangers-on. Finally, you are ushered into his inner sanctum, where he appears very impatient and not at all pleased to see you, unless you are there on a matter of importance to him, such as the signing of a contract.

The Patron *as* Paterfamilias

If you want to keep your workmen, keep your temper.
—South African proverb

In the United States we lead two separate lives, one professional and the other private, and the two are not usually mixed. Business is business, and Americans prefer not to get involved with the private lives of their professional colleagues. In Africa, however, it is the other way around. Professional and private lives blend together as in one big extended family.

In a patriarchal society, the *patron* (boss) of the office is seen as a strict but wise and benevolent parent, a paterfamilias, or head of the family. Like the chief or head of an extended family, the boss establishes trust and harmony in the workplace by taking a personal interest in the lives and families of his employees and by governing by consensus. The flip side is that his subordinates are expected to show him the respect and deference that they would to a parent or chief in a hierarchical system.

Harmonizing hierarchy with consensus can be a challenge for those who are new to Africa. If something must be done, ask your employees for recommendations. These you can always modify before approving them and then say, "Okay, this is how we are going to do it." But, as the boss, you have brought your employees into the consensus and will thereby share with them responsibility for the outcome. For their part, they have been consulted and will be comfortable with your decisiveness and decision.

Maintain an open-door policy. Be accessible to all your employees and make them feel that they are members of the workplace extended family. Show consideration to their families by attending important events such as baptisms, marriages, and funerals. All this takes time, but is well worth it; and it is, moreover, the right thing to do. Employees will have more respect for you, and you will have more appreciation for what these events mean to them. Preparing for a wedding, for example, may involve helping to cook for the guests or paying for clothing and gifts. If asked to be a "parent" for a wedding, you will be expected to cover some of the costs. Weddings are costly, and the festivities can last up to a week.

Once a good interpersonal relationship has been established with members of an office staff, they will be more productive workers as well as good sources of information on what is going on in the office, in the city, and in the country.

Respect, which is something all Africans want and need, can be shown in a number of ways. Show employees that you need them to achieve your objectives. Recognize and appreciate them as professionals, and make them feel part of the organization. Do not jump in with short-term goals before fully assessing the situation. Rather than give orders precipitately, the newcomer should first interview each staff member, from the doorman to the director. Discuss their role in the organization, their aspirations, and their family life. An hour or so spent with each employee will pay future dividends.

The boss must greet everyone when entering the workplace each morning, from the doorkeeper to the floorsweeper, and it should not be just a mere "good morning." You must stop to inquire about their health and the well-being of their families.

Focus on group strength and praise group performance, unless, of course, an individual employee has done something really exceptional. In one business, for example, a ceremony was held to honor a janitor who had stymied a robbery in the office but was beaten up in the ensuing imbroglio.

Friendship is important but can also cause misunderstandings in the workplace. An employer, for example, may invite one of his employees out for a drink, over which they share stories about their youthful escapades. Because of their new relationship, established over drinks, they now "know each other," and the employee may expect his boss to henceforth give him more favored treatment. An American in such a situation would try to separate the two worlds of work and friendship and would not expect favors merely because the boss had invited him or her out for a drink.

Employers are also expected to provide protection for their employees and to help out when needed. A loan request to the boss is considered by employees to be quite normal, a form of assistance from those who have to those who need. As in the extended family, employees also expect sharing to occur in the workplace.

Personal problems, however, rarely come directly to the boss's attention. Employees will band together and try first to solve a problem on their own. If unsuccessful, rather than going to the boss with it, they will inform the oldest staff member and expect him to call it to the boss's attention. But that oldest employee, although available as a mediator, will not come to the boss with his own problems; he will seek his own mediator.

If employees perform poorly, do not get angry and chew them out. Direct talk is acceptable if gentle and considerate, but anger and emotion in the workplace, as elsewhere, are considered infantile by Africans. You might say, for example, "This doesn't quite satisfy my needs, and I would prefer you do it that way." But if you say, "I'm angry because you didn't follow my instructions and I'm going to demote you" (or display similar emotions), you will be seen as childish. Getting angry will only prolong the problem and make it worse.

To deal with such situations, use the indirect African

approach. Talk about the problem with someone whom you expect will discuss it, in turn, with the employee whose behavior you seek to change. Better still, use an African stratagem. Make up a story about some fictitious person with the identical behavior and complain about that fictitious person's behavior to a third person. Everyone will know who the real target is, your message will be transmitted through the third party, and everyone will save face.

Unexpected absences by staff members should be anticipated and tolerated. Employees will call each other "brother" or "sister," and as discussed earlier, there will be frequent absences to attend funerals, weddings, and other important events of coworkers and extended family. Burials are the most common cause of absence, and their legitimacy should not be questioned. Even in South Africa, where business practices are more similar to those of the West, time lost for attending funerals is considered a normal cost of doing business and is often included in annual budgets of business enterprises.

When a government employee dies, an official representative of his or her ministry may have to travel several days to the village where the funeral takes place, and the official attends the ceremony out of concern rather than form. The same holds true for private firms—when an employee dies, the supervisor is expected to attend the funeral.

Relatives and friends may drop by the office to visit and chat with employees, a practice that will be annoying to Westerners. This too is unavoidable but can be held to a minimum by explaining to staff members the need for self-discipline in limiting such visits. One African business executive tells how he was once in an important meeting when his country cousin called to say he had just arrived in town and was at the bus station. The executive had to interrupt the meeting to go pick up his cousin.

Excessive use of office telephones to discuss family matters can also be disconcerting, but the stronger the family network, the more effective the employees will be in their work.

Such networks help to overcome difficulties at work as well as at home.

Be alert to motivational problems. When one Western supervisor talked with a woman who was chronically late for work, he learned that she was bored with her job. When the employee was given more challenging work, she showed up on time and her performance improved.

Hiring and Firing

> There is always a boss above the boss.
> —South African proverb

Just as a member of an extended family cannot be dismissed, so too an employee should not be fired. Transferred, yes, or sent "on mission" somewhere, but to be fired is to lose face, a serious blow to an African's pride and self-respect. Such cultural no-nos are reinforced in countries where labor laws and work codes—a European import—favor employees and make dismissals difficult. In addition, to fire someone an employer may have to pay a separation fee. Employees know these laws and codes and can be very litigious. As a result, incompetent people may be encountered, in private enterprise as well as government offices.

Various strategies are available, however, to purge people with below-par performance. Some are promoted to higher positions that may not be so sensitive to operations, a practice not unknown in the West. Others may be sent somewhere to study on a stipend. And in a novel approach, when Kenya Airways downsized to cut its losses, it asked employees to resign and then reapply for their old jobs.

Western managers should understand, however, that in firing one person they may be affecting the welfare of as many as twenty or more others who are being supported in some way by that one wage earner. For all these reasons, care should be taken in terminating employees.

Hiring new help also has its hazards. Some expats will give preference to anyone who speaks English or French well and wears a shirt, tie, and jacket. But such surface indicators can be misleading. Instead, study letters of reference carefully and check out applicants with someone who knows them from previous employment. Request a resumé but be explicit about what you want it to include. If you do not ask for specific responsibilities and achievements in previous jobs, you are likely to get a laundry list of past employment which tells little about the applicant.

Do not promote employees too fast, counsel Africa veterans. Go slowly in augmenting their duties and developing skills in order to carefully prepare them for increased responsibilities. When promoting staffers, think twice before making a public announcement. Most Africans are reluctant to stand out among their colleagues—the group ethic again—and prefer to play down their gains and advantages. In the Central African Republic, one Western supervisor did not announce staff promotions but let the promoted staffers themselves decide how they wanted to make known their advancement.

Job performance may also be affected by a family and its financial needs. Family members will assume that employees of Westerners are well paid. Expats will agree and often take the view that since their African employees are well paid, at least in comparison with others in the country, they should perform better, in other words, higher expectations and greater demands may be placed on them. But such an attitude overlooks the obligations to extended family members which employees must shoulder and which may affect their job performance. Failure to consider these burdens and responsibilities can cause discord.

To give a job to a relative or someone from the same clan is called nepotism in the West. In Africa it is both a duty and an obligation, as well as the smart thing to do. Success and prestige in Africa depend, to a great extent, on the number of people whose loyalty is assured. As Lamb explains,

For a politician or military leader to choose his closest advisers and his bodyguards from the ranks of his own tribe is not patronage, it is good common sense. It ensures security, continuity, authority.[11]

It may seem logical for Western supervisors to ask their African deputies to suggest whom to hire. But deputies will likely propose persons from their own family or clan, and as a result, most of a staff could come from one ethnic group and be related to each other. Other employees will see this as favoritism, and it may cause discord within the office and with outsiders.

Interpersonal staff conflicts, as noted above, are often settled without the involvement of supervisors, and some problems will be resolved without the supervisors knowing how. In one office car jacks were being stolen from company vehicles. The expat manager discussed the problem with her African administrative officer who said he would deal with it. He did, in his own way, and the thievery ceased.

Wait six months before making changes; advise old Africa hands. Changes may indeed be necessary, but too many made too soon can create morale problems that will affect job performance. In any event, they may not be the correct solutions for Africa.

African staffers are accustomed to seeing Western managers come and go and having to explain everything to each new arrival. They know that you will soon be replaced by another expat, and they are not likely to be upset by any mistakes you may make.

Working with Africans

The cure for poverty is work.

—Yoruba proverb

Africans work well when motivated and can become trusted, loyal, and productive workers. New employees settle in easily and will work Sundays and evenings if necessary, provided they get overtime. One common complaint, however, as earlier noted, is failure to understand the importance of time. In Africa, time is not money. One foreign foreman in Malawi says he spends most of his workday making certain that production targets are met and deliveries made on time. He solves the problem by providing good supervision and enforcing rules.

If employees seem listless, lethargic, or inept, look for underlying health problems. In regions where malaria, bilharzia, or other maladies are endemic, the cause may be medical. It therefore makes good economic sense for employers to pay the medical costs of their business and household employees.

Arriving late, as noted earlier, is not considered rude or a violation of office discipline. So what does the boss do when his senior management team shows up late for staff meetings? A new managing director of Kenya Airways solved this problem by locking the doors to his meeting room and starting his meetings without the latecomers. The tardy ones were embarrassed and soon began to show up on time.[12]

Africans can be very innovative, and Westerners are amazed by what they can do with so little. Travelers marvel at the ingenuity of roadside mechanics who make complicated auto repairs without spare parts, adequate tools, diagnostic equipment, or even a workshop. Family members turn wood, rocks, and scrap metal into playthings for children. Resources are scarce, and everything is hoarded, to be used at a later date when needed. Foreigners are astonished when the most complex problems are resolved in a uniquely African way, as an American in Mali learned when a cow collided with her car, a frequent experience on African roads.

The woman had parked her car at the side of a road in Bamako, and a cow came past and kicked in one of the car's rear lights. When the police came to investigate, it turned out that the cow belonged to the local electric cooperative, and the question arose as to who was responsible for replacing the broken light. Since the domestic cow was worth much less than the imported light, it would not do to sell the cow to reimburse the woman for the damage done. What to do? After some discussion, the head of the co-op agreed to accept responsibility but asked for time to find a solution. A few weeks later he appeared at the woman's home with a new light even though there was no dealer in Mali for her make of car. In the usual African way, a friend of a friend had purchased the light in another African country and sent it on to Mali.

Rather than give their own opinions, Africans will often defer to higher-ups in the workplace, particularly when the boss is a Westerner. When faced with a problem not seen before, they may not attempt to solve it by themselves and may even set it aside without telling the boss. When the problem comes up again, they will expect the Big Man to solve it. One American who represents a PVO (private voluntary organization) in Africa found that when he took his vacation in the United States, he had to run his office from a distance, receiving questions from his staff by fax every day and returning instructions by fax.

In such an environment, how do Westerners serve effectively as consultants and provide the expertise for which they are hired? Rather than parachuting in with a know-it-all attitude, they involve Africans in the process and build consensus. Africans know their countries well and should be asked how they have approached similar problems in the past. You should value their input and contributions and learn from their experience. Be authoritative but do not use your position of authority to impose solutions without achieving consensus. Solutions that are imposed will be ignored.

In building a consensus, take your time. Decisions are usually arrived at through informal discussions before a meeting actually starts, so plan your meetings accordingly. Silence during a meeting does not mean that no one has anything to say. As a Mauritanian proverb puts it, "Talk little, listen much."

Just wait and it will all come out. Try to convince your employees that you value their opinions, and a two-way discussion will follow. Everyone involved in the decision making should be satisfied before proceeding with implementation.

Bring Africans in during the planning stage of new projects, advises a foreign consultant who worked in Lesotho for an international agency which had designed a teacher training project without local participation. When the project was presented to the Basotho (as the people of Lesotho are known), they agreed it would be useful but refused to adopt it because they had not been consulted during the planning stage.

And if you are sent to an African country on a short-term assignment which requires support from the local staff of your organization, show your appreciation by giving them a lunch or providing some special treat like cake with the customary tea or coffee. Your thoughtfulness will pay off.

Forward Planning?

> Do not worry about tomorrow.
>
> —Bantu proverb

Much has been written, by Africans as well as foreigners, about the difficulties Africans have in planning for the future. Mazrui describes traditional African societies as cultures of nostalgia rather than of anticipation, and he writes of "contemporary Africa's apparent incapacity to plan ahead."[13] Others, however, question whether such conclusions are warranted.

Cultivators of land plan ahead, as do pastoralists preparing to move their herds to better grazing grounds. People who are financially strapped must plan ahead, and villagers running out of food before the next harvest learn to eat every other day. Parents select their brightest child for advanced schooling so that he (and it is usually a "he") can get a job that will help to support the extended family. Urban residents and businesspeople also understand the need for forward planning, and women who are busy around the clock at work and at home must also plan their daily activities. So, why the criticism about African failure to plan ahead?

Levels of planning ability vary from culture to culture, but Africans, in general, plan for need and not desire, says one Western businessman who has worked in South Africa for many years. But, he adds, the need for strategic objectives and ways to achieve them may not rate very high, and this can be one of the most frustrating aspects of working in Africa.

The lack of strategic objectives can be traced to the culture of the village and its traditions. In the village it was difficult, and still may be, for Africans to improve themselves or even to think about doing so, especially if they must conform to the customs of the clan.

Nepotism may also limit planning. "How can I plan ahead," asked one government official, "when I have to hire the minister's brother-in-law, who will certainly bring with him members of his clan?"

"Where do you see yourself in five years?" is a question often asked of job applicants in the United States. But such a question would mean little to Africans, who must cope with urgent day-to-day demands—health problems, job security, financial difficulties—all of which may be uncertain. (Such a question may also mean little to lower-income Americans who are struggling to meet the demands on their own limited finances.)

The African concept of time may also be a factor in the alleged failure to plan ahead. Time management skills in Africa, as noted earlier, are not strong, and someone may agree to do something but not specify when. An African's ability to plan may not translate into getting to the workplace at 9:00 A.M., and "tomorrow" may mean the next day or the next month. In Tshiluba, a language of Congo, the same word is actually used for tomorrow and yesterday, and only the context of the sentence permits one to distinguish between the two. So, when discussing tomorrow with employees and colleagues, be sure to make clear which tomorrow you are talking about.

One woman mentions her husband, a skilled craftsman, as an example of a man who fails to figure time into his forward planning. He makes jewelry, she explained, but in the months before Christmas he simply does not plan to make more items that he could surely sell in the preholiday weeks.

In business, the culture of the village and its "time factor" may also play a role. Most African entrepreneurs have a short-term rather than long-range perspective—show results quickly rather than build for the future. In development, as Dia points out, "Acceptance by the population will be maximized if the expected benefits...are easily identifiable and quantifiable and can materialize shortly, and if the reform does not lead to drastic changes in the traditional social and cultural fabrics of the community."[14]

Failure to plan ahead may also be a legacy of the colonial and early postcolonial years, when Africans were trained to a certain level above which expats took over. And some Africans, again reflecting the short-term outlook, may not be accustomed to working within yearly budgets or quarterly spending plans and may proceed instead on a day-to-day basis.

In much of Africa, the present and the past are more important than the future, which may also explain the failure to plan ahead. As Mazrui points out, most indigenous African cultures have refused to regard the past as bygone or the present as transient. "The ancestors are still with us in Africa, and we ourselves are would-be ancestors."[15]

"African ideas of time concern mainly the present and the past," says John S. Mbiti, "and have little to say about the future...."[16] And in traditional societies, adds Francis Mading Deng, a former Sudanese ambassador to the United States,

> ...religions aim at the well-being of human beings in a living society rather than at individual survival after death.... The focus of their concept of immortality is in this world, through procreation and...lineage continuation, which leads to ancestral veneration."[17]

With such beliefs, planning for the distant future becomes speculative, since it has no prospects for showing immediate tangible results.

Climate, theorizes Mazrui, also plays a role in the African failure to face the future. In most of Europe, he points out, seasonal changes of weather and the recurrence of cold winters forced people to plan ahead—for food, clothing, and shelter—which in later years provided the experience and habits necessary for resource accumulation and manufacturing. In Africa, suggests Mazrui, the absence of cold winters reduced the need for advance planning.[18] Clothing and shelter needs were minimal, and while food was not always plentiful and there were periods of hunger, subsistence farming provided self-sufficiency except during periods of drought, blight, or strife. Life was far from idyllic, but there was little people could do to effect change. Africans, as a consequence, have sought to accommodate themselves to their environment rather than combat it.

Others see an explanation in the African struggle for survival. The needs of the present—food for the hungry and medicine for the sick, for example—are more important than saving for the future. The more precarious a person's position, due to finances, illness, or family obligations, the greater the difficulty in planning ahead. People living on the edge of survival simply do not have the resources to think about the future.

A Senegalese who works for an international bank has pointed out other constraints that inhibit forward planning.

Access to scholarly journals and other material needed to design a good plan is limited, as is the time and solitude to prepare one. Trained personnel, moreover, are sometimes so scarce in government offices that it may be difficult to find a colleague who is working on a similar problem and with whom ideas can be shared.

Critics of these theories counter that the fault may lie with foreigners themselves, who often think in terms of the culture of their home country and its standards. A novice expat may impose plans which are simply not appropriate to Africa or which Africans may not fully understand and on which they have not been consulted. Once the "why and wherefore" of forward planning is understood, these critics say, Africans are perfectly capable of preparing for the future. If something makes sense and is important, it will be done. If not, it may indicate that they either do not understand or they believe it is not important, and you will have to go back to square one to explain its import or reconsider and reorder your priorities. What to do?

Play to African strengths and go for the group. A team approach will likely show better results than an individual endeavor. As a Vais proverb says, "What is mine goes; what is ours abides."

Bring employees together in staff meetings and go over what has to be done. Invoke the group ethic and use a team approach and peer pressure to instill discipline and promote productivity. One businessman in Malawi teams up his foreign and African employees to enhance training and help them to work together. Also helpful are monthly wall planners, for all to see, which list due dates for the teams and their tasks.

To be avoided are plans imposed solely by management, whether in private business or government. As noted earlier, anything imposed unilaterally by an outsider, particularly a Western institution or expat, is likely to be ignored.

Age, Experience, and Gender

Does the chick teach the hen to scratch?

—African proverb

A hierarchical pecking order is followed in meetings, observes an executive who works for a large international corporation in South Africa. "Young blacks," he explains, "defer to older blacks, young whites to older whites, all blacks to all whites, young women to older women, and all women to all men." The "all blacks to all whites" is changing in the new South Africa, but age and gender are still grounds for deference.

As the African proverb about the chick tells us, the young do not teach the old, and apparently, women do not enlighten men, at least not in public. This too has its roots in African traditional society, which, as Deng tells us, "...was organized and stratified on the basis of descent, age, and gender, with clearly differentiated roles for chiefs, elders, warrior age-sets, and women."[19]

Age earns the highest respect. As in other traditional societies, great deference and maximum courtesy are shown to elders (as they once were in the West). In many African languages, elders and more senior persons are addressed in the formal third person. When passing an object to someone who is older, higher in rank, or a foreign visitor, Africans, as earlier noted, may proffer the object with their right hand while supporting the right arm with their left hand.

Older people, both men and women, are assumed to have the wisdom and experience which lead to authority and power, and their word is rarely questioned. To call someone in Africa an "old man" or "old woman" is a sign of esteem. Such respect for age can work for Westerners as well, and those with grey heads or bald pates will also be deferred to. So, contrary to what you might do at home, in Africa enhance your age. Try to look older, not younger.

If a foreign firm has a choice, it should send an older representative to Africa. A man will not necessarily be more effective than a woman, since age is more important than gender, although women may have a more difficult time in Muslim cultures. A young female foreigner may find that her age is more of a handicap than her gender. "You are so young," an African might say to a young expat who has come to give advice, "how do you know that it is really so?"

Role assignments between males and females are also strictly defined. There are jobs for men and jobs for women, and they often cannot be interchanged. An American woman who headed a large development project in Kenya decided to give her employees a perk common to U.S. offices—urns of coffee and tea from which to serve themselves when some refreshment was needed. But to her surprise, the employees protested. Their custom, they explained, was to have a (very British) twenty-minute tea break at 10:30 in the morning and another at 3:30 in the afternoon, and during tea breaks they did not work (and in some offices they do not even answer the phone). Also, they added, tea should be served from a cart, not from an urn sitting on a table in a back room. The American supervisor reluctantly agreed.

Her secretary, however, who would normally be given the task of serving tea, was overworked, so the supervisor directed that tea be prepared and served by a driver who had plenty of free time. Again the employees protested, explaining that serving tea is a woman's job. The American supervisor then asked what would happen if the secretary happened to be a man. In that case, rejoined the employees, a woman would have to be hired, and that is what she indeed had to do—hire another female employee whose sole duty it was to prepare and serve tea.

Role assignments between adults and children are also strictly defined. When an adult education program for Africans was established and housed in a school building, the adults balked at entering the school, which, they said, had been built to serve children. They agreed to attend classes only after the organizers assured them that all the children would have left the building before the adult classes began.

Negotiating with Africans

> One does not enchain a bargainer who offers too low a price.
>
> —Yoruba proverb

"Yoruba market transactions are a lively test of wit involving seller and buyer," writes Oyekan Owomoyela. "Since prices were seldom fixed, the understanding was that the seller would ask a price higher than he or she would accept, and the buyer was free to see how low he or she could bring the seller."[20] With such a strategy the assertive and entrepreneurial Yoruba have a well-earned reputation for being among the best negotiators in West Africa.

Negotiation is a process usually associated with diplomats, lawyers, and businesspeople. Two parties meet, each with its own objectives and needs, and seek to work out an understanding that satisfies both sides. In Africa, however, negotiations are not limited to diplomacy, law, and business. Westerners should assume that everything is negotiable, as it indeed may turn out to be.

The African approach to negotiation differs from that of the West. Westerners see negotiation in economic terms—get as much as you can while giving as little as possible. Africans, by contrast, see negotiation as social and personal interaction—a "win-win" situation from which both parties should come away satisfied. Westerners should approach negotiations in Africa in the same way. Relax, enjoy them, and above all take your time. If Africans are hurried through business deals, they will suspect cheating or foul play.

The sharing of resources, a concept basic to traditional communal societies, may also affect negotiations. People are expected to share according to their ability to do so. A person with ten dollars might be expected to pay one dollar for a purchase, but someone with one hundred dollars, as much as ten dollars for the same item. It follows that in an African marketplace a Westerner will be charged a higher price while an African standing next to him may pay much less for the same item. To Africans, this is not gouging, but fairness.

Bargaining over price is the rule in the African market-place and in small shops (but not in hotels, restaurants, and upscale stores), and those who do not bargain will be thought somewhat strange, even out of their minds! The sellers look over the buyers and ask whatever they believe they might pay. The buyers, in turn, have an idea of what an item is worth and what they are willing to pay. A buyer's opening bid, therefore, is always lower than the asked price, and the objective, as in a Western stock market, is to narrow the difference between the "asked" and the "bid." Experienced Africa hands usually bid less than half the asked price and try not to pay more than half.

It's a friendly and sociable contest, but at some point, to see how far off your bid really is, you may want to throw up your hands in disappointment, turn your back, slowly walk away, and see if you are followed by the seller and asked to submit a new bid. Another tactic is to ask with a smile, "Is this the white man's price?"

In the give-and-take of bargaining, push as hard as you can, and don't be afraid to make a scene, albeit a polite one. Above all, do not appear anxious to buy. Sellers will point out the virtues of their wares, but buyers should look for flaws, breaks, or a little dirt as incentives to reduce the price. Such bargaining tactics may not be for every Westerner, and those who are uncomfortable with dickering can purchase their gifts and souvenirs from a state or cooperative store where prices will be higher but fixed.

Haggling over price may indeed win a Westerner a measure of respect as well. Wole Soyinka, Nigeria's Nobel laureate in literature (and a Yoruba), notes that "All over the continent...a recognized foreigner who defeats a market trader in a haggling contest will be spoken of in terms of admiration, even by the defeated trader."[21]

The sellers, however, must not lose face. Do not say that the goods are not worth what the sellers are asking. Rather, concede that the value of the goods may be what they say, but the asking price is simply not within your means. Make it clear that you want to settle on a price that you can afford but one that will also leave them a margin of profit.

Such haggling in the United States is usually limited to larger purchases like houses and cars. But buying a used car in Africa has a curious twist that makes it a very different process and affirms an important aspect of the African approach to serious negotiation. In the States, if Jones buys a car from Smith, the conversation might go like this:

"How much do you want for this car?" asks Jones.
"Ten thousand," replies Smith.
"No, that's too much," responds Jones, and they continue to negotiate until they reach a mutually acceptable price.

In Malawi, the conversation between a buyer and seller might go this way:

"How much do you want for the car," asks Banda.
"Whatever you want to give me," answers Phiri.
"Five thousand," offers Banda, and they agree or do not.
If not, Banda asks, "Why is it too little?"

The offer comes from the buyer in many African cultures so that the seller does not lose face. The buyer recognizes the seller's needs, and, in turn, the seller hopes that his own needs will be recognized through a proper offer. Each party tries to get the best possible deal but also wants the other party to get a good deal.

Willingness to compromise is therefore essential. If you insist on getting the price as low as possible, you may lose your purchase. Africans respect firmness and decisiveness, but a sense of fairness is also expected. When bargaining over a bag of tomatoes, for example, you will know that the seller appreciates your negotiating style when she adds a few tomatoes after the price has been agreed upon. In return, you should give a few extra coins.

All Westerners are assumed to be wealthy, especially Americans, and will be at a disadvantage in negotiating prices. From the African point of view, an American always seems to have money to purchase anything he or she wants. Americans, consequently, should not flaunt their money. Africans do not flaunt theirs, and the African wearing a shabby boubou may have a weighty wallet under his long gown.

To conclude a deal as quickly as possible Americans will often display their affluence by accepting the first price offered, or the second. Africans, by contrast, are prepared to dicker as long as necessary to get the best possible deal, and they will be in no hurry to disclose their bottom line. Neither should Americans be in a hurry; the experience of one American when hiring an African official to manage a business he had just purchased is a good example.

In negotiating his salary, the African explained that his government was paying him the equivalent of $1,200 per month but he needed $2,000 to make ends meet. The American, knowing what his other expenses would be and how much he expected to earn from his new business, made a quick mental calculation and immediately accepted the African's price, since $2,000 was not too much to pay for a good manager. But the African would have been willing to bargain, and the American should have proposed, at the very least, to think it over and call back the next day, thereby giving the impression that he would check the going rate for salaries and consider the higher figure.

In business negotiations, if your bid is not the lowest but Africans are interested in what you have to offer, explain how you arrived at your price and why your bid is the best one. Be direct and honest.

The soft sell is always better than the hard sell and is more likely to produce the desired results. Try to convince your interlocutors that you are there to listen and that their views will be given serious consideration. They may have work experience in the West and even a Ph.D. from a Western university, but they will be wondering whether you really understand their views and needs.

Form and ritual are important in negotiating. Where you sit carries weight, and how you sit. How you speak is also important, as is the level of your voice—lower is better than higher. Knowledge of local rules and accepted practices gives a negotiator status. Try to learn them.

In some countries Africans will say "Yes, that's a great idea" but then nothing happens and months of delay follow. Nothing may indeed be happening, or a consensus to accept your proposal may not have been reached. As discussed in an earlier chapter, a local intermediary may be able to clarify the situation or move the negotiations forward.

Observe the hierarchical ranking in bureaucracies. Go through proper channels, and do not jump over officials in rank. If you do, the official you jump over may do you in. If you should make a courtesy call on a higher official, for example, notify the lower-level official so that he will not be offended. Follow established procedures. Bureaucrats will know what can and cannot be done, and they will tell you.

In a negotiation, try to identify the key persons who are the decision makers. They may be sitting in the background and not taking part in the negotiation, but others will consult with them before making a decision. In a village it is the chief or headman who must give final approval, even when his authority is traditional rather than official. In government offices it will be some senior officials, although they may have to check out an agreement with the minister before making it final.

In most countries these senior officials take into account the recommendations of key subordinates before approving or disapproving a project. Try to learn who advises the authority figure or Big Man, and spend some time convincing or negotiating with that person or bringing other midlevel people on board. If you are a pharmaceutical manufacturer, for example, and want to sell drugs to the ministry of health, you should first see a lower-level official and get his support. Then, go to the Big Man for the final decision. Bear in mind though, as earlier noted, that in Africa it is customary to approach someone of high status through an intermediary.

The African top-down system of decision making should not be challenged. Do not embarrass a midlevel bureaucrat by asking why he himself cannot make the decision. You may be pressed for time, and you may believe that the official is more likely than his boss to approve your proposal. But if you push for a midlevel decision you will be seen as arrogant and disrespectful, and doors may be closed to you in the future.

Get to know the families of your African counterparts. Drop in to see them from time to time and show interest in their lives. In the West, time is money, but in Africa, as we've said before, leisure may also mean money. Take the time to ask about art objects in people's homes or offices and the clothes they are wearing, particularly any intricate embroidery. Bear in mind, though, that if you admire something too much it may be presented to you as a gift.

For business activities in rural areas, you must also establish rapport with the local chief, who can make life easy or difficult for you. Make a courtesy call on the chief or headman, and show the respect due him. For real estate matters, you must also get his oral agreement on use of the land and the boundaries of your plot. Then go to the civil authorities and tell them you have the chief's approval.

When a negotiation has been concluded and agreement reached, be sure to make clear what each party is expected to do, and when. Read the text carefully; you may find some errors or typos that will have to be corrected before the document can be signed.

Contracts are not always respected, and what you have agreed to may or may not be carried out. Government personnel can change. The official you reached agreement with may not be around when the time for implementation arrives, and his successor may ask, "What agreement?" If your negotiating partner is still there but has done nothing to carry out the agreement, do not remonstrate with a "But you promised!" That will be seen as offensive and will get you nowhere. Back off, start all over again if necessary, and be patient.

Before leaving a country, go back to the Big Man to review what you have accomplished and the follow-up steps to be taken. When setting up the appointment, make clear how much time you will need or you may be given only five minutes sandwiched in between two other callers.

The number of witnesses and hangers-on present when an agreement or contract is signed will surprise Westerners. In the village, where agreements are oral and unwritten, it is customary to have others present—often a father, brothers, or other members of the extended family—to legitimize an agreement by their presence. In case of default or violation of the agreement, the witnesses can be summoned to confirm exactly what had been agreed to. This tradition continues in the city, where witnesses provide the formality that reinforces commitment and obligation.

Also, as discussed earlier, there may be an unstated expectation of a quid pro quo in negotiations—some dash or a bribe. It is not given directly, but months after a deal has been completed you might unexpectedly be the recipient of a goat or lamb and expected to give something more substantial in return. Race and color may not play a role, but in business negotiations the color that Africans most respect is green.

African Law

One does not decide a case after hearing only one side.
—Yoruba proverb

As the colonial era in Africa was coming to a close in 1959, Lord Denning, a noted British jurist, described the legal systems of British Africa as a jumble of pieces much like a jigsaw puzzle.

> One group of pieces is founded on the customs of the African peoples, which vary from territory to territory, and from tribe to tribe. Another group of pieces is founded on the law of Islam, with all its many schools and sects. Yet another group is founded on the English Common Law. Another on the Roman Dutch law, another on Indian statutes and so forth.[22]

Some thirty years later, the parts of the puzzle were falling into place, but two U.S. legal scholars were perplexed. As Thomas H. Reynolds and Arturo A. Flores wrote in their highly regarded reference book on foreign law, "All legal systems in operation in the world today qualify as 'mixed,' but those in Africa present admixtures that almost defy penetration."[23]

African law is indeed an amalgam of coexisting legal systems, which are, however, penetrable. This legal pluralism, as it is called, includes traditional tribal law and Islamic law (*Sharia*), in existence long before the arrival of the colonists; "customary" law, based on tribal laws and customs as restructured and recognized by the colonialists; and, finally, the various legal systems carried over from the colonizing countries, which also have their differences.

In most former British colonies, judicial systems are based on English common law—the case method and the decisions of judges which are the bases of Anglo-American jurisprudence. In the former colonies of France, Belgium, Portugal, and Spain, the legal systems are based on civil law—the laws passed by legislatures and defined by the regulations of executive authorities. Further differences exist in the systems of South Africa and its neighboring states of Botswana, Lesotho, Namibia, Swaziland, and Zimbabwe, which are based on old

Roman-Dutch law as modified by English law. Sudan has adopted Sharia as the law of the land, although special exceptions can be made for non-Muslims in the application of Islamic penalties and in personal matters such as marriage and divorce. In Sudan, moreover, despite the Islamization of the legal system, most judges and practicing attorneys are products of common law education, and their legal culture is still mainly Western. Ethiopia and Liberia—two countries with a longer history of independence—have their own systems. Ethiopia, where there was no system of foreign law to be inherited from a colonial power, created modern legal codes based on European civil law systems but with procedures drawn from common law. It also retained its Islamic and customary courts. Liberia adopted American-style common law.

Which system of law will apply in a specific case? That will depend, of course, on the country in question, the parties involved, and the issues in contention.

In Nigeria, for example, in a case between two Nigerians, the customary law applies (with some exceptions such as the sale of goods) unless the two parties have decided that English law should govern or that the issue is unknown to customary law. In a case between a Nigerian and a non-Nigerian, English law will apply unless it can be shown that its use will substantially harm one party or the other, in which event customary law will apply, or the non-Nigerian voluntarily submits to the authority of the customary court. In a case between two non-Nigerians, English law will automatically apply. To further complicate matters, customary law can also vary between different states of the country, and Muslim law may apply in Islamic districts of the northern states.[24]

"African law with African roots plays a major role in some parts of most African legal systems...," especially in family law, according to Peter W. Schroth, a U.S. attorney and law professor with business experience in Africa. But for international business matters and foreign investment, "this sort of African law plays virtually no role at all."[25]

The law of contracts, commercial law, and company law, says Schroth, are among the areas most likely to survive even radical changes of government. Accordingly, to understand those aspects of a country's legal system that relate to international business and foreign investment, Schroth advises foreign investors to learn something about the former colonial power's legal system, especially as it stood some decades ago, when independence was achieved. That legal system is most likely to apply in commercial cases.[26]

Africa's legal systems are undergoing development and adjustment as governments seek accommodations among their various legal systems that will enable them to better meet the challenges of changing domestic societies and an increasingly interdependent global economy. The new judicial systems, however, are likely to give some recognition to African customs which may have been denigrated in the past.

All African cultures possessed procedures for deciding disputes and disciplining delinquents. Both parties to a dispute argued their case before the local chief and his council of elders. Witnesses could be called by both plaintiff and defendant and could be cross-examined. After consultation with the elders, the chief rendered his decision, which could, however, be appealed to a higher court, where one existed, or overruled by public opinion. The court was open to the public, and any adult could testify. Although the law was unwritten, procedures were well established and the rule of law prevailed.

Many of those traditional courts still exist today in countries where there are two parallel systems of law, the customary and the European-based, and the plaintiff and accused can decide which one to use. Many choose the customary court, believing it will be more considerate as well as more lenient. However, some women, young men, and modernized Africans who seek emancipation from the traditional order may prefer the civil court. The civil court may also be preferred in jurisdictions where lawyers are not allowed to represent clients in customary courts.

Contributing to this belief in the consideration and leniency of the customary court is its flexibility and its aim of promoting social harmony. Decisions are based not on a strict code of law but rather on the circumstances of each case and the pertinent precedents.

Traditional tribal law, therefore, emphasizes not punishment but reconciliation and the restoration of communal harmony and stability. Courts try to make amends for whatever damage has been done to the common good or to the wronged individual, and instead of incarceration, a transgressor will likely be put to some socially useful task or made to pay some compensation that will help to mitigate the harm done.

Compromise, accordingly, is more important than litigation, and in traditional courts the judge seeks—you guessed it—consensus, a negotiated solution acceptable to all parties, which ends a conflict and restores harmony. The traditional judge, writes Dia,

> ...is more intent at reaching a consensus than at litigating from the "book." He devises a negotiated solution acceptable to all parties. In legal as well as political matters, the Africans seek unanimity and are prepared to engage in interminable discussions to achieve it. In the same spirit, the judgments handed down in African law seek to establish a broad area of consent and to lead the parties to it."[27]

Such a "win-win" solution, in which both sides agree, is the complete opposite of the spirit of Western law, continues Dia, where the judge interprets the law and pronounces a sentence to which the parties must submit, whether they agree or not.

The African has a totally different concept of law, says anthropologist Colin M. Turnbull, "...and thinks of a court's function not as being one of conviction and punishment, but as an attempt to find a solution to any problem brought before it...to establish justice, not simply to apply the law."[28]

More important than the punishment of the guilty is the protection of the innocent. Truth is not absolute, as in the West, nor are right and wrong or yes and no. In traditional African cultures there can be many versions of verities and many varieties of extenuating circumstances.

Other practical problems may present themselves in enforcement of laws and contracts. Mechanisms for enforcement may be weak, and pursuing them may prove to be prohibitively expensive. Laws may be enforced unevenly and irregularly, and some may conflict with other, equally valid laws. Government decrees can be issued to circumvent laws. And some laws may appear irrational, especially when they apply to you and you find you need a lawyer's advice.

Foreigners in Africa may indeed need legal counsel, as they do in their home countries, in cases involving automobile accidents, in defending themselves in other lawsuits, or in adopting children. But the most common cause of legal action against expats concerns household and office employees who have been fired. As we have noted, employees know the labor laws of their country well, and they do file lawsuits when they believe their rights have been violated. Africa, moreover, like the United States, has its share of "ambulance chasers," lawyers who seek out terminated employees and convince them that they have a case no matter what the grounds for dismissal may have been—stealing, drinking on the job, or, in the case of guards, abandoning their posts. Lawyers will take such cases on contingency, in other words, exacting a high percentage of whatever their client may receive in a court judgment.

When in doubt, consult a counselor.

1   These statistics are from Gerald M. Feldman, "Sub-Saharan Africa: The Overseas Business Challenge of the 21st Century," *Business America* 118 (January/February 1997): 7.

2   Dia, *Africa's Management*, 221.

3   Robert Klitgaard, *Tropical Gangsters: One Man's Experience with Development and Decadence in Deepest Africa* (New York: Basic Books, 1990), 29.

4   Ibid.

5   *New York Times*, 19 October 1995.

6   Susan Blake, *Letters from Togo* (Iowa City: University of Iowa Press, 1991), 86-87.

7   Mamadou Dia, "Indigenous Management Practices," in *Culture and Development*, edited by Serageldin and Tabaroff, 184-85.

8   Chester A. Crocker, "Why Africa Is Important," *Foreign Service Journal* 72, no. 6 (June 1995): 28.

9   George B. N. Ayittey, *Africa Betrayed* (New York: St. Martin's Press, 1992), 68.

10   This version of the three sons parable is from W. Penn Handwerker, *Social Dimensions of Entrepreneurship in Africa*, a study prepared by the Institute for Development Anthropology for the U.S. Agency for International Development, March 1990.

11   Lamb, *Africans*, 9.

12   *Financial Times*, 22 March 1996.

13   Mazrui, *Africans*, 217.

14   Dia, "Indigenous Management Practices," 187.

15   Mazrui, *Africans*, 77.

16   Mbiti, *Introduction to African Religion*, 37.

17   Francis Mading Deng, "Cultural Dimensions of Conflict Management and Development: Some Lessons from Sudan," in *Culture and Development*, edited by Serageldin and Tabaroff, 481.

18   Mazrui, *Africans*, 220-24.

19   Deng, "Cultural Dimensions of Conflict Management," 496.

20   Oyekan Owomoyela, *A Ki i: Yoruba Proscriptive and Prescriptive Proverbs* (New York: Lanham, 1988), 179.

21 Wole Soyinka, "Culture, Memory, and Development," in *Culture and Development*, edited by Serageldin and Tabaroff, 207.

22 Lord Denning, quoted in Christopher Y. O. Adei, *African Law South of the Sahara* (Clayton, MO: International Institute for Advanced Studies, 1981), 1-2.

23 Thomas H. Reynolds and Arturo A. Flores, *Foreign Law: Current Sources of Codes and Basic Legislation in Jurisdictions of the World*, vol. 3 of *Africa, Asia and Australasia* (Littleton, CO: Fred B. Rothman, 1993), 1.

24 Richard W. Danner and Marie-Louise H. Bernal, eds., *Introduction to Foreign Legal Systems* (New York: Oceana Publications, 1984), 178.

25 Peter W. Schroth, ed., *Doing Business in Sub-Saharan Africa* (Chicago: American Bar Association, 1991), xiii, xvi.

26 Ibid., xvi.

27 Dia, "Cultural Dimensions of Institutional Development," 7.

28 Turnbull, *Lonely African*, 207.

Regional Differences

The African heritage is rich, but it is not uniform. It has similarities, but there are also differences from time to time, from place to place, and from people to people.
    —John S. Mbiti, *Introduction to African Religion*

As mentioned earlier, in the Introduction, some variations in the cultural characteristics described above will be found among peoples of the different geographic regions of Africa as well as within those regions. Those whose ancestors were agriculturalists in Coastal West and Central Africa differ from those in East and Southern Africa, who are descended from pastoralists. People of the semiarid Sahel and the Horn of Africa are different from inhabitants of the humid rain forests of Coastal West and Central Africa and the temperate highlands of East and Southern Africa. And within these regions, Muslims differ from Christians.

To discuss these differences, we next examine six geographic regions and, within the limits of these pages, some selected countries and peoples.

175

Coastal West and Central Africa

Here is located the dense tropical rain forest of the Congo
River Basin and the Guinea coast of West Africa, able to
sustain relatively high population densities.
                                                —Henry S. Wilson,
   The Imperial Experience in Sub-Saharan Africa Since 1870

Visitors go to East Africa to see the wildlife and the scenery,
it is often said, but to Coastal West and Central Africa to see
the people, visit the markets, and hear the music. If action is
what you are seeking, West and Central Africa are the places
to be. Here, trade is more traditional, markets more ani-
mated, life more lively, the sound more vibrant, and the
people more assertive. How so?

Anthropologists point out that the peoples of Coastal West
Africa were agriculturalists long before the arrival of the
Europeans.[1] In these regions, sedentary societies seeded crops
and began to develop specialized occupations; market towns
thrived; money was used and the arts and crafts were highly
developed. As a consequence, Africans of these regions were
culturally closer to the colonialists, whose agricultural economies, trading traditions, and pecuniary practices were more
comparable to their own. Coastal West Africa had been in
contact with Europe since the sixteenth century, which gave
its people a head start in understanding Europeans and en-
abled them to adapt more easily to their ways. The colonial
experience, moreover, was generally more benign than in
other parts of Africa, which helps to explain why West Africans are more cordial toward Europeans and are less suspicious of their purposes.

Heavy rains, however, and the resultant mosquitoes, tsetse
flies, and the diseases they cause kept the Europeans from
settling on the land, and they confined themselves, for the
most part, to coastal cities, leaving the interior largely un-
touched. (The Muslim traders from the north had the good

sénse to confine themselves mainly to the Sahel and avoided the less hospitable zones to the south.)

In these regions, both anglophone and francophone Africans have a well-earned reputation for being lively, loud, and "in your face," which may be due, in part, to the high population density. Nigeria has a population of more than one hundred million, the largest of any country in sub-Sahara. Today every fifth person in sub-Sahara is a Nigerian. Moreover, Nigeria is doubling its population every twenty-two years. In international meetings, Nigeria often sees itself as the flag bearer for African anglophone countries, a role which Côte d'Ivoire assumes for the Francophones.

Because of the high population density, coastal areas have become urbanized in several countries. Abidjan, Accra, and Lagos are big cities in every sense, with ports, commerce, markets, and import and export trade as well as enormous social problems such as overcrowding, squatter camps, crime, and pollution.

Despite these difficulties, Coastal West and Central Africans laugh, joke, dance, party a lot, and are fun to be with. Marketplaces are sites for song, dance, and socialization as well as the buying and selling of goods and produce. At nightclubs, many patrons do not show up until midnight, and nightlife continues until the early morning hours. Debate and discussion are enjoyed—and at great length—and the patience of foreign listeners will be tested. Visitors will have to restrain their urge to say "Get to the point." To interrupt, as mentioned earlier, is considered very rude.

Music, both traditional and pop, is important to all Africans, but in these regions you hear it live in the markets and streets as well as on the radio. And those streets teem with young men and women selling everything imaginable—watches, clothing, T-shirts with U.S. logos, food, and anything else they can buy cheap and sell dear.

Generous and forthright, the people of these regions will share whatever they have with others. But along with their generosity, they can be boisterous, rash, and hot-tempered. The loudest and most direct are said to be the Nigerians of the south, who are not known for self-discipline or restraint. Other Africans charge them with arrogance, calling them the New Yorkers of Africa, and Nigerians would probably agree.

If Nigerians are known as hustlers and con artists, it may be because their culture reflects the traditions of the traders who traveled from North Africa across the Sahara and further south into Africa long before the arrival of the Europeans. In 1997, for the second year in a row, a survey of international business executives by Transparency International, an international organization that seeks to curb corruption in developing countries, found Nigeria the most corrupt country to do business in.[2]

Nigerians, however, will tell you exactly how they feel about everything. In contrast to many other African countries, in Nigeria yes is more apt to mean yes, and no, no, and you are more likely to get a straight story and be told straight away (as the British would say) when you are doing something wrong.

But here we run the risk of oversimplifying, for Nigeria and the other countries in the region are not homogeneous in ethnicity, culture, or religion, and one might indeed ask, "Who is a Nigerian?"

About half of Nigeria's people are Muslims, more than any Arab country. But like most African countries, it also has enormous ethnic diversity, and its people speak more than two hundred distinct languages. Politics, however, has been determined by four major groups. A Nigerian, therefore, may be a Muslim Hausa or Fulani, the two largest ethnic groups of the populous but underdeveloped north, who have dominated politics and the military for most of Nigeria's history as a country. Or a Nigerian may be a Muslim or Christian Yoruba in the southwest, a people who have held the nation's socioeconomic power. Or a Nigerian may be a Christian Igbo in the southeast, who are more economically enterprising and who have the oil. All are Nigerians and Anglophones, but they differ in their cultures and in their willingness to coexist.

Recognizing these differences, the British governed Nigeria as two separate countries, ruling indirectly in the Muslim emirates of the north through a highly centralized, traditional, and hierarchical authority which they had established there. The biggest differences, however, were cultural. As Hoover Institution's Larry Diamond points out, "...Western [European] education and religion were permitted to spread rapidly in the South but heavily restricted in the Muslim North, creating enormous disparities in economic and technological development."[3]

Disparities between these dissimilar cultural zones continued after independence, and regional rivalry led to the secession of the Igbo in 1967 and a thirty-month civil war that caused hundreds of thousands of military and civilian fatalities, with many of the world's major powers taking sides in the bitter and violent struggle. A similar split developed in the 1990s, when a military junta annulled a 1993 election in which a Yoruba had been elected president under a program planned to provide a transition to democracy. The military government dissolved all elected governments and legislatures at the state and local levels, clamped down on dissent, executed some of its critics, and jailed thousands more.

One of the root causes of Nigeria's painful and polarizing political rivalry has been the struggle for control of the federal government and its rich oil revenues. As Wole Soyinka describes it:

> To obtain a basic understanding of today's reality of Nigerian politics, one had better learn about and come to grasp with the phenomenon of the spoils of power. Both quantitatively and qualitatively, in aspects of tenacity and duration, of manipulation of interest groups and the scale of attendant corruption, which is usually understood by such groups as pa-

tronage, the spoils of power continue to take central place in the various internal confrontations that have wracked that uneasy entity, Nigeria, since its fabrication by the British colonial power in 1914.[4]

In that struggle there have been winners and losers, and as a consequence, Nigeria has experienced a "brain drain." Many of its educated elite are driving cabs in foreign cities; in fact, for an update on Nigeria, check out your next American city cabdriver. And when your cabbie tanks up his taxi, especially on the U.S. east coast, or you fill your home heating tank in New England, you may be using fuel refined from Nigerian crude. In 1996 Nigeria was the world's tenth largest oil producer and the fifth largest supplier to the United States, accounting for 8 percent of U.S. oil consumption.

"Nigeria presents at one and the same time conflicting images to the American exporter," writes Alicia J. Robinson, a country officer for Nigeria at the U.S. Department of Commerce,

> a market popularly synonymous with fraudulent business prospects, and a market teeming with opportunity that continues to make it the second largest destination for U.S. goods in Sub-Saharan Africa [after South Africa]. Which becomes the reality for an individual firm depends on careful market development.[5]

The illegal activities of a few, adds Robinson, overshadow the legitimate operations of the majority, and she advises new companies exploring the Nigerian market to check every potential business partner's bona fides as well as each contract's authenticity.

Well aware of their country's economic and political importance, Nigerians are very sensitive to outside interference in their internal affairs. Foreign criticism, from other Africans as well as Westerners, is likely to provoke anger.

Ghana is also anglophone and, like Nigeria, it is one of the more developed African countries in terms of education, skills, and resources. Formerly known as the Gold Coast, in 1957 Ghana became the first sub-Saharan colony to achieve independence. But like Nigeria, much of Ghana's human resources has been dispersed to other parts of Africa and the world, as it has shifted back and forth between authoritarian and democratic rule, neither of which has proven successful.

Ethnically diverse, with some seventy-five languages and dialects, Ghana is populated by peoples with an historic antagonism to each other. But while this diversity has been a divisive factor in national politics, Ghana's traditions of consultation and governance by discussion, in contrast to Nigeria, have not polarized it along ethnic lines in recent years.

Also providing grounds for optimism has been Ghana's active civil society, a nationwide network of associations of intellectuals, medical doctors, engineers, businesspeople, workers, farmers, and civil servants that has created an independent political base of its own. Naomi Chazan, an Israeli scholar, writes of the "...strong participatory and egalitarian components" of the traditional institutions of the peoples of Ghana and "...a deeply democratic tradition ensconced in local political cultures."[6] In an election in December 1996 to choose a new president, 77 percent of eligible voters turned out, and while the leader of the military government that had ruled Ghana for eleven years was reelected, opposition parties won sixty-five of the two hundred legislative seats, promising Ghana's first significant legislative opposition in years. "This election," said Ghanaian political scientist E. Gyimah-Boadi, "represents a consolidation of democracy."[7]

One American veteran of Africa says, moreover, that he has never heard anyone say anything bad about Ghanaians, who are reputed to be among the best and most outgoing of African hosts. And crime there is much lower than in many neighboring countries.

Women in Coastal West Africa have also benefited from

the trading tradition. Throughout recorded history, and as long as they fulfilled their wifely obligations, women were allowed to engage in retail trade. As a consequence, women in Ghana have a well-earned reputation for being independent and self-sufficient. They dominate the markets, where they sell clothing, housewares, and food, and some have become quite wealthy.

Traditional African attire is favored in Coastal West and Central Africa, where both men and women dress with color and style. Not uncommon is the sight of women with off-the-shoulder dresses, stylish hair, and fashionable jewelry. In Abidjan, where office dress is more formal, men wear suits, and women, tailored African dresses. Titles are important and should be used, especially in francophone countries.

Central Africa is francophone except for Equatorial Guinea, where one can *hablar* in Spanish, and São Tomé and Principe, where people *fallar* in Portuguese. Cameroonians converse in English in their western provinces, but both French and English are recognized as official languages, a legacy of the colonial era when Cameroon was divided between France and Britain after Germany lost it at the end of World War I.

Christianity prevails in Central Africa, but Islam is the religion of the northern parts of Cameroon and Central African Republic and the Sahel region of Chad. Almost everywhere, however, animism mixes easily with both Christianity and Islam.

The Democratic Republic of the Congo dominates Central Africa, with its vast expanse and rich resources. As the second largest country in sub-Sahara after Sudan, the former Zaire is the size of the United States east of the Mississippi River, and its population of forty-five million is sub-Sahara's third largest, after Nigeria and Ethiopia. Kinshasa, the sprawling capital, alone has more than five million inhabitants and is still growing.

The people are Bantu, similar in culture to other Bantu-language people who predominate south of the equator in

Central, East, and Southern Africa. French is the official language of the former Belgian Congo, but in this vast country with more than two hundred fifty ethnic groups, four local languages are recognized—Lingala, Kikongo, Tshiluba, and Kiswahili. Of the four, Lingala is the most prominent, since it is the language of the capital and the military as well as the language of lyrics for the country's Latin-like music, which is popular throughout sub-Sahara. More than three-fourths of the people are Christian, with Catholics the largest denomination, followed by Protestants and Kimbanguists, an independent African church; some 20 percent of the people practice traditional African religions. Despite the country's past difficulties its people are known for their irrepressible spirit, extroversion, and cultural creativity. Their art is highly decorative and flamboyant, and Democratic Republic of the Congo is a great place to buy traditional African face masks and wood carvings.

Incredibly endowed with enormous mineral and energy resources, fertile farmland, timber stands, and a people known throughout Central Africa for their drive and entrepreneurial spirit, the new Democratic Republic of the Congo is potentially the richest country in Africa. That potential, however, has not been realized in the past. Many of the failings described in earlier chapters applied, only more so—extravagant expenditures, mismanagement, corruption, crime, repressive rule, and misuse of U.S. largess during the Cold War. Moreover, the infrastructure needed to hold together such a vast country was poorly developed, and the authority of the central government had deteriorated precipitously. All this came to a head in 1997.

Taking advantage of the weakness of the central government, the copper- and cobalt-rich Shaba (formerly Katanga) province in the southeast, rebellious in the past, rekindled its ambitions for autonomy by strengthening economic ties with Zambia, Zimbabwe, and South Africa, the anglophone countries to its east and south.

In the northeast, ethnic Tutsis resident in the provinces of North and South Kivu for more than two hundred years rebelled in late 1996 after local Zairian officials announced a plan to deport them to Rwanda. Joining other anti-Kinshasa dissidents and supported by Rwanda, Burundi, Uganda, Zambia, and Angola, the rebels routed the Zairian army along a broad front and swept west to Kinshasha in seven months. Zaire's Big Man and Africa's longest reigning ruler, Mobutu Sese Seko, a Cold War favorite of the United States and France, was forced to make a hasty exit from the country he had dominated for almost thirty-two years and was replaced as head of state by Laurent Kabila, leader of the rebel forces. It is unclear, however, whether the country will be a new Democratic Republic of the Congo or the old Zaire under a new name, but the consequences for all of Central Africa are potentially profound.

With the decline of central government authority, regional autonomies have been emerging in the provinces, and a dynamic civil society is developing. Informal economies have been prospering, and the rich copper, cobalt, and diamond extraction industries as well as cash crops are doing well. In the absence of a functioning central government, people have learned to survive on their own. At this writing, however, it is difficult to predict how much authority the new central government will be able to reassert and how it will deal with the country's ethnic and regional diversities.

The Sahel

> When it rains, we all prosper. When there is drought, we all suffer.
>
> —Sahel saying

The countries of West Africa extend geographically from north to south, but its culture zones stretch from west to east in disregard of political borders. One such culture zone is the Sahel—Arabic for "shore" or "edge"—the semiarid and less developed broad expanse between the sands of the Sahara to its north and the coastal rain forests to its south.

Stretching from Mauritania and Senegal in the west across Mali, Burkina Faso, Niger, northern Nigeria, and on to Chad in the east, the Islamic culture of the Sahel differs much from the Christian West and Central African culture zone to its south. Moreover, the cultural differences between Muslims and Christians within the Sahel are far greater than those between Francophones and Anglophones within the same region. Such cultural divides have caused political rifts and military strife. Nigeria, as we have seen, has a north-south cultural, political, and economic divide, and Chad has had three decades of conflict between its Arabic-speaking Muslim northerners and its Christian and animist southerners.

The Sahel was the terminus for trade routes from North Africa south across the Sahara after the Muslim conquest had given the region economic and cultural unity. Gold and salt were the staples of the trans-Saharan trade—gold going north, and salt, south.

Also moving south has been the Sahara, which, due to erosion and overgrazing, has been encroaching southward at a rate of more than one hundred miles each year. The Sahel, consequently, has a long history of drought, famine, and depopulation going back centuries. In more recent times, successive years of subnormal rainfall, starting in 1969, have caused recurrent droughts which have claimed the lives of millions of Sahelians. Described as the poorest of the poor in Africa, the well-being of all Sahelians depends on the weather, as the saying goes.

Although the Sahel is predominantly Muslim, Islamic tenets are layered over earlier beliefs which persist, such as the cults of spirits, magical practices, sorcery, witchcraft, and divination. Foreigners should take care to respect local customs, traditional as well as Islamic. Also to be respected are the Muslim customs of personal cleanliness and sensitivity to bare skin, and special attention should be paid to grooming and dress. As in other Muslim regions, foreign women should be conservative in what they wear.

Almsgiving is a pillar of Islam, and in the Muslim lands of Africa it is advisable to always carry a few small coins to give. If you don't have small change, just say "the next time" (*la prochaine fois*). Some expats advise adopting a particular beggar and giving to that one on a regular basis, but only after chatting a bit each time. Every African language has an expression which indicates "I have already given." Learn it, and use it with other beggars.

Typical of the Sahel is Mali, one of the poorest countries in Africa but one of the few that can boast a vibrant democracy. A large state, francophone Mali is twice the size of Texas, but 65 percent of its land is desert or semidesert, 25 percent is meadowland and pasture, and only 2 percent is arable. Most of the population is engaged in subsistence farming or food processing and is concentrated in the south along the area irrigated by the mighty Niger River. Ninety percent of the people are Muslim, 9 percent practice traditional religions, and 1 percent are Christian. French is the official language, but numerous African languages are also spoken. Bambara, the major language, is spoken by some 80 percent of Malians.

The herders, nomads, and farmers of Mali are more calm and controlled, more introspective, and less assertive than most West Africans. Their reticence and reserve, however, should not be mistaken for a lack of self-confidence, for they are also noted for their dignity, integrity, and pride. In addition they boast a reputation for hospitality to strangers, including expatriates. Smile and chat with them, and you will be made to feel welcome and may even be invited home for lunch. But do not ask personal questions, which Malians will not appreciate. Wait until you are offered the information.

Visitors to Mali should try to see the old trading city of Timbuktu on the Niger River at the edge of the Sahara. Famed throughout the Islamic world six hundred years ago as a center of Islamic culture and learning, its Grand Mosque dates from 1327.

Less typical of the Sahel is Senegal, whose people have a reputation for being assertive—so assertive that many Africans regard them as arrogant. To others, they may seem snobbish, perhaps because they are the most frenchified of all the Francophones—especially in the coastal cities of Dakar and St. Louis and on Gorée Island—and very proud of it. But the Senegalese can also boast a politically stable and multiparty democracy that has been free of military coups since independence in 1960 and a French elitist system of education that has produced a well-trained bureaucracy. Senegal, moreover, has some of the best commercial facilities in West Africa, and although its industrial base is smaller than its rival Côte d'Ivoire, many foreign companies use Senegal as a regional center for their West African operations.

Wolofs, who number some 40 percent of the population, are the dominant ethnic group in Senegal, and while French is the official language, Wolof is the language of communication for most of the population. As a trading people, Wolofs emphasize getting their share of whatever they believe is due them. Being clever—*moos*, it is called—is an important cultural value, and Wolofs must be clever enough to get what they want and to land on their feet no matter what the circumstances. This explains why others see the Senegalese—both male and female—as so assertive.

The population is close to 90 percent Muslim, which provides a unifying factor that helps to avoid ethnic strife and fosters stability. Although in the French tradition there is complete separation of religion and state, religious leaders are nevertheless influential in governmental affairs and public life.

Senegal has been more influenced by French culture, and for longer, than any other sub-Saharan country. Its capital, Dakar, was the governmental seat of colonial French West Africa and the major port of entry to sub-Sahara from Europe. As *New York Times* correspondent Howard W. French has written, "For anyone who has traveled around West Africa, the strongest impression on returning to Dakar...is likely to be that nowhere has the marriage between Europe and Africa been as thoroughly consummated."[8] With its mix of African and European ambiance, architecture, and cuisine, as well as its refreshing sea breezes and moderate climate, Dakar is a favorite of foreigners.

Not a favorite of foreigners, however, are the street traders of Dakar. "Senegalese street traders, *les banas-banas*," writes British businessman Peter Biddlecombe, "are the best—or the worst—in the world."[9] They follow foreign visitors on the streets, relentlessly hawking their fake Rolex watches, pirated cassettes, and bogus objets d'art. Street traders are encountered all over Africa. "At best they are part of the scene, an integral part of the noise and hassle of Africa. At worst, they are a pain in the neck. In Dakar they are the commercial equivalent of a *maladie exotique*."[10] Often called the New Yorkers of Africa with a French accent, the Senegalese have in fact brought their aggressive selling style to the Big Apple, where they may be found today as street vendors on the sidewalks of New York.

The Horn

> The Horn of Africa is the back door to the Persian Gulf.
> —Herman J. Cohen, "U.S. Policy toward Africa"

The Horn of Africa, so called because of its projection into the Indian Ocean, overlooks the southern approaches to the Suez Canal and is an area of high strategic importance.

Ethiopia, Eritrea, and Somalia were hot spots during the Cold War, caught up first and foremost in their own age-old rivalries but also entangled in the competition between the superpowers as they switched their support from one side to the other and then back again in "revolving door" diplomacy, as a brief recap will explain.

Ethiopia was strongly pro-Western under Emperor Haile Selassie, the last of a long dynasty that claimed descent from the union of the Hebrew King Solomon and the Arabian Queen of Sheba of biblical fame, and whom the Ethiopians claim as one of their own. Ethiopia fought with the Allies in World War II, was a founding member of the United Nations, contributed troops for U.N. interventions in Korea and Zaire, and signed a mutual defense assistance pact with the United States in 1953.

Internally, however, the political system was archaic, the economy feudal, and all powers vested in Emperor Haile Selassie. Open opposition to the emperor's rule surfaced in 1974, led by a small educated elite and young military officers and triggered by the regime's failure to request foreign aid to end a famine caused by drought during the previous two years. A military coup deposed the emperor in 1974 and abolished the monarchy one year later. Next, a revolutionary movement driven by Marxist ideology took power and ruled ruthlessly in a disastrous experiment with communism, which devastated the country. Supported by Soviet arms and Cuban troops, the regime fought insurgencies in Tigray province and in Eritrea, which it had annexed in 1962, and repelled an invasion in the Ogaden region by Somalia, Ethiopia's traditional adversary.

The Ogaden, inhabited mostly by Somali nomads, borders on Somalia and is regarded by Somalia as part of its historic homeland. In a Cold War scenario, Muslim Somalia, previously supported by the Soviet Union in its conflict with Christian Ethiopia, switched sides and became staunchly anticommunist and an ally of the United States.

But when the Cold War ended in 1991 and the Soviets withdrew from the Horn, Ethiopia's Marxist regime, harassed by rebels, was forced to flee and was replaced, first by a provisional government led by a coalition of rebel forces, and then by an elected government which restored order to most of the country. Relations with the United States improved, but internal strife heated up again—in Ethiopia between rival ethnic groups and in Somalia between competing clans.

Eritrea, which became self-governing after the fall of the Ethiopian Marxist regime, formally declared independence in 1993, and Somalia's central government collapsed in 1991, when rival clans began to war with each other from their rural fiefdoms. U.S. military forces, numbering 28,000, served in Somalia from 1992 to 1994 as part of a United Nations peacekeeping and emergency famine relief mission but were withdrawn after thirty-six of them were killed.

The volatile Horn is where Africa and Arabia meet, and the peoples of the region reflect the influences of both. Although there is great diversity among its inhabitants, most are of mixed Arab-African descent and are very proud of their heritage. Muslims predominate in the coastal areas and the eastern lowlands of Ethiopia, and Christians, in the western and central parts of Ethiopia and the highlands of Eritrea.

Climatically, the Horn's narrow coastal strip is hot and humid, but the rest of the region is high and dry, and its livelihood depends on the weather. As in the Sahel, when rain falls there is enough to eat. When rain fails to fall, there is famine and hundreds of thousands die, as occurred in Ethiopia and Somalia in the 1970s and 1980s.

Ethiopia has symbolic importance for Africans because of its three-thousand-year tradition as a unified and independent state, having over most of that period a written language, a recorded history, and an independent Ethiopian Orthodox Church dating from the fourth century, long before the arrival of European missionaries in Africa. During the European "scramble for Africa" Ethiopia managed to maintain its independence by annihilating an invading Italian army in 1896. This lustrous legacy, as well as imperial Ethiopia's conquest of neighboring nations, has nourished a deep sense of national pride but has also given its Amhara and Tigrean elites a superior perspective which neighboring nations, as well as Ethiopia's other ethnic groups, do not appreciate.

With a mean altitude of 8,000 feet, Ethiopia is the highest country in Africa, and its mountains and arid deserts have helped to isolate and protect it from predatory neighbors. For most of its history, Abyssinia, as Ethiopia was formerly known, has been ruled by two Christian, Semitic-speaking peoples, the Amhara and the Tigreans. The Amhara, living mostly in the northern and central highlands, controlled what eventually became the city of Addis Ababa and gradually extended their rule over adjacent areas. The Tigreans, also a northern people, prevailed in the province of Tigre and the Eritrean highlands. Together, the two groups comprised some 40 percent of the population and constituted the country's elite, although Tigrean resentment of the Amhara was strong and lay behind the insurgencies in Tigray province and Eritrea.

One of the most ethnically diverse of African countries as well as one of the world's poorest, Ethiopia's estimated fifty-five million people vary in physical appearance and culture and speak a dozen or more languages and many more dialects. Amharic is the official language, but English is the language of secondary school education and is widely spoken, especially in business, government, and academic circles. The vast majority of the people depend on subsistence farming or herding and live with recurrent cycles of drought and famine.

With the end of colonialism, Addis Ababa, with its long history of independence, was a natural choice in 1963 for the site of the founding meeting of the Organization of African Unity (OAU), which is permanently headquartered there. Encompassing the entire continent, the OAU is a forum for cooperation and the resolution of disputes between and among its members and has helped to give sub-Saharans a sense of unity and Africanness, and Ethiopians another reason to be proud. Addis, as it is commonly known, also boasts an ideal climate—mild and sunny; the average temperature remains at 59 degrees Fahrenheit year round. September through June is the season of best weather.

Despite its poverty, Ethiopia is the fifth largest U.S. export market in sub-Sahara. Agriculture, consisting mostly of peasant farms, accounts for 40 percent of the nation's output, 85 percent of is exports, and 85 percent of total employment. Coffee, which originated in Ethiopia, is the most important crop, constituting some 55 percent of exports. Coffee is an integral part of Ethiopia's way of life, and its preparation for visitors in homes is accompanied by a traditional ceremony.

The diet staple is *injera*, a flat sourdough pancake made of a local grain called teff, which is very nutritious and contains its own yeast. A traditional meal involves a gathering of people who sit around one circular plate and eat by tearing off a small piece of injera and using it to pick up pieces of meat and sauce. Ethiopian food is very tasty, and you can eat well almost everywhere in the country. Remember, however, to eat only with the right hand and to wash your hands before eating, using the soap and jug of water which are provided.

Also proud are the Eritreans, whose culture today is strongly influenced by their 1991 victory over Ethiopia in a thirty-year war for independence in which they were outnumbered ten to one and outgunned by Soviet arms. Eritrea, whose name is derived from the Latin for the Red Sea on which it borders, was a part of Italian East Africa from 1890 to 1941, and vestiges of Italian architecture, cuisine, and culture remain in Asmara, the capital city. At 7,600 feet above sea level, Asmara's climate is dry and cool, and residents, in the Italian style, go on evening strolls and sip their cappuccinos at sidewalk cafes. A resolute people, as indicated by their long struggle for independence, they celebrate their deeds of war in music, theater, and dance. Out of respect for its nine ethnic groups, Eritrea has no official language, but Arabic, English, and Tigrinya are used in government work, and English is the language of instruction in all schools from the sixth grade on. In religion, Eritreans are equally divided between Christianity and Islam, with some animists. About one-third of Eritrea's freedom fighters were women, and women today play an active role in the political, social, economic, and cultural life of the country. Although it was devastated by thirty years of warfare and recurring droughts and is one of the world's poorest nations, Africa's newest nation appears determined to avoid dependence on others and to maintain complete control over its development.

Somaliland, as it was known in the colonial period, was divided into three parts—Italian in the south, British in the north, and French in the northwest. With the end of colonialism, British and Italian Somaliland were joined and became present-day Somalia; French Somaliland became Djibouti, one of the smallest of the new states of Africa.

Six clans predominate in Somalia, four of them nomadic pastoralists and the other two cultivators. Northerners tend to be taller, thin-boned, lighter-skinned, and physically similar to Arabs, from whom they trace descent. Southerners, for the most part, are darker and resemble Bantus. Although Somalia is predominantly Muslim, there is a small Catholic minority in the south.

A gregarious people, the Somalis spend most of their waking hours with others. Less conscious of social status than many other Africans, the egalitarian Somalis are pleased to invite foreigners to their homes irrespective of differences in position or economic status. Despite their generosity and hospitality, they also have a deep suspicion of foreigners as well as members of other Somali clans. British anthropologist I. M. Lewis, a leading Western authority on the Somalis, writes of the nomadic Somalis: "...aggressive self-confidence and...open contempt for other people" as well as a "...guarded approach to the outside world, coupled with a politician's gift for seizing the advantage, [which] makes the Somalis formidable adversaries.... Displays of superior force earn only temporary respect as these most ungovernable people bide their time. One can argue with them, one can cajole them, but one cannot securely command them."[11]

Sudan, although geographically not part of the Horn, is often included in the economic and development context of the region, bordering as it does on Ethiopia, Eritrea, and the Red Sea. Nearly half the size of the United States, Sudan is the largest country in Africa and has one of the world's most heterogeneous and poorest societies. Its more than twenty million people include some six hundred tribes, which speak no fewer than four hundred languages and dialects and practice a variety of religions including Islam, indigenous beliefs, and Christianity, in that descending order of magnitude. "Sudan is a country with an obvious crisis of identity," writes Francis Mading Deng.[12]

The Sudanese identity crisis has been exacerbated by its north-south cultural divide and deep-rooted animosity which fueled a civil war that has been going on for more than thirty years. The north is Muslim by religion and Arabic by culture and language; the south is animist and Christian, African by culture, and English speaking. Moreover, from its earliest history the south has been the target of slave raiders from the north. Little wonder that the two halves of the country do not get along.

Decades-long coups, insurgencies, and wars have devastated the economies of the Horn and left many of its people impoverished and demoralized. Visitors should tread cautiously and be sensitive to the passions that can be aroused by history, religion, and culture.

Swahililand

> The Swahili have stood apart from neighboring groups by virtue of having a literate and Muslim culture with economic and political ties both within Africa and across the Indian Ocean. Their civilization has a long history of unusual cultural efflorescence and character; it has been and remains unique, with a documented history as long as any possessed by those who came to conquer it.
> —John Middleton, *The World of the Swahili*

Swahililand, as we will call it here, is the narrow coastal strip along the Indian Ocean stretching from southern Somalia down through Kenya and Tanzania to northern Mozambique and across the Indian Ocean to the offshore Comoros. This long littoral is peopled by the Swahili, literally "People of the Coast" in Arabic. Exposed to overseas influences from its earliest history, this coast attracted traders from Arabia, India, the Malay Archipelago, and even China. They came in search of gold and ivory, and later, slaves, but they brought from their homelands creative impulses that took root and thrived in the African soil. The Swahili coast was the setting for the tales of the *Thousand and One Nights*, and it was to that shore that the fabled Sinbad the Sailor set forth from Arabia.

Arab traders began to settle there more than a thousand years ago, bringing Islam, a written language, and a mercantile culture. Next came the Catholic Portuguese at the end of the fifteenth century, who ravaged and ruled the coast for two hundred years until ousted by the Dutch, English, and French. In our time, the British came to Kenya and the Germans to Tanganyika, as Tanzania was then known. With the British came the Indians, whom the British needed to build the railroads and support the infrastructure for their colonies and who are today so prominent in business and trade throughout East Africa.

All of these people intermarried with each other and with the indigenous Bantus, and the result was a new civilization built on trade between Africa and Asia, based in a string of thriving coastal port cities and offshore islands with such exotic names as Mogadishu, Mombasa, Pemba, Zanzibar, Dar es Salaam, and Kilwa. Although of disparate origins, the people are all Swahili, and their civilization is distinguished by a number of traits and virtues, admiringly described by John Middleton, a U.S. social anthropologist:

> ownership of permanent and very private houses; the claiming of real or assumed direct lineal ancestry to descent group founders...marriages of daughters with trading partners elsewhere and with those owning land...literacy and importance

given to learning; transformation of wealth into reputation and prestige; the giving of public charity; forms of lavish display and consumption; the acquisition and continual renewal of male honor and female purity; and various forms of dignity, sagacity, and courtesy.[13]

Not all Swahili possess all these traits, cautions Middleton, and they are not limited to the Swahili, but "all the Swahili see the entire complex of traits as distinguishing themselves from other peoples."[14]

With the new civilization there also evolved a new language, Kiswahili, literally the language of the Swahili. Originally spoken only along the coast, Kiswahili eventually moved inland with the traders in ivory and slaves and is now a lingua franca in most of East Africa, where it is spoken by more than twenty million people as far west as Uganda and eastern Congo as well as in Mozambique and the offshore Comoros.

Past debates about Kiswahili have been spirited, but linguists and ethnographers now generally agree that it is an eastern Bantu language with many loan words from Arabic and English. Written today in the Roman alphabet, it is easy to learn and can be useful to expats throughout East Africa. The Bible can be read in Swahili (as the language is commonly called), along with works by Shakespeare, Molière, and many other renowned Western writers.

East Africa

Looking back on a sojourn in the African highlands, you are struck by your feeling of having lived for a time up in the air.... Up in this high air you breathed easily, drawing in a vital assurance and lightness of heart. In the highlands you woke up in the morning and thought: Here I am, where I ought to be.

—Isak Dinesen, Out of Africa

The highlands of East Africa are a study in contrast with the lowlands of Coastal West and Central Africa. In the East—in Kenya, Uganda, and Tanzania—the air is drier and lighter, the population density lower, and the pace of life slower. People are more reserved and soft-spoken, perhaps because there are far fewer of them. Queuing up in orderly lines without pushing and shoving, they keep their distance and show more respect for personal space. And, in contrast to West Africa, criticism in the East is seldom direct—your staff there is less likely to tell you when you are doing something wrong. "In East Africa," observed one Western businessman, "they will let you make mistakes and allow you to walk off the plank."

A recent visitor arriving at airports in East Africa was surprised to find that young men approached him offering assistance with baggage and taxis but did not do so aggressively. This was in contrast to Nigeria and Senegal, where he had to have his elbows out to stop youngsters from grabbing his bags and passport so they could earn some money by "expediting" his arrival. In Kenya, Uganda, and Tanzania he had his elbows out, but it wasn't necessary.

East Africa was settled by Nilotic pastoralists from the north and Bantu farmers from the west, both of them seeking fertile land and adequate rainfall. Barter was the principal means of exchanging goods before the arrival of the colonialists, since markets are not indigenous to East (and Southern) Africa and were, in fact, introduced there by the colonial powers.

The absence of a trading tradition inland from the coast explains the paucity of markets, and visitors comment frequently on the limited variety of goods sold in those markets. Indians dominate small business and the retail trade, and where markets are run by Africans, men rather than women predominate, in contrast to West and Central Africa.

European settlers were more numerous in East Africa because of its fertile land, comfortable climate, and more favorable health conditions. In the highlands, the settlers cultivated cash crops for export, using Africans as cheap labor. With the colonialists came Christian missionaries of all denominations.

In religion, Kenya and Uganda are two-thirds Christian, equally divided between Catholics and Protestants, and there are smaller numbers of animists, Hindus, and Sikhs. Tanzania is one-third Christian, another third Muslim (along the coast), and the remainder, traditional African religions or Hindu—the religion of its Asians. Among Christian converts, as elsewhere in Africa, many practices of African traditional religions continue to be observed.

Rainfall is a major determinant of survival and well-being in much of Africa, and East Africa is no exception. The economies of the region are agriculture-based and heavily dependent on rainfall. In Kenya and Tanzania, population is concentrated in the 25 percent of the land with adequate rainfall, and the rest, dry or semiarid, is sparsely settled. Coffee is one of the chief crops, and it is very good indeed, although the cup you order locally may be made from instant or mixed with chicory.

Despite the location on or near the equator, the climate in all three countries, especially in the highlands where days are warm and nights cool, can be quite comfortable. Coastal areas, by contrast, are hot and humid but tempered by torrential rains and refreshing sea breezes. Lake Victoria and its environs, as well as most of adjacent Uganda, where the population is concentrated, have seven to ten months of heavy rain.

Concentrate on Uganda, wrote Winston Churchill in 1908, "...from end to end one beautiful garden, where the staple food of the people grows almost without labour....Does it not sound a paradise on earth?"[15] Fertile Uganda was indeed a most pleasant place to live until Milton Obote and Idi Amin, two tyrants who ruled in succession for sixteen years, made it an international pariah with their despotic, destructive, and brutal regimes. In 1986, President Yoweri Museveni came to power, restored order, and began a program of national re-

construction based on economic liberalism and decentraliza-
tion, which has made Uganda an African success story. Foreign investment is increasing, the economy is growing, infla-
tion has been kept in check, and there is hope for the future
in this country that has so recently seen incredible chaos.
English is an official and business language of Kenya,
Uganda, and Tanzania, but Kiswahili is the language most
widely spoken and is also an official language in Kenya and
Tanzania. Kiswahili is spoken as far west as the eastern provinces of Congo, which are geographically and culturally a
part of East Africa.

Kenya is the most developed country in East Africa. It was
a favored British colony, and telecommunications are dependable, roads are good, the postal system is reliable, train
service is excellent, and its capital, Nairobi, is a hub for air
travel in East Africa. Nairobi is also a friendly and cosmo-
politan city, although street crime and carjackings have been
increasing, and there are parts of the city where it is not
advisable to walk at night.

Kenya has the potential to be a success story, with its
educated workforce, key location, and exceptional tourism
opportunities. Yet, the challenges it faces are considerable,
including poor management of public institutions, a slowing
pace of economic reform, widespread corruption, deepening
poverty, and a continuing political struggle between an authoritarian, heavy-handed government and an opposition
which seeks constitutional and electoral reform and increased
civil liberties.

Tanzania, known as Tanganyika until it merged with Zanzibar in 1964, is popular with foreigners. Tanganyika had few
European settlers under both German and British rule, and
this perhaps accounts for the warm welcome Westerners receive there.

Tanzania owes much—for good and for bad—to its founding father, Julius Nyerere, who served as president from 1961
to 1985, when he stepped down voluntarily. A graduate of
Makerere and Edinburgh universities, Nyerere is known to-

day as Africa's elder statesman, but his countrymen still call him *Mwalimu* (Swahili for teacher), a profession he practiced before entering politics. Inheriting a pitifully poor country, Nyerere chose the path of socialism for his country's development. The economy was nationalized and people were herded together into village farming cooperatives called *ujamaa*, intended to combine traditional African communalism with modern socialism. By the 1980s Nyerere's economic program was seen as a colossal failure; transportation was in ruins, food production was down, and industrial production had been halved. Nyerere, however, had made major gains in education and health and had kept the peace for thirty years, while neighboring nations were strife-ridden. But his greatest achievement, he points out, "...is building a nation out of this collection of tribes."[16]

In the 1990s, in its drive for development, Tanzania has abandoned idealism for reality. Economic reforms have begun, investment has been encouraged, development assistance has increased, and recovery is progressing.

Tourism is big business in Kenya and Tanzania, bolstered by wildlife game parks, safaris, ocean beaches, and a good supporting infrastructure. Kilimanjaro, Africa's highest mountain at 19,340 feet, is in Tanzania, just south of its border with Kenya. Both countries are well worth a visit, although crime against foreigners has been on the increase and visitors should exercise caution.

Southern Africa

Historians know that the various parts of the subcontinental region that we call southern Africa—roughly all the lands of the central-southern plateau and its coastal peripheries down to the Cape of Good Hope—have possessed since remote times an underlying unity of culture and economy.
—Basil Davidson, *The Search for Africa*

Southern Africa, not to be confused with South Africa, is larger than China and encompasses thirteen countries— Angola, Botswana, Comoros, Lesotho, Madagascar, Malawi, Mauritius, Mozambique, Namibia, South Africa, Swaziland, Zambia, and Zimbabwe. In this region the climate is temperate, the people are friendly, and the scenery is spectacular.

Like East Africans, Southern Africans are more reserved and less assertive than West Africans. The region has had its share of violence but has seen far fewer military coups and palace revolutions. Prior to the arrival of the British in the middle of the eighteenth century, it had been relatively tranquil (except for the Arabic and Asian slave trade, which was very violent). As Davidson describes the people,

> Though living within many political entities, they clashed little with each other until new circumstances arose in the eighteenth century, or, when they clashed, their wars were little more serious than a throwing of spears, by chosen champions, among countless communities spread thinly across the skylines of countless hills.[17]

Today, the population of Southern Africa is still spread thinly, and the sparsely settled region has a total population of only one hundred twenty-five million. (Readers will recall that Nigeria alone has a population of more than one hundred million.) Most of the people are speakers of the Bantu family of languages.

In many parts of Southern Africa, residents are mostly women and children due to the absence of men working in the mines. In olden days, the region's mineral wealth—gold, copper, and iron—was well known throughout the Arab world and as far away as India and China. In our day, however, the mineral industry has been extracting not only ore from the incredibly rich but deep and costly gold and diamond mines of the region, but has also been extracting men from their homes for work far from their families. In Lesotho, with a population of less than two million, some 40 percent of the men are working in South African mines at any given time.[18] Intercountry networks are strong in Southern Africa. The countries are mostly anglophone, with the exception of Angola and Mozambique, which are lusophone, and Comoros and Madagascar, which are francophone. For most of the countries, membership in the British Commonwealth and the Southern African Development Community (SADC), formed to enhance trade among its members, has provided a basis for close collaboration. This explains why it is easier to conceive and implement regional development and business networks in Southern Africa than elsewhere in the continent.

West African-style marketplaces are also rare in Southern Africa. Traditionally, as in East Africa, there was neither money nor markets, and in the colonial period trade was dominated by whites and Asians. An American who was advising community garden projects in Lesotho was surprised to learn that there were no weekly community markets in which to sell the produce.

Zimbabwe, the former Southern Rhodesia, was also once a bastion of white supremacy, like South Africa. Independent since 1980, after a sixteen-year war of liberation, Zimbabwe encouraged many of its white settlers to remain, and the country now boasts an easy mix of races in contrast to the racism of its past.

Doris Lessing, the British writer who lived in Zimbabwe for twenty-five years, writes,

> The best of the Zimbabwe story is the vigour, the optimism, the determination of the people. You may return from a several-weeks' visit to Zimbabwe and realize...that you have been day and night with people, white and black, who talk of nothing else but how to make Zimbabwe work....[19]

Rich in mineral resources, self-sufficient in foodstuffs, and with a good road and rail network and a well-educated workforce, Zimbabwe has great economic potential. Performance, however, has been modest, constrained by a severe drought in 1992 and a continuing reluctance to reduce government controls over the economy. Agriculture is the mainstay of the economy, with 70 percent of the population dependent on it for income. But Zimbabwe also has the second most developed manufacturing sector in the region, after South Africa, and is a leading member of SADC. With a population of eleven million and a territory the size of California, it plays a key role in the economy of Southern Africa.

English is the language of government, business, and the cities of Zimbabwe, but some 85 percent of the people speak Shona, the language of the high plateau, while the other 15 percent (mainly in the southwest) speak Ndebele, a language derived from and mutually intelligible with Zulu. In religion, Zimbabwe is predominantly Christian, with Catholicism the largest denomination. Traditional religions, however, prevail in rural areas, and many Zimbabweans practice a mixture of Christian and traditional beliefs.

An open, friendly, and courteous people, Zimbabweans esteem humility and frown on loud, showy behavior, sarcasm, and pomposity. Patience and courtesy are important in conversation, and visitors who listen carefully, avoid direct eye contact, and attempt to understand their hosts will create a good impression. Smartness in dress is also considered important and is almost a requirement in top hotels and restaurants. In conducting business, a suit is preferred for men, and in some city social spots a jacket and tie are required. Women wear long and short dresses, in both Western and traditional styles.

The scenic wonders are spectacular, the climate is Mediterranean-like but without humidity, and the tourism potential is enormous. At world-famed Victoria Falls, the broad and placid Zambezi River suddenly plunges with a roar into a mile-wide chasm, throwing up a billowing spray visible some forty miles away. Hundreds of species of tropical wildlife can be seen in the many game parks. And the ancient ruin of Great Zimbabwe, sub-Sahara's largest stone monument and a source of Zimbabwean national pride, is testimony to the quondam capital of a powerful and prosperous empire of the twelfth to fifteenth centuries.

South Africa, an Exception

> This is a time to heal the old wounds and build a new South Africa...all South Africans must now unite and join hands and say we are one country, one nation, one people, marching together into the future.
> —Nelson Mandela, *Long Walk to Freedom*

The Republic of South Africa, always cited in Africa as the exception par excellence, deserves special attention here. For expatriates, city life in South Africa is almost like that of Europe or the United States, with first-class communications, medicine, and transportation. A network of good highways crisscrosses the country, and air and rail transport are excellent. Suburban malls are a shopper's paradise, and credit cards are accepted widely. Checking accounts can be opened at local banks, and cash is readily available at ATM machines. Satellite TV brings choice channels into living rooms, including the major U.S. networks and coverage of U.S. professional sports teams. South Africans wear Levis and Nikes, savor their Big Macs, drink Coke and Pepsi, enjoy American films and music, and eat Kellogg's Corn Flakes and Rice Krispies for breakfast. For expats, it's almost like living in the West.

But because of years of apartheid and international isolation, many of the changes in the West since the 1960s bypassed South Africa. "Despite rapid political change," reports the *New York Times*,

> [South Africa] remains for now much like 1950s America, for better or worse. At least that's the way it can seem to a newly

arrived American, particularly a white more likely to encounter a cocoon of white privilege in daily life than the hard lot of the black majority...."[20]

Almost anywhere in South Africa, continues the *Times*,

...an American can pull off a perfectly paved road into a time warp. It's called a petrol station, and several smiling attendants will converge on the car, one washing the windows, one checking the oil, one filling the tires, one carefully topping off the tank with premium. The bathrooms are spotless, and a 56-cent tip—not necessarily even expected—leaves everyone beaming.[21]

Five times the size of Britain, South Africa has a population of only 41.2 million (according to 1995 estimates). Blacks number some 31.5 million; whites are another 5.2 million; and "Coloureds," of mixed African, Indian, other Asian, and European origin, 3.5 million. Rounding out this ethnic mix are one million Asians, mostly Indians, whose ancestors originally came to work the sugarcane fields. More than 80 percent of the population is Christian.

The differences among these groups, however, lie not in their numbers but in their economic status. Blacks now have the vote, the majority, and the government, but economic and social inequities continue.

Apartheid's legacy is devastating, reports the *Washington Post*:

Adult blacks today have had half the educational years of whites; their salaries are barely a third of whites' salaries; and their unemployment rate is eight times higher. Although blacks run the nation's government, whites still run the economy; whites are 13 percent of the population but own 90 percent of the nation's wealth, according to government statistics.[22]

The Afrikaners, numbering nearly 60 percent of the whites, are descendants of the original settlers, the Dutch Calvinist Boers (farmers) who were long predominant in South African agriculture. Recent generations of Afrikaners, however, have become urbanized and middle class. Prior to 1994 they controlled the government and the army, but today their numbers include entrepreneurs, technocrats, professionals, writers, and other intellectuals. The other whites, mostly of British origin but including a large Jewish community, are mostly urban and are predominant in business, finance, and the professions. Also active in business and the retail trade are the Asians.

Due to inequities in the division of resources and wealth, racial tensions exist not only between blacks and whites but between blacks and Asians as well. Caught in between are the Coloureds, most of whom live in the western half of the country, where in some districts they are the majority. Although the Coloureds were subordinated to white rule under apartheid, they were privileged in comparison to blacks.

Unlike other sub-Saharan countries, urban and rural populations in South Africa are almost equal, with a 48-52 ratio. The largest city, Jo'burg, as Johannesburg is popularly called, has the appearance of a big U.S. metropolis except that it is surrounded by gold mines. Pretoria, the administrative capital, looks like the government center of a midwestern state except for a large nearby diamond mine. Cape Town, where the parliament sits and where more than one million Coloureds live, has the ambiance as well as the climate of San Francisco.

The business culture is also Western, and negotiations are first-world style—yes will mean yes, and no, no. Long-term business relationships, however, are not the rule, and most entrepreneurs have a short-term perspective—get in and out as quickly as you can. Most of private industry is controlled by a handful of superconglomerates so that there is little competition and even less incentive to hustle. If South Africa's markets are ever opened up, major changes will have to be made in how it does business.

What is unlikely to change is the politeness of interpersonal relations. In business meetings, visitors can expect to be treated most courteously and be offered the customary cup of coffee, tea, or soda.

South Africa's earliest inhabitants were the Khoikhoi and San, known today as Khoisan collectively but also once known respectively (although not respectfully) as Hottentots and Bushmen. Next came Bantu-speaking blacks, who began to migrate southward from Central Africa some two thousand years ago. European settlement, initially Dutch and later English, dates from 1652 and was the earliest in Africa. The Dutch, moreover, came in large numbers and took the most fertile land. Their descendants, the Afrikaners and their National Party, came to power in 1948 and ruled until 1994, when the apartheid system they had created was finally ended with a government elected with full black suffrage and headed by Nelson Mandela as president.

"The discovery first of gold and then of diamonds," writes South African journalist Allister Sparks, "was the watershed event in South African history. Overnight it turned a pastoral country into an industrial one, sucking country folk into the city and changing their lives."[23]

Whites created the richest and most industrialized country in Africa and maintained for themselves a standard of living as high as anywhere in the world. Having lived for so long in Africa, they consider themselves Africans, not expatriates, although the end of apartheid has changed the power structure of the country.

The end of apartheid laws, however, has not ended apartheid economics, reports the *New York Times:*

> Almost all blacks still live in the townships [black enclaves]. The first glimpse of Soweto, for an American expecting something like Harlem or Watts, can be startling. The city, just down the highway from Johannesburg...resembles nothing in America so much as it does that postwar icon, 1950s

Levittown: row after row of identical houses with neat yards on curving suburban streets, all governed by strict zoning.[24]

But Soweto (an acronym for Southwest Township) and the other townships where blacks were forced to live also have shocking shantytowns and unemployment close to 45 percent. A major task of the new government is to provide housing, jobs, health care, and social services for people who were long considered second-class citizens. As legal underpinning for the changes to be made, a new constitution, adopted in 1996, renounces racism and guarantees to all South Africans equal rights and broad freedom of speech, movement, and political activity.

English is a unifying factor and is spoken almost everywhere, although South Africa has eleven officially recognized languages, including Afrikaans, the Dutch-based creole spoken by the Afrikaners and many blacks and Coloureds. Spoken Afrikaans is difficult for English speakers to understand, but for those who know some Dutch or German it is fairly easy to read.

Of the nine local languages, Zulu is the most commonly spoken, but many South Africans without formal education are fluent in several languages, which they need to communicate in the multilingual townships. In Soweto at least one-quarter of the residents are said to speak five or more languages.

Despite the racial tensions, there is no emphasis on "Africanness" among blacks. As Mamphela Ramphele, vice-chancellor of the University of Cape Town, explains, "Blacks here have always known that, come rain or shine, they are the majority here; there is a security and a rootedness which flows from that."[25] This rootedness, say South Africans, accounts for the lack of bitterness on the part of most blacks, their spirit of reconciliation, and their patience. Respect and deference to seniors is shown by both blacks and whites, the heritage of an authoritarian culture based on strict religious leaders and parents.

But after decades of disciplinarianism, a culture of violence has been emerging in the black townships as well as downtown city centers, where street crime in broad daylight is common. Since Nelson Mandela's victory in South Africa's first all-race elections in 1994, political violence has declined while criminal violence has soared. Carjacking is endemic and often accompanied by mindless violence. According to government crime statistics released in 1996, an average of fifty-two people are murdered each day in South Africa, which makes its murder rate nearly ten times that of the United States.

Knowledgeable observers, nevertheless, are optimistic about the outlook and regard South Africa as the future "engine" that will drive the economies of Southern Africa. A major resource is South Africa's large pool of educated and skilled people, who lack not training but investment, finance, and access to new technology.

Optimistic predictions for the future, however, depend on improving the status of blacks, which means providing sufficient housing, improving health services, and increasing job opportunities. What gives hope is that blacks and whites recognize that they need each other and now appear willing to work together. And perhaps most important, pragmatists now run the country.

How should Westerners react to all these changes? Newcomers should not think they know it all, advises a South African businessman. "Don't come to teach, but come to listen. Walk slowly, don't run. The best advice is not to give it. We'll work it out by ourselves."

Botswana, Another Exception

[The Tswana people] commemorate the virtues of propriety, tranquility, and a peaceful approach to interpersonal relations. The peacemaker, the wise man of words, and the conciliator are as likely candidates for herodom as the warrior

...physical and verbal aggression...is sanctioned in very few contexts in current communal life.

— Hoyt Alverson, *Mind in the Heart of Darkness*

Another exception must be mentioned here—Botswana, an oasis of economic and political stability, and one of the few places in Africa where multiparty democracy works. One of the poorest countries in the world when it achieved independence in 1966, Botswana has nevertheless experienced three decades of phenomenal growth due to good leadership, prudent fiscal management, a government decision to pursue a market-oriented economy, a well-trained and effective bureaucracy, and an army that has stayed out of politics.[26]

Lying to the northwest of South Africa, Botswana is the size of Texas but is mostly desert and has a population of only 1.5 million, some 70 percent of whom are Tswana, the dominant ethnic group. But in addition to its ethnic tranquility, Botswana has another blessing—it sits atop one of the world's richest stores of diamonds. Yet, despite its stable currency and enormous foreign currency reserves, the country's leaders have not enriched themselves at the expense of their people but have sought instead to improve their well-being. A good part of the annual budget goes to programs that affect the bulk of the population—education, health, social services, and small-scale regional development projects. Every village of size has a well-equipped school. Health clinics are within walking distance of most villagers, and mobile health units serve the others. During the 1980s, per capita income rose fivefold.

The Tswana are quiet, mild-mannered, and rather reserved for Africans, but they are not subservient and can be firm when necessary. They also have a reputation for civility and allowing others to have their say although they may disagree. Foreign visitors will be allowed to speak their piece even when the Tswana know that they are wrong. Consequently, you may believe you have agreement when there actually is none.

Politics is consensual and based on a tradition of bringing people together to resolve issues in town meetings, the *kgotla*. Held before the house of the chief or village headman and presided over by him, the meetings have been customarily used to discuss new initiatives and reach agreement. Today, they are used by government officials to discuss new policies before local implementation. "They also seek to get a consensus behind their proposals," says John Holm, a political scientist from Cleveland State University. "If one does not emerge, the program is likely to be reformulated or sometimes terminated."[27]

Rule of law is also traditional, and Botswana is one of the most law-abiding countries in the world, says Holm. "If you are driving in a car full of Batswana and you make an illegal U-turn, everyone gets very quiet. They feel guilty for you."[28]

Cultural ties to home villages are strong, and although many men go abroad to labor in the South African mines, most of them return home. For those who study abroad, the return rate is also high, as much as 90 percent.

But all is not perfect in Botswana. Society is stratified, with a very large low-income group, a small middle class, and a much smaller group of wealthy cattle ranchers. Unemployment is high. Politics, moreover, is dominated by a privileged elite which takes a paternalistic approach to governing. Yet, Botswana can boast of being the only country in Africa with an unbroken string of free local and national elections over the past three decades, consultation and moderation based on tribal traditions, government officials with modest lifestyles, a low level of corruption, and no political violence.

Almost everything in Botswana is as it seems to be except for the pronunciation of the name of its capital city, written as "Gaborone" but spoken as "Haborone," with a strongly aspirated *g*. The confusion results from an inaccurate transliteration from the Setswana language into English many years ago.

1 In this chapter the authors have drawn on the works of anthropologists, including, among others, Herskovits, *Human Factor*.

2 *New York Times*, 3 November 1997.

3 Larry Diamond, "Nigeria: Pluralism, Statism, and the Struggle for Democracy, in *Democracy in Developing Countries*, vol. 2, Africa, edited by Larry Diamond et al. (Boulder, CO: Lynne Rienner Publisher, 1988), 35.

4 Soyinka, *Open Sore*, 62.

5 Alicia J. Robinson, "Doing Business in Nigeria, Distinguishing between the Profitable and the Questionable," in *Business America*, November 1995, 26-28.

6 Naomi Chazan, "Ghana: Problems of Governance and the Emergence of Civil Society," in *Democracy in Developing Countries*, vol. 2, edited by Diamond et al., 130.

7 *Washington Post*, 12 December 1996.

8 *New York Times*, 3 March 1996.

9 Biddlecombe, *French Lessons in Africa*, 313.

10 Ibid., 314.

11 I. M. Lewis, *Somali Culture, History and Social Institutions* (London: London School of Economics and Political Science, 1981), 40.

12 Deng, "Cultural Dimensions of Conflict Management," 469-70.

13 John Middleton, *The World of the Swahili: An African Mercantile Civilization* (New Haven: Yale University Press, 1992), 199.

14 Ibid., 199.

15 Winston Churchill, *My African Journey* (New York and London: W. W. Norton, 1990), 57.

16 *New York Times*, 1 September 1996.

17 Basil Davidson, *The Search for Africa: History, Culture, Politics* (New York: Random House, 1994), 292-93.

18 *New York Times*, 16 January 1996.

19 Doris Lessing, *African Laughter: Four Visits to Zimbabwe* (New York: HarperCollins, 1992), 10.

20 *New York Times*, 17 September 1995.

21 Ibid.

22 *Washington Post*, 14 July 1996.

23 Allister Sparks, *The Mind of South Africa* (New York: Ballantine Books, 1991), 119.

24 *New York Times*, 17 September 1995.

25 Mamphela Ramphele, cited by Paul Taylor, in *Weekly Mail and Guardian*, 6-12 January 1995.

26 For Botswana, the authors have drawn from John Holm, "Botswana, A Paternalistic Democracy," in *Democracy in Developing Countries*, edited by Diamond et al.

27 Holm, "Botswana," 195.

28 Holm, quoted by Harden, in *Africa*, 296.

Working the Workshops

Listen carefully and you will learn.

—Kikuyu proverb

Workshops, a familiar feature of the African business and development scene, can take a variety of forms, such as a full-day meeting to train business employees in a new sales strategy, a several-day course in personnel management, and a multiweek training session for rural health workers. In these intense yet intimate environments, cross-cultural differences can easily come to the fore. How to avoid such misunderstandings will be the subject of this chapter.

Preparing the Ground

To make preparations does not spoil the trip.
—Guinean proverb

Workshops usually begin with the obligatory welcoming remarks by a government representative or other high-ranking dignitary, and the opening will be delayed until the honored guest arrives. Next comes a coffee or tea break to allow the notables to make their unobtrusive departure. The break is

215

likely to be followed by the also often obligatory discussion of per diem (or "sitting fee," as it is called in some anglophone countries) and other financial arrangements for participants, if they were not settled beforehand.

The amount of per diem to be paid and what it covers is of intense interest to those workshop participants, most of whom have large extended families to support with their low salaries. They will also want to discuss the details, such as how reimbursement for transportation to the workshop will be calculated, because in some places more will be paid if the roads are bad. And such discussions are not limited to low-level participants, as Togo television viewers once learned. In coverage of a national conference in Togo called to debate a new constitution, TV viewers were surprised to see the conferees discussing the details of their per diem. First things first!

In another African country, women at a workshop complained when per diem was not given to them directly but was used by the sponsors to cover the participants' hotel and meal costs. As the women explained, their spouses had objected to their attending the workshop and relented only when told that any unspent per diem would be brought home. If they returned home without some of their per diem there would be dire domestic discord.

Such difficulties stem from how Africans regard per diem. Most see it not as money paid to cover expenses, but rather as payment for their time and attendance, and for them to take home at the end of the workshop.

Per diem is a creation of donor organizations, an incentive to get people to attend workshops they were not truly interested in attending. Today, these same donors are trying hard to backpedal on per diem, and some are asking for participant fees. The participants, however, realize that they are on to something good and are reluctant to relent.

Also leading to discord can be the selection of workshop participants. Because per diem is so highly desired, an African supervisor may select a friend, someone to be rewarded, or even him- or herself rather than the most qualified candidate. Such favoritism can be avoided by meeting in advance with those charged with candidate selection and agreeing on the criteria for participation.

Avoid selecting the so-called "darlings of development"—those who are always invited to donor-funded workshops, in part because they speak English well and move easily in bicultural situations. At a recent workshop in Ghana, one participant had been in training for six consecutive weeks at sessions funded by different donors.

Underestimating the time needed to present and discuss the topics to be covered is a familiar failure in preparing a workshop or meeting agenda. Africans need sufficient time for in-depth discussions, but trainers, pressed by donor agencies to achieve maximum results in a minimum of time, may unrealistically try to cover too much during long workdays, with shortened lunch hours, insufficient tea breaks, and evening sessions. In such cases, it is far better to cover less but to do it well. Participants, moreover, are likely to be more willing to work longer hours, even under uncomfortable conditions, if they understand the extent of the workshop program and the time needed to treat it adequately. Trainers should try to reach a consensus with the participants to either arrive early, work late, or reduce the amount of material to be covered.

Evening sessions, if scheduled, should include a light program with participatory projects such as the sharing of experiences as well as some recreational or informal activities. Africans appreciate the opportunity to network, a key component of any workshop. In the absence of cheap and available telephone service and other modern means of communication, workshops afford an opportunity for friends and colleagues to share information and build relationships. Informal evening sessions also enable trainers to get feedback from participants, which may be more difficult to do during formal daytime sessions.

The African way of organizing workshops may also present some surprises to expat trainers. In the African mode, a workshop organizer determines the general purpose of the workshop and prepares a loose agenda around the objective. The organizer then calls his or her friends to ask if they will be available to make presentations. However, unless an effort is made to coordinate the various presentations, the workshop can easily become a series of unrelated lectures.

Be prepared for unforeseen logistical problems. Where there is no air-conditioning during the hot season, it may be necessary to schedule sessions in the mornings and at night to avoid the hottest part of the day. Classroom light may be insufficient because hosts will often use low-wattage bulbs to save on electricity. Veteran trainers always carry a few high-wattage bulbs.

Residential workshops, where participants live at the workshop site away from their workplaces and families, are more productive than those where they return home in the evening. In the latter, you are less likely to have their full attention as they come and go during sessions, responding to work needs and family responsibilities.

Ground Rules

Before shooting, one must aim.

—Nigerian proverb

Rules of procedure are important to Africans and should be discussed in detail and repeated to make sure they are fully understood. In the United States such procedures are usually summarized by the chairperson or included in a handout, after which questions are taken from the floor. In Africa, however, a facilitator will often read the procedures aloud, line by line, while interpolating personal comments. And when the plenary session breaks up into small discussion groups, each group leader may again read the instructions.

Some of this repetition results from language and education differences among participants and the consequent need for sufficient time to digest instructions. Foreign language study in school may not have prepared participants for absorbing a long string of complicated instructions in a foreign language. While they may understand the language of the workshop—usually English or French—they may not have full fluency. Moreover, facilitators may have accents that are difficult to comprehend. Some Africans find British accents easier to understand than American, but with others it can be the reverse, although the idiomatic English spoken by some Americans may be puzzling.

To avoid such problems, after the initial presentations in English or French someone should repeat the instructions in a local language, where appropriate. When instructions are for work to be done in small groups, they should be included in a written handout for review within the groups.

In preparing an agenda, do not schedule too tightly on the first day. Allow some slack in each component for late arrival of dignitaries, late-arriving participants, and malfunction of equipment.

Allot at least as much time for the discussion as for the presentation. Lengthy discussions should be expected, although participants may only be repeating what has already been said. The more prestigious the speaker, the longer the speech is expected to be, because in a traditional African setting a short speech may indicate that the speaker does not know what he or she is talking about. Presenters may also have difficulty observing a time limit, and questioners may not limit themselves to a single question.

Francophone formality can show up in workshops. At the start of a meeting, Francophones will likely want to go through the rules of how they are supposed to interact with each other, and they may spend considerable time in selecting their presiders and rapporteurs. Rules are also likely to be repeated at the start of each session, and one participant is usually assigned to jot them down even though they may be routine and participants will have heard them many times before.

The group ethic usually prevails over the individual approach. In preparing for a workshop you may find it necessary to go through each step with the entire group rather than dividing them up to make better use of available personnel and time. An American consultant, for example, was once working with three African trainers to prepare a program for traditional birth attendants. They had only a few days before the workshop was to begin, and the consultant suggested that they divide up the tasks and give each person an assignment. But that tactic was not acceptable to the three Africans, who wanted to go through each step in the program together. The group ethic won out, but they also ran out of time for preparation.

The Search for Solutions

Even an experienced man will try something new.
—Somali proverb

Solutions should not be imposed without a consensus being reached among those concerned with the problems, whether in a workshop or office setting. Western consultants, reports a Mauritanian physician, come with solutions for Africa's many problems, but they don't always look for answers that Africans themselves may have developed. Foreigners may indeed have answers to some of Africa's problems, but only by working with Africans will they generate solutions that are appropriate to the local scene and acceptable to the people.

"This is the way we do it in the States" is an approach guaranteed to turn off Africans. Such an approach gives the impression that everything American is superior, and everything African inferior. More likely to succeed is a tactic that presents options but does not identify them with a particular country.

To introduce a new procedure that has been tested and shown to work well in another country, test it first as a pilot project in the country where you are working. If an agricultural extension worker, for example, should want to introduce a new crop or technique to a village, he or she should keep in mind that the villagers may not adopt it until they have seen with their own eyes that it actually works. The Sahel countries, with their traditional Muslim cultures, would not have implemented family planning programs without first conducting small pilot projects to determine whether their conservative constituents would accept such services.

In attempting to persuade Africans to change established procedures, outside examples may not work. To get over this hurdle, advises one Western trainer, you might say, "I know that you are more advanced than your neighbors, but here is a procedure from country X of how a different approach might work." But use an example that is relevant. In West Africa, a West African example would be best. Next best would be an example from another part of Africa. Less useful would be something from a developing country in another part of the world, and least useful, an example from the United States or Europe.

"Treat Africans with respect" is an admonishment often voiced by Africans. First-time visitors can rub Africans the wrong way with the condescending attitude, "I know best, and I'm here to tell you what to do and how to do it." Rather, advisers should assume that the Africans with whom they are working are where they are because they have education and experience. Talk with, and not down to, the participants.

To persuade Africans to consider a particular plan or procedure, one Western trainer advocates an indirect approach. "You may find this procedure useful," she says, "and here are the key steps and why we believe they are important. But you should look at the problem from your own experience and perspective, and then we will see how we can combine our two viewpoints." Another expat trainer says that he is not at all embarrassed to tell an African counterpart, "I don't want to commit a faux pas. What should I do in this situation?" An even better approach, and one which will help build local proficiency, is to pair a Western consultant with an African trainer who does most of the actual speaking to the workshop participants.

Consensus, Again

> The one who talks thinks. But the one who does not talk, thinks more.
>
> —Baganda proverb

Don't expect to change things overnight. Building consensus, as we have seen in earlier chapters, is necessary in Africa, and often nothing happens to change the course until everyone has been brought on board. Don't try to speed up the process, even when Africans seem to be repeating themselves in a form of catharsis. To the foreigner, it may appear that nothing is happening, but something may indeed be in the making without being readily apparent. Africans are a very reflective people and will want to think things through before taking action. Workshops, accordingly, should provide time for reflection and internalization. This can best be accomplished in a group setting.

Africans have their own methods for reaching consensus, and those methods may not be apparent to Westerners. At one workshop, participants were divided into four small groups, each of which was assigned a problem to solve. The participants went to their groups and seemed to be shouting at each other, each person insisting adamantly on how the problem should be resolved. But after twenty minutes of shouting, consensus prevailed, and each group had come up with an appropriate solution.

When small groups return to the plenary session to report the results of their deliberations, Africans will often give lengthy presentations which, according to their traditions, should represent the thoughts of all so as not to offend anyone in the group. To avoid long, boring speeches, facilitators should be as specific as possible on what should be included in the presentations, and summaries should be limited to the main points. To save time, have the first group give its report in full, and ask other groups to add only what is new or to comment on the previous presentation.

Participatory Training

> Seeing is different from being told what to do.
>
> —Kenyan proverb

Africans are unaccustomed to workshops where participants are encouraged to speak up, question, and criticize. At an early age, they are taught to observe, reflect, and imitate. In schools, teaching at all levels is largely by lecture, and rote is routine, as might be expected in societies where the oral tradition is still strong. In cultures where age and experience are esteemed, it is not considered appropriate to question or challenge a teacher, supervisor, or trainer.[1]

How, then, does one encourage participants to speak up and provide feedback in a workshop (or office, for that matter) where questions may be considered intrusive, especially when put to older persons or strangers?

As previously recommended in these pages, a group strategy will be more productive than an individual approach. Africans perform well in team efforts, and a group approach that draws on their communal heritage will provide the time they may need to reflect before reaching a conclusion.

In group sessions, advises Gérémie Sawadogo, a trainer from Burkina Faso, Africans should be clustered according to age, social class, and gender:

[O]ne might start by forming small homogeneous groups of two to three people and progressively move from small groups to medium-sized groups involving four to eight people while still taking into consideration factors of gender, age, and social class.[2]

Because of the hierarchical nature of African society, the more homogeneous the group according to age, experience, and gender, the more they will interact. The younger and lower in status will speak up more readily and you will learn more, not of what is on the mind of some individuals, but rather what they together think as a group.

Alternatively, each small group might be led by a skilled facilitator who uses methods that encourage everyone to speak without embarrassing those who are shy. One such method would be to rotate the chance to speak systematically, one-by-one through the entire group.

Another technique is to conduct feedback sessions in appropriate sequences or stages. "In the first stage," suggests Sawadogo, "feedback is devoted to identifying and discussing positive aspects of the training session; in the second stage, the trainer might gradually move on to solicit recommendations."[3] If all else fails and you still get no feedback, be provocative, advises an experienced U.S. trainer, a tactic that will surely get a response.

Music can also be used to encourage participation. Africans love to sing, and every culture has its music, so try to slip some songs into the sessions. In one workshop for laboratory technicians, the trainer had them compose songs about their work. They enjoyed being songwriters, their songs made them feel they were a part of the learning process, and the singing helped to break up a long day.

As with other innovations, the best way to accustom people to participatory training is to involve them in the planning. Africans are the best interpreters of their own societies, and by sharing their knowledge they will surely suggest culturally appropriate methods to be incorporated into the training agenda.

Resistance to participatory training, however, may be found among university graduates who believe they will merely be playing games and not accomplishing anything. "Just tell us what you want us to know," they might say. To get around such objections, co-opt them by having them help with the training.

Whether to use foreign or local experts is a question that often arises. Africa has experts who may be just as good, if not better, than those from abroad. An African will know the local culture and how to present pertinent information. But the foreigner, as with many other imports, has a special cachet that may have its own attraction, whether justified or not. As an African saying sarcastically puts it, "The expert is a foreigner who comes with slides."

---

[1] In this section, the authors have drawn, in part, from Sawadogo, "Training for the African Mind," 281-93.

[2] Ibid., 285.

[3] Ibid., 288.

Tips for Travelers

Travel with open eyes and you will become a scholar.
—Swahili proverb

"Keep quiet" is the advice most often given newcomers to Africa. Listen and observe before offering an opinion, advise veteran Africa hands, and suspend judgment on Africa and its ways for your first six months. It will be so different from anything you have experienced that the best course is simply to take it all in before rushing to judgment.

"Don't complain" is another piece of advice. You may be bothered by weather that wears you down, bugs that bite, roads that jar your innards, corruption and crime that shock you, and shops that don't have what you most want. Electricity often goes out at night, and water may stop flowing just when you are preparing to take a shower. With close African friends you can complain about such shortcomings but not with others. Africans have little or no control over such failings, and expats often forget that their home countries may have some of the same problems.

Africans will ask many questions about a foreigners's home country, but since most have an imperfect understanding of the differences between Americans, Canadians, and Europeans, we are all *mzungu* (*wazungu* in the plural and Kiswahili for "white person"). Some of their questions, moreover, may be considered personal—your religion, ethnic origin, the size of your salary. Decide in advance how you want to deal with such questions. Also, be sure to bring photos of your family and home, always subjects of interest to Africans.

The conventional wisdom often given to newcomers is to avoid discussion of politics and religion, at least until you get to know an African well. Such discussions can often lead to disagreement, but dodging them may also make Africans believe you have something to hide or are ashamed to discuss. A better approach is to answer questions factually but try to avoid expressing opinions until you know the person well. When controversial issues arise, give both points of view, such as "Some people say this, and others say that. What do you think?"

Race should not be seen as a barrier to interactions with Africans. Expats are more polarized on racial lines than are Africans, who tend to be color-blind. As Susan Blake says, "In Togo, my students are conscious of race, but to them 'white' seems to have the neutral sense of 'outsider' rather than the politically charged sense of 'oppressor.'"[1]

But for one expat in Africa, the first thing that stood out was that he himself stood out, especially in the countryside. Compared to villagers, he was overdressed, overeducated, and upper class. Whatever he might do, he would never blend in. He had gone to Africa with the attitude of some Westerners that he was going to be one of the *people*. But that is just not possible in Africa. It's not just the color of your skin but your education, finances, upbringing, and culture that make you different. When one of the authors was the subject of attention while visiting a community center in a rural Botswana town, he asked his local escort, "Why is everyone looking at me as if I were a man from Mars?" To which the escort replied, "Here, you *are* a man from Mars."

Be streetwise, especially in large cities. Street crime in

Africa, with some exceptions, is no worse than in many large U.S. cities, and residents of New York, Los Angeles, and the authors' hometown of Washington, D.C., will know what "streetwise" means. Try not to look like a typical tourist, and if you must carry a bag, daypack, or fanny pack, be aware that you may literally be ripped off. Keep valuables in a safe place, preferably a hidden money belt or pouch hanging from the neck inside your shirt or blouse. Carry three passport-size photos with you, and make a copy of your passport page with the photo, number, and place and date of issuance; if you should lose your passport, these will facilitate your getting a new one at your nearest consulate. Never leave anything of value unattended, even for a few minutes. Don't wear your wealth by flaunting jewelry, carrying an expensive camera, or brandishing foreign currency in public. Beware of scams and con artists, the kinds of which are too numerous to mention. Ignore anyone who approaches you on the street with a "deal" involving money that sounds too good to be true. It probably is, and you will be deftly deceived.

Street justice in Africa can be swift and brutal. A pickpocket caught by a crowd can be killed on the spot. "One cry of 'thief,'" a Hausa proverb tell us, "and the whole marketplace is on the lookout." As the *New York Times* reports from Nairobi, "Because the underfinanced police force is ineffective, unmotivated and often corrupt, mobs have become enforcers of social norms. Street justice is Kenya's most common form of crime...."[2]

Harassment and rape of expatriate women is rare in Africa provided normal precautions are taken, but rising unemployment has increased the incidence of purse snatching and other forms of theft, especially in large cities. Before leaving your hotel, ask the concierge for an update on crime in the area.

Travel in some countries can be potentially hazardous at times because of banditry, lawlessness, terrorism, or civil strife. (For an update on the travel situation and other useful information on individual countries, call the U.S. Department of

State's Consular Affairs Automated Fax Service, tel. (202-647-3000.)

Finally, in relating to Africans be as polite as you can, but don't try to be an African. Be true to yourself and who you are.

Staying Healthy

Once you have been to Africa the bug gets into your system.
—Edward Heath, *Travels, People and Places in My Life*

It's not clear which "bug" former British Prime Minister Edward Heath was referring to, but most Western visitors to Africa know that they should drink bottled or boiled water, eat only cooked vegetables, and peel all fruit. Equally important is to wash your hands before eating and to not eat anything that has fallen on the ground. Those nasty bugs are everywhere and they love foreigners whose systems are so sterile that they succumb to any bacterium, parasite, or virus that they have never previously hosted. Experienced expatriates always carry bottled water when traveling up-country.

Malaria is prevalent in many African countries but is especially severe in West and East Africa, which have strains that have become resistant to some of the traditional and relatively safe drug treatments. The falciparum strain, the most drug-resistant, is the one most likely to cause serious illness and even death.[3]

Almost one of every hundred visitors to West Africa contracts malaria, and while the disease is not necessarily fatal, early treatment is crucial. Symptoms may include fever and chills, headache, sore joints, diarrhea, and general malaise, which result in many of the potentially fatal cases being misdiagnosed as flu. If you get a fever, assume it is malaria and see a doctor within twelve hours. And if you have such symptoms after return to your home country, be sure to tell your doctor that you were recently in Africa.

Prophylactic antimalaria drugs are a *must* in high-risk areas, and qualified physicians will know which one to prescribe, how far in advance of travel to begin taking it, and how long to take it after your return. Avoid mosquitoes wherever possible; the anopheles mosquito, which carries the malaria parasite, starts biting at dusk and continues through the night (but may also bite during the day), and it may take only one bite to contract the disease. Wear long-sleeved shirts and trousers when outdoors, use a repellent containing DEET (diethyl-toluamide) on exposed areas of the body (in a concentration no higher than 50 percent), and sleep under a treated net. DEET also repels the dengue-carrying mosquito, which bites during the daytime. Carry the repellent with you at all times, on your person and not in your checked luggage, and use caution when applying it to children's faces and hands. Malaria can be dangerous to travelers, but with proper precautions it is preventable and treatable.

Bilharzia, which causes schistosomiasis, is another parasite to beware of. Transmitted by snails in freshwater lakes, rivers, and streams, especially along shorelines and in stagnant waters, its early symptoms include weakness and slight fever which lead, however, to a more serious illness. The only complete prevention is to avoid skin contact with fresh surface water. Skin contact between your feet and the ground should also be avoided to guard against worms and chiggers. Youngsters accustomed to going barefoot back home will have to learn to wear sandals or shoes.

Other diseases prevalent in Africa include yellow fever, dengue fever, typhoid fever, cholera, hepatitis A, rabies, and AIDS. So, before traveling to Africa, visit a travel clinic or a specialist in tropical medicine. (For up-to-date information on these and other illnesses in countries to be visited and to learn which immunizations you may need, call the International Travelers' Hotline at the U.S. Centers for Disease Control and Prevention, tel. [404-332-5449].)

Although AIDS is prevalent throughout Africa, visitors

should run no risk of becoming infected unless they engage in high-risk behavior, such as unprotected sex or the sharing of infected needles. New arrivals in Africa should seek advice from their embassies on what to do in case a medical emergency should require a blood transfusion.

Medical care varies considerably across the continent. Physicians may be well trained, but hospitals often have inadequate facilities, outmoded equipment, and shortages of supplies, particularly medicines. Travelers are advised to bring their own prescription drugs and preventive medicines. Not all medical insurance provides coverage outside the country of origin, and African providers may expect cash payment. Supplemental medical insurance with overseas coverage and a medical evacuation provision is advisable.

Rules of the Road

> Traveling may bring bad luck for travelers abroad, as well as for those they leave behind.
>
> —Dama proverb

Driving in Africa can also be hazardous to your health. Roads are replete with reckless and inexperienced drivers, some of whom may also be under the influence. To reach your destination, you must drive defensively.

There are other dangers as well. On roads, cars compete for space with scooters, bicycles, pushcarts, pedestrians, and animals, both domestic and wild. Cows are a constant hazard, and if you hit one, you and your car will know it. Main roads can be very good in some countries but teeth-rattling and bone-crunching in others. Minor roads are likely to be unpaved, replete with potholes and impassable after heavy rains. Blind curves and excessive speed contribute to a high accident rate, and driving at night should be avoided when possible.

"It is difficult to find a satisfactory explanation for the

Africans' propensity to pass on blind curves and drive at out-of-control speeds," writes Lamb.[4] Lamb speculates that an African does not conceptualize a potential problem the way a Westerner does. If an African passes on a blind curve without a head-on collision, he may do it again because he got around such a curve once before without a mishap.

Police roadblocks can be another obstacle. You must stop, and even when your documents are in order and you have done nothing wrong, a bribe may be solicited before you can proceed. How much to pay or what to give will vary, but most experienced travelers suggest you pay or present a small gift and get it over with. Do not, however, pay the amount requested or attempt to negotiate the price. Negotiating may only raise the cost. Bribery is illegal, of course, and the police will want to get it over with as quickly as you do.

To avoid such hazards hire a driver who knows the rules of the road, how much of a bribe to give, and how much to pay if you hit an animal. If you are involved in an accident, it will be the driver's legal responsibility, not yours.

In most anglophone countries driving is on the left, which is fairly easy to become accustomed to until you get to a "roundabout" (rotary circle). In some countries the car entering the roundabout has the right of way, and in others it may not. When you step off a curb, look right, not left, for oncoming traffic.

Happy motoring!

Getting from Here to There

> When you travel in the rain, you think the journey will never end.
>
> —Cameroonian proverb

Everyone has a favorite story about African taxis. Ours is about a cab with no windscreen (windshield, to Americans), driving through a downpour in Conakry. By itself, this does not sound unusual in Coastal West Africa, but this driver was steering with one hand and with the other was holding a large umbrella through the opening where his windshield should have been.[5]

Public transportation in most African cities is inadequate; so inadequate, says Nigeria's Wole Soyinka (speaking of his home country), "...that it provides a study in collective masochism, degenerating often into a contest of the fittest at the arrival of the lone tumbril."[6] Travelers who give up on public transport must resort to private transport—taxis, jitneys, minivans, and even trucks—to get around within and between cities. But getting from here to there by private means is also chancy, and it can be downright dangerous.

Vehicles are poorly maintained, including taxis, many of which were wrecks in Europe before they were exported to Africa. Exceptions are the so-called "London taxis," which visitors to England will recall for their roomy interiors, jump seats, and space for luggage up front next to the driver. Many of the older models of the London taxi fleet have ended up in Africa, where they command a premium fare but are well worth the higher price.

Taxis must often be shared with strangers and can get quite crowded if you are seated cheek-to-cheek and with another passenger's baby or child on your lap. If a taxi has no meter or a broken one, negotiate the fare in advance and be prepared to bargain. Westerners, however, should be resigned to paying more than Africans for the same ride.

An American anthropologist, who has extensive experience in Africa, reports sharing a bush taxi in Niger on a long trip of several hundred miles and, as often happens, in the company of several fellow passengers whom she did not know. The taxi was rather decrepit and the woman wondered if she would make it safely to her destination. Also giving her pause was the fact that Nigeriens, as Muslims, may feel that their fate is in the hands of Allah, so why drive slowly or carefully.

The taxi appeared to have a tire problem, and our wary

woman kept urging the driver to stop and check it. With each of her urgings the driver would chuckle and say, to the laughter of the other passengers, "Are you afraid of dying?" The anthropologist was getting more and more upset and finally retorted, "If I die in this taxi, my husband will have your neck." The driver turned and replied with a grin, "Madame, a woman is like an old shirt. When it wears out you replace it." Everyone laughed, the American included, and she gave up trying to get the tire checked and became a convert to Kismet.

Less expensive than taxis are local minibuses, called "matatus" in East Africa and *cars rapides* in francophone West Africa. Custom-built on a truck chassis, they are usually packed with many more people than they can legally or even illegally hold. Passengers sit literally on top of each other, and sometimes in the driver's lap, as they tear through city streets at speeds of seventy-five miles an hour or more.

The high speeds, overcrowding, poor maintenance, and reckless, overworked, and even drunk drivers all contribute to a very high accident rate. Kenya, reports the *New York Times*, has a traffic death rate several times higher than Europe or the United States, with one death for every 166 vehicles per year, compared with California's one fatality for every 6,200 vehicles.[7] Even more dangerous are the trucks used for intercity travel. Overloaded, unregulated, and misused as buses, they are often involved in crashes that kill dozens of passengers.

Travel by rail is very good in South Africa, Kenya, and a few other countries, but in much of sub-Sahara it can be quite challenging, as one American experienced on a not atypical trip up-country from Bamako, the capital of Mali. To be sure of a seat, our intrepid traveler boarded the train for her ten-hour trip well in advance of the scheduled departure at 8:00 A.M. But 8:00 A.M. came and went with no departure, which is not unusual. Accustomed to "African time," our patient passenger perched in her seat for a few hours until someone finally told her that the morning train would not be leaving until evening. A full day had been lost, but what's a day in Africa?

When the train finally departed in the dusk of evening, meaning much of our patient passenger's trip was after sundown, she learned that the train's interior lights did not work. For most of her journey she sat in the dark, reading a book with a flashlight propped on her shoulder, proving again that a flashlight (along with a Swiss army knife) is one of the most important pieces of equipment to take to Africa. Without it, she might also have fallen into the toilet, which was a mere hole in the floor of the lavatory.

Food service on many trains is nonexistent, but whenever a train stops in a town or village, whether by night or day, passengers can expect to be greeted on the platform by women bearing trays on their heads and vending a variety of food and drink. If you don't like what's for sale at one stop, just wait until the next one, where a higher or lower elevation and climate change may result in different produce.

For long-distance travel within Africa, air is the fastest and most expedient means of transportation, although flying on African national carriers also has its hazards, as *New York Times* correspondent Howard W. French reports:

> For passengers of almost all these carriers, flying in Africa has for years been a special experience, one far beyond the vagaries of San Francisco fog or flight congestion at Heathrow or O'Hare. It has meant lost baggage, abrupt changes in flight times, poor on-board service and high fares.[8]

Other perils have appeared as air travel has increased and accident rates have risen sharply. According to a report by the International Federation of Air Line Pilots Associations, air traffic infrastructure is inadequate and most of Africa lacks the necessary equipment and personnel to meet minimum standards of aviation safety.[9]

Reconfirm your reservations in each country, more than once. African airlines will often overbook, and some passengers may be bumped at the last minute for politicians and other VIPs. Passengers should ask for a printout of their flight data and the name of the clerk confirming a reservation. They may be needed later at check-in, when a passenger could be told that there is no record of the reservation.

Flying from the United States to Bamako via Abidjan, an American woman was told on arrival in Abidjan that her scheduled connecting flight to Bamako had been canceled and there would be none for three days. The airline, moreover, was unwilling to cover her hotel costs, although she pleaded that she did not have enough money to pay her expenses for three days. Determined to wait them out, she sat down in the airline office and said she would not leave until they agreed to put her up at a hotel, which they eventually did.

If you are told to do something at an airport before exiting a country, do it and don't be difficult about it. One passenger recalls being asked to pass through a metal detector, but when he pointed out that the metal detector was unplugged, that made no difference. Regulations called for him to go through it, and he did. And if you are advised that check-in time is two hours or more in advance of scheduled departure, believe it and even allow a little more time for unexpected eventualities, as a traveler discovered in Lagos, Nigeria's main city and the most populous in sub-Sahara.

Lagos is known for its chaotic and monumental traffic jams, and the traveler was advised by her embassy to leave her hotel at 6:00 P.M. to check in at Murtala Muhammed airport for a midnight flight. It actually took two hours to make it across Lagos by taxi from her hotel to the airport in bumper-to-bumper traffic along a major highway, and another two and one-half hours at the airport to complete exit formalities, even with the help of an embassy expediter.

Lagos's Murtala Muhammed Airport was a free-for-all for

sellers and swindlers, money changers, panhandlers, and touts offering all kinds of services to passengers. Once described as the most customer-unfriendly airport in the world, its riotous reputation was reversed in 1995 after a government crackdown. Equally hazardous for travelers is Kinshasa's Ndjili International Airport, the Congo capital's port of entry. As you descend the plane's stair ramp,

> running through your head are all the sordid tales told by those who have braved this adventure before you: The hand luggage that disappeared with the guy who said he was a porter. The visa that evaporated from inside a passport at the immigration counter; pay $300 here for another. The passport grabbed and held for ransom by a soldier who said it was invalid but he would overlook the problem for $50.[10]

One sure way to avoid such harassment, say experienced travelers, is to hire an expediter who knows the airport obstacles and can run interference for you. Embassies use them as well as major corporations and international agencies.

---

1 Blake, *Letters from Togo*, 129.

2 *New York Times*, 5 October 1995

3 The information on malaria here is from Roger Collis, in *International Herald Tribune*, 10 December 1993.

4 Lamb, *Africans*, 228.

5 From Paul Rippey, *Travel Notes from the Interior* (Conakry: Paul's Vanity Press, 1994), 4.

6 Soyinka, *Open Sore*, 124.

7 *New York Times*, 16 April 1996.

8 *New York Times*, 21 March 1996.

9 *New York Times*, 29 December 1996.

10 *Chicago Tribune*, 25 December 1996.

In Conclusion

Africans, Americans, and African Americans

The first step [in developing an African policy] is to recognize that the United States and the American people have enduring interests on the African continent. These interests are economic, political, strategic, humanitarian, and, above all, practical.

—Sanford J. Unger,
Africa: The People and Politics of an Emerging Continent

Americans came to Africa early, as traders, slavers, explorers, missionaries, teachers, and engineers. More recently, they have also come as peacekeepers, negotiators, investors, and providers of humanitarian aid and technical assistance. All have left their mark on Africa and have been equally influenced by their experiences there.

New England whalers fished the waters off African coasts, and Yankee clipper ships made port in Africa to replenish supplies and take on water for their long voyages to China. In the decades prior to the Civil War, merchants from Salem, Massachusetts, dominated the Indian Ocean trade, and a "most favored nation" agreement in 1833 between the United States and Zanzibar, then the commercial center of the entire East African coast, gave the Salem traders predominance in the commerce of that port state. American interest in Africa was awakened by the Yankee traders and the slavers (discussed later in this section) who followed them.

It was Henry Morton Stanley, an explorer and foreign correspondent for the *New York Herald*, who "found" David Livingstone, the Scottish missionary physician who was believed lost (leaving to literature his celebrated greeting, "Dr. Livingstone, I presume?"). Stanley later made the first East-West passage down the Congo River to the Atlantic, thereby preparing the way for Belgian's King Leopold II to establish his so-called Congo Free State, subsequently the Belgian Congo, later Zaire, and now Congo. American mining engineers came with the latest technology to help develop the gold and diamond mines, which are today the economic mainstay of South Africa.

Liberia, the strife-ridden country on Africa's west coast, was settled in 1821 by freed American slaves (backed by New England abolitionists) and became an independent state twenty-five years later. Its capital, Monrovia, is named in honor of President James Monroe, and the country has traditionally enjoyed a special relationship with the United States. Although the descendants of the original American settlers numbered no more than 5 percent of the population, they ruled Liberia as an oligarchy until ousted by a coup in 1980. Since then, Liberia has seen much strife and violence as various warlords, some with degrees from U.S. universities, have vied for government control.

African Americans have always known where their roots lay, but slavery broke all contact with their ancestral homelands. To correct that disconnection and to rekindle interest in Africa, several prominent African Americans played key roles.

W. E. B. Du Bois, American author, philosopher, poet,

scholar, teacher, and NAACP founder, was also an organizer and leader of the pan-African movement from which modern African nationalism can trace descent. In 1919 Du Bois led a delegation to the Paris Peace Conference, where he attempted to place Germany's African colonies under international supervision, an effort that later bore fruit in the mandate system of the League of Nations and the trusteeships of the United Nations. Du Bois also organized a series of pan-African congresses, and by 1945, when the fifth and final congress was held in England, the Africans were ready to take over its leadership with men such as Kwame Nkrumah of Ghana and Jomo Kenyatta of Kenya, who were soon to become leaders of the African independence effort. Du Bois became a citizen of Ghana in 1963 and was buried there.

Marcus Garvey, a charismatic black nationalist, founded his Universal Negro Improvement Association in 1914 in Jamaica but soon moved it to New York, where he sought to unite black people everywhere behind a drive to liberate and develop a homeland in Africa and establish a United States of Africa. Although the movement fizzled out in the early 1920s, "Garveyism" was influential in arousing interest in Africa and its nascent independence movement.

Booker T. Washington and his Tuskegee Institute were instrumental in introducing agricultural and industrial arts along with teacher training to schools in anglophone Africa. Many of the practical training schools described in an earlier chapter were based on the examples set by Tuskegee and Hampton Institutes, where many Africans were trained.

Lincoln University in Pennsylvania, Howard University in Washington, D.C., and other black colleges pioneered the education of Africans in the liberal arts. Sponsored by American missionaries, African students began to study in the United States in significant numbers in the decades following the Civil War. During the 1920s and 1930s their numbers increased, and they grew substantially after World War II, assisted by scholarships from foundations and Fulbright funding. Among Lincoln's more prominent graduates were Kwame Nkrumah, Ghana's first president, and Nnamdi Azikiwe, the first president of Nigeria, who also studied at Howard. Malawi's founding father and former president, Hastings Banda, was a graduate of Meharry Medical College in Tennessee.

U.S. foundations were also active early on in Africa. Phelps-Stokes, Carnegie, Wenner-Gren, Rockefeller, Ford, and Guggenheim, among others, provided training and technical support in agriculture, education, health, and the social sciences, and provided scholarships for Africans to study in the United States. Humanitarian assistance and relief have been given by nongovernmental organizations such as Africare, CARE, Catholic Relief Services, the International Rescue Committee, Save the Children, World Vision, and many other nonsectarian and church-affiliated groups.

The U.S. government, through its Agency for International Development (USAID), has also been active in Africa for decades, although during the Cold War it tended to see Africa through the prism of competition between the superpowers. Today, the five key elements of its longer-term approach to African development are (1) promoting broad-based economic growth, (2) stabilizing population growth and improving health conditions, (3) protecting the environment, (4) fostering democracy, and (5) providing emergency relief to help nations make the transition from crisis to sustainable development.

Foreign assistance, however, is not popular among U.S. voters when Congress is cutting domestic programs. USAID funding for sub-Saharan Africa declined 25 percent (in constant dollars) from fiscal year 1992 to 1996, and the United States, in total dollars spent on foreign aid, had dropped by 1996 to fourth behind Japan, France, and Germany. As former Secretary of State Lawrence S. Eagleburger and retired Ambassador Robert L. Barry point out, U.S. government development assistance worldwide in 1996 was only one-tenth of

U.S. gross domestic product, which they describe as "...a sum that makes the United States the most miserly of the industrialized countries."[1]

With and without government funding, many U.S. citizens are traveling to Africa today as advisers, consultants, business representatives, and distributors of humanitarian aid. Since the inception of the Peace Corps in 1961, more than 57,000 of its volunteers have served in forty-five sub-Saharan countries in such fields as agriculture, education, health, and small business development. Peace Corps alumni provide a rich resource for U.S. expertise on Africa, and many of them have returned to Africa, where they are active in development work.

The many misconceptions that Americans, white as well as black, have of Africa have been described by one of them who travels often to Africa on business. Many Americans who have never been to Africa, he says, go there with a feeling of pity for Africans, largely because of how the U.S. media portray Africans as helpless and hopeless people who fight with each other a great deal. Other Americans, he adds, believe that Africa is all grass huts and no tall buildings, and that women all go bare-breasted and have long, stretched earlobes.

Western media coverage of Africa indeed has its critics. As Beverly G. Hawk, a U.S. specialist on Africa, writes:

> Africa is truly "covered" by the Western press in the sense that important stories go unreported.... Most African events are simply ignored by the media in its spotty coverage of the continent. Those aspects of African life covered by the foreign media are stories easily reported in brief dispatches and comfortably understood by the American audience...racial stories, coups and wars, and famine and disease. Stories communicating African history, culture, and values never reach the American public.... The confusing barrage that results has a common theme: Africa is a failure and needs our help.[2]

Coverage of the United States in the African media is

similarly sparse. Most Africans know more about Europe than the United States, and Francophones, in particular, are Euro-oriented. Moreover, with little access to the print media, Africans know America mainly through films and television, and those that they see are often violent action movies which portray the United States as crime-ridden. Also causing concern is racism in the United States, and Africans will surely ask about it.

But these negatives notwithstanding, Africans are mainly positive about the United States and its people. Life in the States is assumed to be easy, all Americans are believed to be rich, and a visit to the States is a dream of many. In interactions with Africans, moreover, North Americans have a built-in advantage over Europeans. Because they do not share with Europeans a colonial experience in Africa, North Americans are perceived by Africans as being different from other outsiders and are placed in a separate category. And, as whites in a black continent, most Americans visiting Africa for the first time will learn how it feels to be a member of a minority.

One American traveling to Africa for the first time was concerned about how Africans would react to him as a white man. In Europe, if he dressed like a European he would not stand out and be taken for an outsider. In Africa, he surmised, because of his white skin, blending in would simply not be possible. But as he later learned, Africans are more concerned with differences in dress, education, social status, and wealth than with color.

Study abroad, and the advancement it brings, is a goal of most African students. Half of all foreign students in France, as earlier noted, are Africans, and an estimated 50-60,000 are sub-Saharan. Another traditional place of study is the United Kingdom, which has close to 10,000 sub-Saharans. Study in the United States has been increasing, and in the 1994-95 academic year some 17,000 sub-Saharans were enrolled in U.S. colleges and universities. The number of U.S. students in sub-Saharan Africa is still small but has also been increasing in recent years; 1,546 studied there in 1994-95.[3] But here too, as with foreign aid, U.S. government funds for student exchanges have been reduced by a White House and Congress bent on balancing the budget.

Africans did come to the United States in the past, and in large numbers, but as slaves to fill the demand for plantation field hands in the growing agricultural economy of the antebellum South. Indeed, Africa's first major export to the Americas was men and women, sold into slavery from the west coast of Africa, from Senegal in the north to Angola in the south.

From the early sixteenth century when the Atlantic slave trade began until 1870 when it finally ended, some ten to twelve million Africans were transported to the New World, and under appalling conditions. The vast majority of those who survived the arduous voyage ended up in the Caribbean and Latin America, but an estimated 500,000, the ancestors of most of today's U.S. African Americans, came to the English colonies north of Florida. One of every five people of black African ancestry lives in the Americas, some thirty-three million in the United States.

Many of those involuntary immigrants arrived in the holds of ships from Newport, Rhode Island, and Salem, Massachusetts, in a triangular trade of molasses, rum, and slaves. Molasses was brought from Caribbean plantations to New England ports, where it was distilled into rum that was shipped to Africa to be exchanged for slaves who were then brought to the Caribbean to work on the plantations that grew the sugar cane from which the molasses was made. It was a lucrative trade and brought fortunes to families of New England port cities. In a quirk of history, Massachusetts and Rhode Island, along with Pennsylvania and its Quakers, were later to become centers of the abolition movement which helped to abolish slavery in the United States and end the African slave trade.

Many African Americans who go to Africa in search of

their roots expect to be treated like Africans and are disappointed when they are not. "If you think you're African," says U.S. writer Stanley Crouch, "then I invite you to go to Africa. You'll find out very quickly that you are an American."[4]

Paul A. Burns, a Peace Corps volunteer who served in Lesotho 1990-1992, writes, "As a black American, my reception by Africans was, for the most part, open and welcoming. In fact, I experienced a level of acceptance that my white counterparts could never achieve." However,

...I too, like my white counterparts, stand outside the door of African society simply because of who I am. I dressed Western and spoke differently. To the average African, it is culture that defines identity. Therefore, I was viewed and often classified as *lokhoa*, or white person, although with my Native American and Creole ancestry, I would have been classified as Colored had I been born in London.[5]

Whites may not encounter a color barrier in Africa, but American blacks sometimes do. African Americans report that upon arriving at African airports, they are more likely to be singled out for customs inspection, to be snubbed when hailing taxis, and given less favorable treatment than whites in the marketplace, where they may be mistaken for Africans.

Such treatment can annoy African Americans who believe that they should be able to relate to Africans because Africa is indeed their motherland. But while most Americans can identify a specific country from whence came their ancestors, few African Americans can trace their roots.

Maya Angelou writes of an "...unceasing parade of naive travelers who thought that an airline ticket to Africa would erase the past and open wide the gates to a perfect future..." and who saw their first visit to Africa as a homecoming but did not understand that "...they had not come home, but had left one familiar place of painful memory for another strange place with none." As one African American in Angelou's book says, "...if you expect Africans to open their arms and homes to you, you'll be in for a terrible shock. Not that they will be unkind. Never unkind, but most of them will be distant."[6]

Nevertheless, on leaving Ghana, where she lived with a group of American "returnees," Angelou wrote,

> Many years earlier I, or someone very like me and certainly related to me, had been taken from Africa by force. This second leave-taking would not be so onerous, for now I knew my people had never completely left Africa. We had sung it in our blues, shouted it in our gospel and danced the continent in our breakdowns. As we carried it to Philadelphia, Boston and Birmingham we had changed its color, modified its rhythms, yet it was Africa which rode in bulges of our high calves, shook in our protruding behinds and crackled in our wide open laughter.[7]

Despite the disappointments, African Americans do identify with the continent of their origin. "I am an African, too," declared Colin L. Powell during a visit to Africa in 1992. "I feel my roots here in this continent."[8]

Until recently, the United States looked at Africa through the prism of the Cold War, and it had to make friends with some rather unsavory regimes as African states gave their support to the higher bidder in the superpower rivalry. With the end of the Cold War, the United States can now deal with each government on its own merits, and one factor considered today is how it treats its own citizens.

President Franklin D. Roosevelt played a role, largely unknown, in Africa's pursuit of independence. In 1943, en route to his meeting with British Prime Minister Churchill in Casablanca, Roosevelt's plane refueled at Bathurst (now Banjul) in Britain's African colony of The Gambia. Appalled by the misery, poverty, and disease he saw there, Roosevelt wasted no time in telling Churchill about "that hell-hole of yours."

Roosevelt expressed his hopes for African freedom after the war, and in the remaining two years of his life he pursued his goal of independence for the colonies by ensuring that his views were taken into consideration in plans for the United Nations, which were then taking shape. At Yalta, in 1945, he won agreement from Churchill and Stalin for the trusteeship principle in the United Nations Charter, which eventually led to full independence for the people of Africa.[9]

Americans and Africans also have a cultural connection. "Just as Afro-Americans share a racial inheritance from the British Isles with Euro-Americans," write Bohannan and Curtin, "all Americans share a cultural inheritance from Africa."[10] From Africa are derived our jazz, blues, gospel, rock, and rap as well as our rhumba, samba and calypso. Africa has also had a profound effect on the language we use, and much of our cooking, especially in the American South, has its origins in Africa whence come our gumbos, jambalayas, and in colonial times, our rice, yams, okra, peanuts, sesame, and cumin. "Every 'southern' cookbook silently exhibits its debt to those heartsick slaves who recreated a bit of home in their stews and cornbreads and greens and fritters."[11] In return, Africans are indebted to Americans for cassava, maize, manioc, and peanuts, staples of the diet in many parts of their continent but brought from South America to Africa by the Portuguese.

Succeeding in Africa

We fear Africa because when we leave it alone, it works.
—Patrick Marnham, *Fantastic Invasion*

Success in Africa can be elusive. To succeed, you must not exactly leave Africa alone but rather adapt your behavior to the African scene. You won't get Africans to change unless you yourself change, as a recap of some of the main points of this book will show.

Show patience and take the long view. Learn to wait to see people, present your views calmly and dispassionately, listen when Africans express theirs, establish a good interpersonal relationship, nurture that relationship with follow-up visits, and never lose your cool.

All this takes time, but it works. Do not expect to fly in for a few days, sign a contract or agreement, and leave with a done deal. As a Somali proverb puts it, "The slow climber does not fall."

Learn how Africans see their own problems. Don't open a meeting with your solutions, but rather introduce them at some point later in the talks. Africans are interested in learning about Western approaches to their problems but will want to be shown first that those approaches really meet their needs. In the meantime, they can show strong survival skills and seemingly unlimited patience.

Do not underestimate the sophistication of Africans. Africans who speak English or French will also speak several local languages and often several dialects as well. They represent an old culture and are worldly-wise in ways unknown to Westerners. And they are wondering how wise you are.

When disagreement is unavoidable, repeat your position for the record and then concede. Another opportunity to restate your case will likely occur. In the meantime, continue to collect your facts and marshal your arguments for future use.

Africans can be determined in their inaction, believing that if they delay a response, the person making the request may forget it or eventually give up. But when they do respond, Africans will often avoid a direct no and will use various formulations to delay or obfuscate. To avoid giving offense, they may also resort to saying no through a third party.

Governments in Africa are centralized and hierarchical, in the European tradition. Decisions are usually made at the highest level and are a long time in the making. Not allowed the luxury of failure, bureaucrats tend to avoid risks. Governments change often, and officials will not want to be on the wrong side of their new superiors. Getting it "right" in Africa is not the most important thing. More important, for expats, is to act as role models, to build trust and confidence, to set an example. When Africans have confidence in and trust you, your example may be followed.

For consultants, establishing trust and confidence and accomplishing anything in so little time may prove difficult. To realize your objectives, it may be necessary to extend a stay or return for a second or third visit.

Don't expect to make big changes, but, rather, look for pockets of hope. Work with a small group that is prepared to accept change—the "early adapters"—and use them as role models. Have realistic expectations and make much of small successes.

Change, however, must be made in a way that is culturally acceptable. African development must accord with local cultural traditions, says Francis Mading Deng, or it will not be accepted in Africa, where

> there is an urgent need to develop a formula that can politically, economically, socially, and culturally utilize the values and institutions of traditional society by recognizing them and building on them in a manner that reconciles them and makes them partners with the forces of modern science and technology, the magic tools of development.[12]

But the best or least expensive science and technology may not be best for Africa if it does not build on indigenous values, social organizations, and patterns of behavior. As Deng concludes, "...there is no clear demarcation between what is traditional and what is modern; they constantly interplay and are potentially mutually reinforcing and reproductive."[13]

"Sitting in"—working as a foreigner in a government min-istry—is important, counsels one American who worked as an adviser to an African government. Until you do so, you may never understand why Africans do things the way they do. Success may seem elusive but can become evident in surprising ways, says the former adviser. Uncertain whether he had accomplished anything during his two-year tour, he was pleasantly surprised when his African counterpart made him a consummate compliment in a predeparture farewell. "You were so helpful to me in so many ways," he said. "I hope you understand that I was testing you during the first year."

Don't be afraid to ask your African colleagues for the "right" way to open a meeting or make a proposal. African cultures, despite their similarities, do differ, and what works in one place may not work in another. Check out the local culture before you begin.

Listen to the local people, advises Kofi Annan, the Gha-naian who became U.N. Secretary General in 1997. In de-scribing his first experience with winter as a student at Macalester College in Minnesota in 1959, Annan relates how he bundled up in heavy clothing but drew the line at earmuffs, which he thought looked ridiculous. But after his ears nearly froze one day, he bought the biggest pair of ear-muffs he could find.

"I learned a very important lesson," Annan explained. "You never walk into a situation and believe you know better than the natives. You have to listen and look around. Oth-erwise you can make some very serious mistakes."[14]

The U.S. Peace Corps advises its volunteers to use a four-step approach in Africa: listen and observe, discuss and de-cide, try something, and if it doesn't work, listen and observe again.

"Some people are not born to set foot on the African continent," counsels an American who was born and raised in Congo and speaks several local languages. "You need radar to sense the obstacles lying ahead, to set realistic goals, and

252

to be flexible and sensitive. Just because you have the dollars does not mean you can do what you want." Be reconciled to learning more from Africa than you will be able to contribute. And no matter how well you know Africa, there will always be a surprise awaiting you.

1 Lawrence S. Eagleburger and Robert L. Barry, "Dollars and Sense Diplomacy," in *Foreign Affairs* 75, no. 4 (July/August 1996).

2 Beverly G. Hawk, "Introduction: Metaphors of African Coverage," in *Africa's Media Image*, edited by Beverly G. Hawk (New York: Praeger, 1992), 6.

3 Foreign study statistics are from Todd M. Davis, ed., *Open Doors 1995/96: Report on International Education Exchanges* (New York: Institute of International Education, 1996).

4 *New York Times*, 25 March 1996.

5 Paul A. Burns, "A Lesotho Peace Corps Memoir," *Foreign Service Journal* (June 1995): 43.

6 Maya Angelou, *All God's Children Need Traveling Shoes* (New York: Vintage Books Edition, 1991), 40-42.

7 Ibid., 208.

8 Colin L. Powell, *My American Journey* (New York: Random House, 1995), 349.

9 Donald Wright, "That Hell-Hole of Yours," *American Heritage*, October 1995.

10 Bohannan and Curtin, *Africa and Africans*, 14.

11 Tami Hultman, *The Africa News Cookbook* (New York: Viking Penguin, 1986), ix.

12 Deng, "Cultural Dimensions of Conflict Management," 508.

13 Ibid., 506.

14 *New York Times*, 7 January 1997.

Afterword

It is only the fool who needs a proverb explained to him.
—Akan proverb

Appendix A

Countries, Capitals, and Languages

Country	Capital	Official Language
Angola	Luanda	Portuguese
Benin	Cotonou	French
Botswana	Gaborone	English
Burkina Faso	Ouagadougou	French
Burundi	Bujumbura	French
Cameroon	Yaoundé	French and English
Cape Verde	Praia	Portuguese
Central African Republic	Bangui	French
Chad	N'Djamena	French
Comoros	Moroni	French
Democratic Republic of the Congo	Kinshasha	French
Congo (Brazzaville)	Brazzaville	French
Côte d'Ivoire	Yamoussoukro	French
Djibouti	Djibouti	French
Equatorial Guinea	Malabo	Spanish
Eritrea	Asmara	none
Ethiopia	Addis Ababa	Amharic
Gabon	Libreville	French

Country	Capital	Official Language
The Gambia	Banjul	English
Ghana	Accra	English
Guinea	Conakry	French
Guinea-Bissau	Bissau	Portuguese
Kenya	Nairobi	English and Kiswahili
Lesotho	Maseru	English
Liberia	Monrovia	English
Madagascar	Antananarivo	French and Malagasy
Malawi	Lilongwe	English
Mali	Bamako	French
Mauritania	Nouakchott	Arabic and French
Mauritius	Port Louis	English
Mozambique	Maputo	Portuguese
Namibia	Windhoek	English and Afrikaans
Niger	Niamey	French
Nigeria	Abuja	English
Rwanda	Kigali	French
São Tomé and Principe	São Tomé	Portuguese
Senegal	Dakar	French
Seychelles	Victoria	English
Sierra Leone	Freetown	English
Somalia	Mogadishu	Somali
South Africa	Pretoria	English, Afrikaans*
Sudan	Khartoum	Arabic
Swaziland	Mbabane	English
Tanzania	Dar es Salaam	English and Kiswahili
Togo	Lomé	French
Uganda	Kampala	English
Zambia	Lusaka	French
Zimbabwe	Harare	English

* South Africa also recognizes nine African languages as official.

Appendix B

Recommended Readings

> The cultural patterns of recent Africa and the historical patterns of the African past are a necessary introduction to the Africa of today and tomorrow.
>
> —Paul Bohannan and Philip Curtin,
> *Africa and Africans*

Chinua Achebe. *Things Fall Apart*. New York: Doubleday, 1994. An African classic, this novel by a leading Nigerian writer tells of the changes brought by colonialism to an Igbo village.

Better Health in Africa: Experience and Lessons Learned. Washington, DC: World Bank, 1994. The experiences of the past and a plan for the future are set forth in this study by the staff of the World Bank, prepared in close cooperation with the World Health Organization and UNICEF. Numerous tables and figures provide data on the state of health in each country.

A. Adu Boahen. *African Perspectives on Colonialism*. Baltimore: Johns Hopkins University Press, 1987. In a departure from the Eurocentric viewpoint, a leading African historian describes how Africans regard their colonial past.

Paul Bohannan and Philip Curtin. *Africa and Africans*. 4th ed. Prospect Heights, IL: Waveland Press, 1995. An anthropologist and a historian combine their expertise to write a readable and

informative work about the African past and its culture, and
how these can be a guide to understanding the African present
and future.

Basil Davidson. *Africa in History*. Rev. ed. New York: Macmillan,
1974. A "broad brush" but comprehensive and sensitive treatment of Africa from its earliest years, by a prolific British writer
on Africa.

Blaine Harden, ed. *Africa: Dispatches from a Fragile Continent*. Boston: Houghton Mifflin, 1990. The *Washington Post* bureau chief
in sub-Saharan Africa from 1985 to 1989 writes stirringly of the
human cost of political change.

Health Information for International Travel. Washington, DC: Government Printing Office, 1997. Published by the U.S. Centers
for Disease Control and Prevention, the "Yellow Book," as it is
commonly known, is a basic reference for travel clinics and gives
recommendations for disease protection, including inoculations,
dosages, and timing. Orders may be placed by telephone at (202)
512-1800 or fax at (202) 512-2250. It is also available on the
Internet at http://www.cdc.gov

Jan Knappert. *African Mythology*. London: Diamond Books, 1995.
A treasure trove of myths and legends that explain African
beliefs, arranged in alphabetical order for easy access, by a Dutch
professor who spent thirty-five years collecting the oral religious
traditions of Africa.

David Lamb. *The Africans*. New York: Vintage Books, 1987. A
political and social survey of all countries of sub-Saharan Africa,
by a former African bureau chief of the *Los Angeles Times*.

Lonely Planet Travel Survival Kit series. Volumes on East Africa,
Central Africa, West Africa, Southern Africa, and individual
countries. Hawthorne, Australia: Lonely Planet Publications. A
wealth of detail, background, and practical tips on Africa's regions and countries, written for the low-budget traveler. Also
available on the World Wide Web at www.lonelyplanet.com

Phyllis M. Martin and Patrick O'Meara, eds. *Africa*. 3d ed.
Bloomington, IN: Indiana University Press, 1995. This readable
overview of Africa from prehistoric to modern times has become
the most popular introductory text for African studies courses in

North America.

Ali A. Mazrui. *The Africans: A Triple Heritage*. Boston: Little, Brown, 1986. Geography, culture, religion, economics, and politics are examined by a leading African scholar who believes Africa is being split by its triple heritage—indigenous traditions, Western culture, and Islamic culture. Mazrui, a Kenyan, is a professor at universities in Africa and the United States.

John Middleton. *The World of the Swahili: An African Mercantile Civilization*. New Haven: Yale University Press, 1992. A social anthropologist takes a new look at the Swahili people, their past history, ethnographic present, and centuries-old mercantile society.

Alan Moorehead. *The White Nile*. New York: Dell Publishing, 1960. *The Blue Nile*. New York: Harper and Row, 1972. The exploration of the sources of the Nile River and the opening of East Africa and the Horn to the West. Two classic studies that are a pleasure to read, and a "must" for anyone interested in Ethiopia, Sudan, Uganda, Kenya, Tanzania, and Congo.

Peter W. Schroth, ed. *Doing Business in Sub-Saharan Africa*. Chicago: American Bar Association, Section of International Law and Practice, 1991. A survey of business law in Africa, with chapters on individual countries written by African lawyers and Western lawyers with extensive African experience.

Allister Sparks. *The Mind of South Africa*. New York: Ballantine Books, 1991. The history, culture, and people of South Africa, black and white, and the background to apartheid as seen by a fifth-generation South African journalist. Called by many the best single book on South Africa.

Robert Stock. *Africa South of the Sahara: A Geographical Interpretation*. New York: Guilford Press, 1995. A fresh look at the geography of Africa, focusing on contemporary sociocultural, political, and economic issues and how they affect Africans in the 1990s. By a Canadian geographer and Africanist at Queen's University, Ontario.

Michael E. M. Sudarkasa. *The African Business Handbook: A Practical Guide to Business Resources for U.S./Africa Trade and Development*. Washington, DC: 21st Century Africa, no. 3, 1996. A useful reference guide for U.S. companies interested in exploring business opportunities in Africa, especially within the private sector.

Tips for Travelers to Sub-Saharan Africa. Washington, DC: U.S. Department of State, Bureau of Consular Affairs, 1994. A handy, pocket-sized booklet with information on health, visas, travel, country profiles, and other subjects, as well as addresses and telephones of U.S. embassies and consulates. It can be purchased through the U.S. Government Printing Office.

Colin M. Turnbull. *The Lonely African.* New York: Simon and Schuster, Touchstone, 1987. The conflict between the traditional Africa of the village and tribe and the Westernized Africa of the city and state, as seen by a noted English anthropologist in a book first published in 1962 but still timely.

Appendix C

Internet, Fax, and Telephone Connections for Information on Africa

African Embassies in Washington, D.C. Embassies will answer questions for travelers to their countries. Only a few now have web sites, but their number is expected to grow. Web site: http://embpage.org

Africa News. Up-to-date information on Africa from the African News Service. Web site: http://www.africanews.org

Africa South of the Sahara. Selected Internet resources. Provides links to Africa-related resources created for the African Studies Association (U.S.). Organized by categories and regions, it is also searchable by key words. Web site: http://www-sul.stanford.edu/depts/ssrg/africa/guide.html

City Net web site. A broad range of information on individual African countries drawn from a variety of sources, including the U.S. government. Web site: http://www.city.net/regions/africa

Daily News Bulletin. News on South Africa distributed by the Embassy of South Africa in Washington, D.C. Web site: http://www.southafrica.net

Demiurge. Host country web sites in Africa and how to find local Internet service providers in individual countries. Web site: http://demiurge.wn.apc.org:80/africa

Flashfax Hotline for Africa. Department of Commerce automated fax system for general, regional, and country-specific reports on trade and investing in Africa. Tel. (202) 482-1064

International Travelers' Hotline at the U.S. Centers for Disease Control and Prevention. Tel. (404) 332-5449; on the Internet: http://www.cdc.gov

State Department Automated Fax System. Information sheets, travel warnings, public announcements, tips for travelers, visa information, and other consular matters for individual countries. Tel. (202) 647-3000

Washington Post. The *Post's* home page has links to a wealth of information and data on all African countries, including country profiles. Web site: http://www.washingtonpost.com/wp-srv/inatl/Africa.htm

The Authors

Yale Richmond is a veteran of thirty years as a cultural officer in the U.S. Foreign Service, with postings abroad in Germany, Laos, Poland, Austria, and the Soviet Union. He has also served as staff consultant to the Commission on Security and Cooperation in Europe (U.S. Congress), and was Senior Program Officer at the National Endowment for Democracy. A specialist in cultural exchanges and international communication, Richmond has written *From Nyet to Da: Understanding the Russians* and *From Da to Yes: Understanding the East Europeans*, among other publications. His latest passion is Africa and its cultures.

Phyllis Gestrin has more than sixteen years of experience in African affairs, including postings in Somalia and Zaire with UNICEF. She has also served as a technical adviser and has designed public health programs in Africa for the U.S. Peace Corps. Currently an employee of the Office of International and Refugee Health in the Office of the Secretary, U.S. Department of Health and Human Services, she is on assignment to the Africa Bureau of the United States Agency for International Development. A graduate of the University of Chicago, she has a Ph.D. in psychology/physiology from the University of Washington, a Master of Public Health from Harvard, and has taught psychology at the University of Texas (Austin). Dr. Gestrin has traveled widely in Africa, which she visits frequently.

Index

A

Abidjan, 28, 177
abortion, 68
Abyssinia. *See* Ethiopia
Accra, 4, 177
Achebe, Chinua, 35
Addis Ababa, 191
African Americans, 239-48
Africare, 242
Afrikaans, 23, 79, 208
Afrikaners, 23, 62, 206, 207, 208
age, respect for, 159-60, 223-24
Agency for International Development (USAID), 242
AIDS, 46, 57, 68-70, 118, 231-32
Ake, Claude, 22
Aku, 19
alcohol, 101
    and AIDS, 118
    See also beer; palm wine
almsgiving, 186
ambiguity, 85-87
Americans, 227, 239-48

R

Ramadan, 32. *See also* Qur'an
Ramphele, Mamphela, 208
Red Sea, 192, 193
religion, xiv, 26, 30-42
    folk, 34-35, 37-41
    in Nigeria, 178
    See also animism; Christianity; Islam; Protestantism; Roman Catholicism; spiritualism; Vodu
Reynolds, Thomas H., and Flores, Arturo A., 168
Robinson, Alicia J., 180
Rockefeller Foundation, 242
Roman Catholicism, 15, 26, 30, 32, 33, 41, 42, 183, 195, 198, 203
Roosevelt, Franklin D., 247, 248
Rwanda, xx, 15-16, 19, 184
    and women, 48

S

Sahara, 178, 184-86
Sahel, 26, 133, 175, 177, 182, 184-88, 221
SADC. *See* Southern Africa Development Community
St. Louis, 187
Salem, Massachusetts, 239-40, 245
Samu, Samu M., 52
San, 207
San Francisco, 206
sangoma, 40
São Tomé and Principe, 182
Save the Children, 242
Sawadogo, Gérémie, 223, 224
Sawyerr, Akilagpa, 3
schistosomiasis. *See* bilharzia
Schroth, Peter W., 169, 170